Understanding, Managing, and Leading

Early Childhood Programs in Canada

JANE BERTRAND
School of Early Childhood
George Brown College

THOMSON
™
NELSON

Australia   Canada   Mexico   Singapore   Spain   United Kingdom   United States

THOMSON

NELSON

Understanding, Managing, and Leading: Early Childhood Programs in Canada

Jane Bertrand

Associate Vice President, Editorial Director:
Evelyn Veitch

Editor-in-Chief, Higher Education:
Anne Williams

Executive Editor:
Cara Yarzab

Senior Marketing Manager:
Dave Ward

Developmental Editor:
Sandy Matos

Photo Researcher and Permissions Coordinator:
Jane Bertrand

Content Production Manager:
Susan Wong

Copy Editor:
Valerie Adams

Proofreader:
Wendy Thomas

Indexer:
Gillian Watts

Manufacturing Coordinator:
Loretta Lee

Design Director:
Ken Phipps

Interior Design:
Tammy Gay

Cover Design:
Johanna Liburd

Cover Image:
Jupiter Images

Compositor:
ICC Macmillan Inc.

Printer:
Thomson West

COPYRIGHT © 2008, by Nelson, a division of Thomson Canada Limited.

Printed and bound in the US
1   2   3   4   10   09   08   07

For more information contact Nelson, 1120 Birchmount Road, Toronto, Ontario, M1K 5G4. Or you can visit our Internet site at http://www.nelson.com

Statistics Canada information is used with the permission of Statistics Canada. Users are forbidden to copy this material and/or redisseminate the data, in an original or modified form, for commercial purposes, without the expressed permissions of Statistics Canada. Information on the availability of the wide range of data from Statistics Canada can be obtained from Statistics Canada's Regional Offices, its World Wide Web site at <http://www.statcan.ca>, and its toll-free access number 1-800-263-1136.

ALL RIGHTS RESERVED. No part of this work covered by the copyright herein may be reproduced, transcribed, or used in any form or by any means—graphic, electronic, or mechanical, including photocopying, recording, taping, Web distribution, or information storage and retrieval systems—without the written permission of the publisher.

For permission to use material from this text or product, submit a request online at www.thomsonrights.com

Every effort has been made to trace ownership of all copyrighted material and to secure permission from copyright holders. In the event of any question arising as to the use of any material, we will be pleased to make the necessary corrections in future printings.

Library and Archives Canada Cataloguing in Publication

Bertrand, Jane, 1951–
Understanding, managing, and leading: early childhood programs in Canada / Jane Bertrand.

Includes index.
ISBN 978-0-17-625180-2

1. Early childhood education--Canada--Administration--Textbooks. 2. Early childhood education--Canada--Textbooks. I. Title.

LB1139.3.C3B47 2007   372.21068
C2007-904747-5

ISBN 10:   0-17-625180-4
ISBN 13:   978-0-17-625180-2

This book is dedicated to Canada's early childhood work force—still struggling, but gaining recognition for its work with young children and their families.

BRIEF TABLE OF CONTENTS

TABLE OF CONTENTS

Chapter 9: Continuous Learning 223

Chapter 10: Advocating for Children, Families, and Communities 245

PREFACE

Understanding, Managing, and Leading: Early Childhood Programs in Canada introduces early childhood educators to Canada's emerging early childhood system that employs members of the early childhood work force.

SECTION 1: UNDERSTANDING EARLY CHILDHOOD PROGRAMS

Research findings continue to conclude that the quality of experiences that children have in the first six years of life has a long-lasting impact on their development, on their future success at school, and on their overall health and well-being. Increased public awareness of the importance of early childhood experiences leads to considerations of the purpose of early childhood programs. Public policy defines the scope of early childhood programs. The quality of early childhood programs is central to their value in meeting the needs of children, families, and society. This first section considers the purpose of early childhood programs, their public policy context, and how the quality of these programs can be measured.

SECTION 2: MANAGING EARLY CHILDHOOD PROGRAMS

The second section presents detailed information about the management and administration of various types of early childhood programs, with a specific focus on regulated child care programs but also including family support programs, kindergarten and other early years programs in the education system, and school-age programs. The Appendix includes several examples of forms and procedures to accompany the material in these chapters.

SECTION 3: LEADING EARLY CHILDHOOD PROGRAMS

The final section of the book explores leadership within early childhood programs, as well as leadership in promoting an early childhood system for families and communities. The scope and size of the work force is expanding as early childhood educators are working in a broader range of program settings. Leadership in this rapidly maturing work force requires attention to roles and responsibilities, pedagogy, and ongoing learning and development. Increasingly, programs are moving towards closer working relationships and, in some instances, dissolving operational boundaries. More recent interest in the importance of early child development presents opportunities to advance early childhood policy, and early childhood educators have a leadership role as a new system emerges.

PEDAGOGICAL FEATURES

The main text is supplemented by three types of feature boxes:

- *From the Past* provides historical examples that offer insight into today's practices.
- *Beyond Our Borders* features international examples that complement or contrast with practices in Canadian early childhood settings.
- *Innovations* are selected examples that illustrate a unique or exemplary practice.

The sample forms and procedures in the Appendix mostly support the material in Section 2 without interrupting the flow of the text. They are set up around a hypothetical early childhood program that is introduced at the beginning of Section 2 and described further in the introductions of Chapters 4 to 7. Blank forms will be made available on the website that supports this chapter.

Throughout the book, Web icons indicate further material (e.g., colour illustrations and maps) and links that are available on the book's website.

ABOUT THE AUTHOR

Jane Bertrand is an early childhood educator who graduated from the ECE diploma program at St. Lawrence College in Kingston, Ontario, in 1975. She also has a B.A. in psychology from Queen's University and an M.Ed. in early childhood from the Ontario Institute for Studies in Education at the University of Toronto. Jane is currently a faculty member in the early childhood program at George Brown College. She has had many opportunities to work across the early childhood sector—in programs, policy development, and research. Recently, she participated on the Toronto First Duty Research and Development team, the research and writing team for the *Early Years 2: Putting Science into Action,* and contributed to the development and revisions of the *Science of Early Child Development,* a multimedia curriculum resource.

ACKNOWLEDGMENTS

Several groups have generously given permission to reprint material for this text. A special thanks to Founders' Network, Council for Early Child Development, Atkinson Centre, Atkinson Charitable Foundation, Childcare Research and Resource Unit,

Human Early Learning Partnership, the Ontario Coalition for Better Child Care, and the Child Care Human Resources Sector Council.

I would also like to acknowledge the assistance of the following reviewers:

- Judith Boyd, New Brunswick Community College
- Dawne Clarke, Mount Royal College
- Barbara J. Duffy, Okanagan University College
- Myrna G. Fox, Portage College
- Maxine King, St. Clair College
- Karin Macaulay, Camosun College
- Maaja Matsoo, Seneca College
- Donna Morrison, Red Deer College
- Diana Nyisztor, Vanier College
- Laura Oyama, Humber College
- Cheryl Park, Cambrian College
- Cindy Piwowar, University College of the Cariboo
- Laila Shah, Seneca College
- Allison Soave, Niagara College
- Karen Troughton, Saskatchewan Institute of Applied Science and Technology
- Pam Whitty, University of New Brunswick

In addition, the editorial team at Nelson contributed to the clarity and design of the text. The efforts of Cara Yarzab, Executive Editor; Sandy Matos, Developmental Editor; Susan Wong, Content Production Manager; and Valerie Adams, copy editor are greatly appreciated.

Jane Bertrand
May 2007

Understanding Early Childhood Programs

Understanding early childhood programs in Canada begins with understanding the context of children's lives. Family life remains at the centre of young children's experiences and is shaped by community, work, values, culture, and society's expectations for men and women. Overall, Canada's social environment is dramatically changing, transforming life inside families and neighbourhoods. The realities of children's lives drive the demand for, and determine the purpose of, early childhood programs.

An explosion of research in the biological and social sciences has deepened our collective knowledge that early environments matter a lot. Attention to the rights of all citizens brings increasing awareness of the rights and entitlements of children to a stable and secure childhood. The convergence of changing circumstances, increased knowledge, and the desire to do the right thing for children is changing how we think about and deliver early childhood programs.

Public policies for early childhood programs in Canada and elsewhere are responding. In Canada, the gap between what we know and what we do as a nation continues, but public investment in early childhood programs has at least doubled since the end of the 1990s.

The quality of early childhood programs is important to parents, practitioners, and policymakers. Measurement and monitoring help make sense out of what is happening in early childhood programs. The basic question of whether investment in early childhood *can* make a difference has been answered and does not need further investigation. But we need to know if Canada's expanded efforts for young children and families *are* making a difference.

THE PURPOSE OF EARLY CHILDHOOD PROGRAMS

CHAPTER OUTLINE

Hon. Margaret Norrie McCain

The NLSCY [National Longitudinal Survey of Children and Youth, a joint project of Human Resources Development Canada and Statistics Canada] data tells us most kids are doing okay. That's good news, but we could make it much easier for families. During the *Early Years Study*, we were confronted by the array of services—child care, drop-in play groups, nursery schools, kindergarten, head start, family resource and parenting centres, among others. It may sound as if the field is covered but, in fact, we were witnessing the fallout of inadequate public policy—a scattering of disconnected, poorly resourced programs. Few parents know what services exist or what they do.

The quality of parenting is paramount for children but parents are under a great deal of pressure. We add to their stress and guilt by loading them with information and then abandoning them to the hunt for quality child care.

What parent of a young child doesn't need help? It is difficult for an individual parent to replicate the stimulation provided by a good-quality child-development program. For example, how many would consider that mucking around in goop is a great sensory experience for a toddler? Or who is prepared to cover their floor in paper every day so a child doesn't have to focus on "being careful" as she develops her fine motor skills with paint and markers?

Mothers are in the work force—over 60 percent will return to work by the time their child is three—and there are plenty of economic, social, and political reasons to support their participation. There is also ample brain research indicating we should be very concerned about the nonparental care their children receive. Now we have to wait for governments to catch up.

Source: Interview with Honourable Margaret Norrie McCain, former Lieutenant-Governor of New Brunswick.

Chapter Objectives

This chapter will:

1. Summarize current scientific findings about early child development
2. Discuss children's right to quality early childhood programs
3. Examine views about childhood and early development
4. Review the multiple purposes of early childhood programs

Our understanding of childhood is formed by what we know from researchers who study early human development, our beliefs and commitment to the rights of children, and our image, or ideas, about what childhood is. Our image of the child is influenced by our core values about what is important in our society. Our understanding of childhood defines what we think young children and their families want and need.

Early childhood programs are part of the social infrastructure in neighbourhoods and communities where young children and their families live. Their purposes may be varied, depending on our view of childhood, what we think families want and need, and the historical, social, cultural, and economic context.

Canadian child care programs were first established in the late 1850s as charitable services to provide basic **custodial care** and supervision for the young children of impoverished mothers who had to engage in paid employment to support the family. **Kindergarten** began as part of the public education system in the 1880s in Toronto. Its purpose has always been viewed as the preparation of children for entry into the formal school system. **Family support programs,** intended to confirm and enhance the ability of families to raise their young children, grew out of early public health programs. These are still separate programs; the differences in their origins can still be seen in how they and other early childhood programs are funded, in the training requirements to work in the program, in the status of the work, and in remuneration levels. But their underlying purposes are converging. Kindergarten programs provide nonparental care. Quality child care programs provide early childhood education and support parenting abilities. Family support programs may offer respite nonparental care, build community capacity, and offer early educational experiences for young children.

In this chapter we are going to look at different ideas about children, early development, and early childhood programs. We will then examine the converging and overlapping central purposes of early childhood programs.

 Beyond Our Borders

THEMATIC REVIEW OF EARLY CHILDHOOD EDUCATION AND CARE

In 1998, the Education Committee of the Paris-based Organisation for Economic Co-operation and Development (OECD) launched the Thematic Review of Early Childhood Education and Care Policy. The OECD is an organization of industrialized countries. The goal of the review of early childhood education and care programs is to improve access to and quality in early childhood education and care.

A set of objectives, analytical framework, and methodology was developed for the review, and OECD member countries were invited to participate through their national education ministries. Twenty-one countries volunteered to participate in the review (Australia, Austria, Belgium, Canada, the Czech Republic, Denmark, Germany, Finland, France, Hungary, Ireland, Italy, Korea, Mexico, the Netherlands, Norway, Portugal, Spain, Sweden, the United Kingdom, and the United States), which took place in two rounds. Early in the review process, countries participating in the first round agreed upon the framework, scope, and process of the review, and identified the major policy issues for investigation. A first comparative report (*Starting Strong*), based on the first round of

(continued)

country reviews, was released at an international conference in Stockholm in 2001. *Starting Strong II* was released at an international conference in Bologna, Italy, in September 2006.

The reviews found the following:

- In most Western European countries the majority of preschool children attend publicly funded and publicly delivered early child education and care programs for at least two years before entry into formal schooling.
- Governments and public opinion recognize the need for public investment in early childhood education and care in most Western European countries.
- There is considerable attention to the transition between early childhood programs and the school system, and the need for pedagogical consistency.
- The purpose of the early childhood care and education programs in these programs is twofold: to support optimal child development and to support parents' participation in the work force.
- The United Kingdom, United States, Canada, and Australia have less coherent systems with more emphasis on early child development programs that are targeted to "at-risk" populations. Nevertheless, the overall awareness of, and commitment to, early child development has increased over the past decade.

Sources: Bennett, 2004; OECD, 2001, 2006.

UNDERSTANDING CHILDHOOD

We have come to understand childhood as a distinct period of development during which helpless infants become competent, skilled individuals. The metamorphosis of childhood is a dynamic dance between children and their environments. Understanding the patterns of early development helps early childhood educators plan optimal environments and interact positively with young children and their families.

The science of early development has grown up over the past 150 years. We now know that human development is an interconnected process. Separating out the development of **emotional maturity** from **social competence** or language abilities or **cognition** is an artificial categorization of what is an integrated process. Categories do allow us to think and share ideas about specific aspects of development but it is essential to keep in mind the interconnectedness of **early child development.** Learning to talk is social, emotional, cognitive, and physical.

Children's development happens within the context of children's daily lives in families and communities. A complex array of environmental and biological factors shape early development. Genetic makeup, the quality of interpersonal relationships

Families' values about childhood shape ideas about what's important to know and learn.

within and outside the family, and the quality of early environments and experiences contribute to the pattern and timing of development.

Values and beliefs about childhood influence ideas about child development (Friendly et al., 2006). Children's development happens within families whose own beliefs about childhood will shape childrearing practices and expectations. Understanding child development is shaped by values about childhood, early development, and the role of families and communities. Day-to-day experiences and interactions among early childhood educators, children, and their families should reflect the shared values and an understanding of children's development.

The Science of Early Child Development

Early daily life shapes pathways for lifelong learning, behaviour, and health that are inextricably linked to the development of the whole child. The brain orchestrates physical, social, emotional, linguistic, and cognitive development. It governs capacities to learn, ways of behaving, and immune and hormone systems that influence physical and emotional health (Mustard, 2006).

Genes may set the parameters for the basic structures of the developing brain, but it is a child's interactions and relationships with parents and significant others that establish neural circuits and shape the brain's neural pathways (McCain et al., 2007). The dynamic dance between genetic and environmental variability establishes neural pathways and the biological potential for learning from experience, including the capacity to perceive, organize, and respond. The brain's capacity for higher-level human functions—such as the ability to attend, interact with others, signal emotions, and use symbols to think—build on this platform.

The brain's architecture and a child's skills are built from the bottom up. Neural circuits that process basic information are wired before those that process more complex information. The sequence may be similar for all children, but the rate of development and variety of pathways that emerge varies.

Children begin life ready for relationships that drive early brain development (Greenspan & Shanker, 2004). The abilities of children to regulate their own emotions, behaviours, and attention increase over time with maturation, experience, and responsive relationships. Support for **self-regulation** is a central focus of early childhood because self-regulation skills lead to physical, social, emotional, behavioural, and cognitive competence.

Differing cultural and social contexts—including quality of stimulation, availability of resources, and preferred patterns of interactions within communities—interact with each child's potential for development (National Scientific Council on the Developing Child, 2005; Greenspan & Shanker, 2004). Early brain development benefits from interactions with adults who are **responsive** and from activities that challenge young children. Access to shelter, clean water, and food, and to developmental opportunities

Babies arrive in the world ready for learning.

Innovations

EXPERIENCE-BASED BRAIN DEVELOPMENT

The exponential growth in new knowledge from research in the neurosciences and biological sciences is providing evidence of "how" the social environment of early life gets "under the skin" in the early years of life that shape learning, behaviour and health throughout the life cycle.

- Around 5 million years ago human beings' hominid ancestors descended from the trees and began to walk upright, and the brains of early human species grew larger and larger. In order to accommodate bipedalism and the large brains of modern humans, babies are born "prematurely" with one-quarter the size of an adult brain, but more than tripling in size by the time the child is three years old.

- Billions of neurons, all with the same genetic coding, make trillions of connections with each other to build the neural pathways of the human brain.

- Early sensory stimulation activates specific genes in different parts of the brain to differentiate neuron functions and establish sensory pathways.

- Sensory pathways influence the development of neural pathways to other parts of the brain involved in coping, movement, language, cognition and biological pathways, including the immune and hormone systems.

- Early environments are mediated through relationships with primary care-givers that drive the development of neural pathways and shape the baby's brain to become highly attuned to the quality of early experiences.

- Sensory stimulation in early life influences genetic machinery and differentiation of neurons which in turn affects how neurons function in setting the foundation for lifelong learning, behaviour and health.

Source: Early Years Study II—McCain et al., 2007, p. 17–18. Reprinted with permission.

such as parks, high-quality early childhood programs, and libraries increase families' abilities to be responsive and stimulating. Fewer resources make it more difficult to sustain optimal conditions for development.

The Rights of Childhood

"A right may be defined as that which a person is entitled to have, to do, or to receive from others, and which is enforceable by law" (Arnold, 2004). The idea that children are citizens with rights and are entitled to resources is an understanding about childhood that is as important as the notion that early childhood is the foundation for lifelong learning, behaviour, and health.

Canadian society now recognizes that children are individuals and citizens in their own right and therefore should be assured the same access to resources and opportunities as other citizens. "Action now will put our children and our future on a firmer foundation for the future. This action is necessary, not only to keeping a reasonable standard of living, but also because it is the right thing to do for our young children" (McCain & Mustard, 1999, p. 2).

The notion of a child as a citizen with rights is a prominent part of interest in children's rights (Friendly, 2000). The United Nations adopted the Convention on the Rights of the Child in 1989. The Convention states that children are entitled to citizenship rights and to special care and assistance. It suggests that children's rights should include civil, political, economic, social, and cultural rights that are inherent to the human dignity of the child (United Nations, 1991, cited in Friendly, 2000). In addition, the child's individual rights to resources should be respected, quite apart from the child's value as an asset to society.

The Convention builds on four general principles (Arnold, 2004):

- All actions concerning the child shall be in his or her best interests.
- Children have the right to survive, develop, and fulfill their human potential.
- Children are protected by the state from any form of discrimination (whether based on race, gender, culture, religion, abilities, and political affiliation of their parents).
- Children have the right to participate in their society and in the creation of the shared social fabric and to have their opinions respected in decisions affecting them.

The Convention sets out a legal framework for the protection and well-being of children and is part of the broader human rights system. There are more countries signed on to the Convention on the Rights of the Child than any other international convention. It has significant legal implications because it is legally binding for state governments and is a powerful tool to use to advocate for children (Arnold, 2004). Countries that have signed on are legally bound to honour children's rights. Rights are linked to obligations to meet the needs of children.

Image of the Child

Early childhood programs are grounded in a particular image of the child—a view of what childhood is. The vision, principles, goals, and organization of early childhood programs are expressions of that image. Our image of the child is rooted in what we know about early development and what we value and hope for, as well as our culture and personal histories.

Three different images of the child can be found in Canadian early childhood settings. Early childhood educators in a variety of settings value children as independent, competent, active learners who have rights to the best possible childhood, while recognizing that early development does set a foundation for later life, and early interventions to address small problems can avert big problems. Children are seen as natural explorers: competent, confident, adventurous beings who ask questions, take risks, and make discoveries in their efforts to make sense of the world around them.

Innovations

A CANADA FIT FOR CHILDREN

A Canada Fit for Children is the Government of Canada's response to commitments made at the United Nations General Assembly Special Session on Children in May 2002. Jointly developed by Health Canada and Social Development Canada, and under the leadership of Senator Landon Pearson, *A Canada Fit for Children* reflects the central issues affecting children today and suggests opportunities for action that all Canadians can take to improve the lives of children in Canada and in the world.

A Canada Fit for Children outlines goals, strategies, and opportunities under four central themes: supporting families and strengthening communities, promoting healthy lives, protecting children from harm, and promoting education and learning.

Building upon Canada's collective efforts for and with children, *A Canada Fit for Children* is based on the following principles:

- Recognition that parents (and legal guardians where designated) have the primary responsibility for the care and nurture of children
- Recognition of governments' roles and responsibilities
- Respect for the diversity of children's communities, culture, and background
- Ensuring social inclusion
- Participation of children
- Fostering multi-sectorial collaboration
- Sharing research, information, and best practices
- Recognizing and acting on responsibilities for all the world's children

Sources: Friendly, 2006; Doherty et al., 2003; Social Development Canada, Public Health Agency of Canada and Northern Affairs Canada, 2005.

In other early childhood programs, early childhood educators view children as adults-in-waiting who need to be prepared for academic achievement and later life—the **schoolification** of early childhood (Bennett, 2004). The schoolification approach emphasizes specific **school readiness** skills, such as letter and sound recognition, counting and printing, and willingness to recognize the authority of the teacher. Activities supporting these types of skills are the central driver of the curriculum and daily schedule. Children are usually assessed against a set of specific learning expectations or standards.

Or early childhood programs may view children—and their families—as problems that need to be remediated. This is the **pathologization** of early childhood. When this image of the child dominates, programs are set up to identify deficiencies and programming is viewed as an early intervention to fix the problem. From the pathologization perspective, early childhood educators emphasize the early identification of problems and focus on plans to intervene to address problems.

Read the following description of interactions in an early childhood program. It tells us about Sandra, an early childhood educator, and how she interacts with a group of preschool children. What is the image of the child in this vignette?

> The children in a preschool community-based child care centre are following the construction of a high-rise building next door with great interest. During outdoor times, children line up at the fence and watch the comings and goings of diggers, front-end loaders, and cranes. One day, Sandra, an early childhood educator, moves the tricycles, wagons, and some large empty boxes close to the fence. She notices that four-year-old Pedro sits down on one of the tricycles and moves it back and forth making a *vrrrrr* sound. Before long, Pedro is joined by three other children and they are orchestrating tricycles and wagons around an area they name "the building site."
>
> One day, Sandra joins the children and asks if they would like to put a large fence up around the building site. Pedro says, "Yes, and we will need to make big signs that say 'Danger' and 'Keep Out.'" Sandra extends the time outside and joins in the new developments. A week later, the building site is still a popular area of the playground and now includes a digging area in the sand box; structures made out of blocks, tubes, and boxes; and numerous picture and word signs giving directions for construction vehicles and warning of dangers.
>
> The children are asking more and more questions about how the construction vehicles work and are debating what the proper names for each of them are. Sandra does not know the answers to many of their questions. Today she has brought in several picture books about construction vehicles from the nearby library. Excitement in community events and the children's keen interest are the starting points from which Sandra creates a platform in pretend play to elaborate the children's learning, literacy, and development. Sandra respects their interests and abilities.

The dominant image of the child strongly influences the way early childhood educators interact with children, and how environments are constructed. If it is believed that children are independent, competent, curious, and active beings who have views and perspectives to share, then early childhood educators support holistic growth and development. At the same time, early childhood educators can draw on their knowledge and experiences to enhance and extend learning. The skills necessary for successful school learning become byproducts, not the central focus. Developmental difficulties can be identified and addressed without a focus on deficits. Instead, the emphasis remains on optimal development and learning.

The image of the child is not static—it is always changing in response to knowledge, experiences, beliefs, and aspirations, and according to who participates in conversations about childhood. The views of parents and other family members must be central to these conversations. Early childhood educators can add their voices, bringing knowledge about current research, wisdom from experience, and their personal views. Conversation is about exchanging information, opinion, and passion. Early childhood educators have much to contribute to the conversation.

The remaining sections in this chapter consider the multiple purposes of early childhood programs. The perspective is based on the view of young children as competent, capable human beings who are respected as active learners.

EARLY CHILDHOOD EDUCATION

The provision of early education opportunities that expand children's abilities and enrich their opportunities for learning is often considered the primary purpose of early childhood programs (Moss, 2006). If this is a (or *the*) primary purpose of early childhood programs, the next question is how do young children learn and what should they be learning.

Society's perception of what it wants for its young children is reflected in its approach to early childhood education (Doherty, 2005). The OECD's thematic reviews (see the box on pages 5 to 6) of early childhood education in 20 countries found consensus across countries regarding the following (Bennett, 2004):

- The importance of the holistic development of young children.
- The importance of young children developing a positive disposition towards learning that is characterized by curiosity about the world and how it works, a desire to understand, engagement rather than passivity, the confidence to take risks, and task perseverance.
- The need for programming to recognize that young children's thinking is qualitatively different from that of older children and that they learn in a different way.
- A flexible approach and curricula that can take into account the special needs of individual children or particular groups such as dual-language children and children with special needs.

Pedagogy is about how learning takes place. It is the process of cultivating learning and development. It is sometimes referred to as "education in its broadest sense" (Moss, 2006). A pedagogical approach in early childhood education refers to what early childhood educators do and how they interact with young children. It also refers to what children do. **Curriculum** is often described as the content of early childhood settings (National Research Council, 2001). It includes the organization of the physical space, materials, and activities that are designed to encourage learning processes, skills, and the acquisition of specific information.

Pedagogy and curriculum are terms that are often used interchangeably (Kagan & Kauerz, 2006). In this chapter, we have defined pedagogy as how early childhood education is delivered and experienced, and curriculum as what the content of early childhood education is.

Play Accelerates Early Learning

Early childhood education can offer children an array of opportunities to explore, discover, and create. An environment designed for learning by solving problems through regular, consistent play opportunities with other children provides rich sensory stimulation that the young child absorbs and integrates into core brain development. **Play** is a pedagogical approach that views children as active, independent, and competent learners.

Play is child-centred activity that engages a young child and promotes learning (Berk & Winlser, 1995; Hewes, 2004; Kagan & Britto, 2005; Greenspan & Shanker, 2004). Play is how children make sense of the world and is an effective method of learning for young children. Ideas and skills become meaningful, tools for learning are practised, and concepts are understood. Play engages children's attention when it offers a challenge that is within the child's capacity to master. Effective settings take advantage of play and embed opportunities for learning in the physical environment and play activities.

Children who thrive in primary school and whose pathways are set for later academic success are those who enter Grade 1 with strong oral communication skills, are confident, are able to make friends, are persistent and creative in completing tasks and solving problems, and are excited to learn (Shonkoff & Phillips, 2000; Bennett, 2004; National Research Council, 2001; Sylva et al., 2004; Maggi et al., 2005). These are the same qualities that children strengthen through high-quality play during their early years.

The imitating and exploring play of infants and toddlers (and the underlying development and organization of the brain) evolve into **symbolic thinking** and the capacity for pretend or imaginative play. As children engage in **pretend play** with each other, they are learning to get along with each other, make compromises, resolve conflicts, regulate emotions and behaviour, and initiate friendships. Pretend play is a form of communication that requires the pretenders to communicate with each other using language gestures and symbolic objects to tell and retell stories (Berk & Winsler, 1995). Social competence, emotional and attention self-regulation, and the ability to communicate with others are foundational to all types of learning and are best developed in play-based environments (Barnett et al., 2006; Ziegler et al., 2004; Kagan & Lowenstein, 2004).

Pretend play drives early learning.

Pretend play is the primary mode of learning during the preschool years and continues to be important into the primary grades. Pretend play means practice in choosing, generating possibilities, and taking risks. Children use language and thinking skills to compare and plan, problem-solve, negotiate, and evaluate in pretend play. Language shapes and extends their play as they express ideas and tell and retell stories. High-quality pretend play means the child is deeply involved and is acquiring and practising emerging skills.

In pretend play children try on a variety of roles and scenarios that facilitate perspective-taking and later abstract thought. Researchers have studied relationships between pretending and the development of mental representation (e.g., see Astington, 2004; Bergen, 2002; Schwebel et al., 1999).

Pretending involves mental representation. A child's ability for joint planning and assigning roles during pretend play with other children is related to the child's level of theory of mind, or his or her ability to understand that others have beliefs, desires, and intentions that are different from one's own. The understanding that what one believes and what others believe may not be the same is a critical element in the development of theory of mind that is acquired at about four years of age (Astington, 1993). Children expand their abilities for joint planning and role assignments during pretend play (Moses & Carlson, 2004).

Although play is a well-established feature of early childhood education, there is often a lack of general understanding of the important contribution that high-quality play—especially pretend play—can make to children's literacy, numeracy, and inquiry skills in the early years. If the focus shifts from play during preschool years to a strong emphasis on the formal instruction of isolated skills such as learning symbols (letters, sounds, numbers), children's **literacy** skills as well as their **numeracy** and **inquiry** skills may actually be reduced (Bennett, 2004; Nabuco & Sylva, 1996). High-quality play that is mediated by early childhood educators and other adults who are play partners and able to inject small amounts of direct instruction based on the needs of the child into the daily play is an effective pedagogy for **emergent literacy**, numeracy, and inquiry skills (Clarke-Stewart & Allhusen, 2005; Kagan & Kauerz, 2006; Schweinhart, 2006; Siraj-Blatchford et al., 2002).

Cognitive research points to the role of pretend play in **early literacy** (National Research Council, 2001; Neuman & Dickinson, 2001; Ziegler et al., 2004). Symbolic play requires children to determine and carry out tasks and goals, and provides opportunities for narrative recall and use of complex language. In complex pretend play situations, children use more advanced language and have higher levels of narrative structure than they do in other situations. Children become storytellers, creating new versions of familiar stories and composing new stories. The ability to use narrative and more advanced oral language are linked to later reading comprehension and fluency (Roskos & Christie, 2004; NICHD, 2005). When literacy materials are embedded within play settings in preschool, kindergarten, and multi-age programs, studies find increases in children's use of literacy materials and engagement in literacy acts (Ziegler et al., 2004). By using and creating environmental print in their pretend play, children begin to understand what reading is and how print works. Pretend play helps children develop schemas and scripts as organized mental structures that are applied to understanding print.

Understanding numbers begins early in life. Young children begin to understand quantity differences, the role of special numbers like 5 and 10, and the relationships between big and little, large and small, more and less, tall and short, and so forth. The social environment in general, and rich pretend play opportunities with adult coaching in particular, provide counting words and mathematical relationships, including one-to-one correspondence and the various contexts in which numbers are used—to put things in order (ordinality) and to count "how many" (cardinality). Play can consolidate understanding about numbers and children can then begin to use a number line that is a prerequisite for addition, subtraction, multiplication, and division (Case et al., 1999; National Research Council, 2001). Play that involves games that use a number line, one-to-one correspondence, and counting (e.g., simplified variations of

Snakes and Ladders) help children master and integrate understanding about numbers (National Research Council, 2001).

Infants are young scientists (Gopnik et al., 1999). Babies see how objects move and behave, gather information, build patterns of expectations about the world around them, and form general categories. Toddlers experiment with tools and learn to manipulate objects. They learn to solve simple problems they encounter in their environment (e.g., how to get an object out of reach or how to make their desires understood). Preschool children use methods of inquiry including data collection, predicting, recording, and talking about findings. Problems to be solved emerge in preschool pretend play. Also, early childhood educators may introduce problems into the environment that engage children's curiosity and provide opportunities for them to apply and reinforce their problem-solving skills.

In summary, children seem to learn best when they can play, explore the world, and interact with adults and peers. Their explorations require flexibility and inventiveness. Children react to the outcomes of their investigations and create strategies for discovery. Play is the platform for inquiry and exploration. Early childhood practitioners balance opportunities for the child to figure out how the world works and to overcome challenges with the practice necessary to perform skills effortlessly.

Planning for Early Learning

Curriculum in early childhood education is about planning for early learning. In Canada, four common curriculum approaches are Reggio Emilia, emergent curriculum, High Scope, and Montessori.

Reggio Emilia is a curriculum approach that builds on Lev Vygotsky's concept of the social construction of knowledge and skillfully integrates other theoretical concepts, including Jean Piaget's theory of cognitive development, John Dewey's concept of progressive education, Hugh Gardner's theory of multiple intelligences, and Urie Bronfenbrenner's ecological environment theory (Berk & Winsler, 1995). Originating in the Reggio Emilia municipality in northern Italy in the middle of the twentieth century, Reggio Emilia is a curriculum centred on children's interests, reflected in projects that are undertaken in considerable depth and detail. The curriculum is inseparable from its pedagogical approach, which is child-centred, and centres on a spirit of collaboration between early childhood educators and young children in facilitating intellectual discovery through social process. The participation of families is also an integral part of the educational experience (Gestwicki, 1995).

Emergent curriculum incorporates some of the principles found in Reggio Emilia programs. However, Reggio Emilia is not a curriculum model that can be transported from its roots in northern Italy to Canadian settings. It is a way of thinking and interpreting the immediate surroundings (natural environment and social community) and following the lead of children and their families to create a unique early childhood setting. Emergent curriculum is an approach that encourages early childhood educators to really respond to their immediate surroundings—physical place and people—and guide children's natural curiosity about their environment to encourage learning.

High Scope curriculum is based on Jean Piaget's constructivist theories of child development. Learning centres with appropriate materials and small and large group

From the Past

COMPENSATORY PRESCHOOL PROGRAMS

During the 1960s, child development research on the importance of early experiences on later abilities and the growing movements to end racial segregation and poverty in the United States pointed to early childhood care and education solutions. Child advocates, policymakers, and researchers pursued early child development initiatives with high optimism that enriched early childhood experiences could change the life course of disadvantaged children, especially African-American children. **Head Start,** the Perry Preschool Project, and *Sesame Street* are three specific initiatives that attempted to improve disadvantaged children's developmental outcomes and ameliorate the effects of poverty, social marginalization, and racism:

- Head Start was established in 1965 as part of U.S. President Lyndon Johnson's "War on Poverty" to expose young children (ages three to five years) living in disadvantaged environments to experiences that would minimize the effects of poverty and racial discrimination. The purpose of the program was to improve children's health and well-being; develop physical skills, social opportunities, and cognitive functioning; and involve parents in their children's educational experiences. In addition, the program offered medical, dental, and nutritional screening and services for children and social services to their families.

- The Perry Preschool Project was a carefully designed experimental longitudinal study on the effects of compensatory preschool education programs for children three and four years old in the 1960s. Preschool teachers worked closely with child development and educational experts to develop a cognitive-developmental program (known as High Scope) based on Piagetian theory of cognitive development. The findings dramatically endorse the financial and social benefits of compensatory preschool education as an intervention for disadvantaged, marginalized children (Schweinhart et al., 2005). The follow-up studies found that children who attended the half-day program were more successful in school, less likely to be involved in the criminal justice system, and less likely to be on social assistance. The cost–benefit analysis of the results illustrated a seven-dollar savings for every one dollar spent on the targeted program delivered to at-risk children and their families.

- *Sesame Street,* the best-known children's educational show in North America, began in 1969. The Children's Television Workshop produced the daily program to foster intellectual and social development. The initial program proposal stated that *Sesame Street* would respond to "the national demand that we give the disadvantaged a fair chance in the beginning"

(continued)

(Liebart & Sprafkin, 1988, p. 219). The creators drew on both ideology and research to design a show that would bring stimulation and opportunities for learning into disadvantaged children's homes through the television to compensate for resources presumed to be available only to affluent families. Both earlier assessments (Liebert & Sprafkin, 1988) and more recent studies (Wright & Huston, 1999) report positive benefits for low-income children who regularly view the show.

A number of smaller-scale programs based on Head Start and the Perry Preschool Project emerged in Canada during the 1970s. Several of the programs funded by the federal government's youth employment program, Local Initiatives Program (LIP), launched preschool compensatory programs for poor children. Theses programs often adapted the cognitively oriented curriculum of the Perry Preschool Program and a Head Start approach that combined enriched early childhood education experiences with additional family supports.

In 1974, the Moncton Headstart Inc. began as a free day care for a few children whose parents could not afford outside care and were having difficulties in their parenting role (Bradshaw, 1997). It quickly adapted the Perry Preschool Program children's curriculum and included programs to support families. Parent participation in the children's program and in parent sessions was required. Adjunct programs to meet families' basic physical needs (food, shelter, and safety) and adult education activities were also offered.

The University of Western Ontario (UWO) Preschool Project began in 1973 as an experiment to assess the impact of compensatory preschool education on low-income children (Howe et al., 2000). Mary J. Wright, who headed the project, developed a constructivist type of curriculum with an emphasis on cognitive development (similar to the High Scope curriculum created for the Perry Preschool Project, and described later in this chapter) as well as focus on the development of social competence and emotional control (derived from her work with William Blatz at the Institute for Child Studies, discussed later in this chapter). Children from economically disadvantaged families attended the UWO Preschool for one or two years alongside children from middle-class families. Low-income children who attended the program for two years demonstrated greater cognitive and self-management skills than low-income children who only attended for one year. Follow-up assessments after Grade 3 found that 82 percent of the low-income children who attended for either one or two years were at grade level, compared to only 58 percent of a low-income control group of children who had not attended any preschool program. According to Howe et al. (2000, p. 226),

> Overall, the findings of the UWO Pre-school Project supported the idea that compensatory education can have long-term beneficial outcomes for low-SES [low-socioeconomic-status] children, particularly if

the preschool experience is two years in length. A word of caution is in order: the study was based on a very small number of subjects, and it is difficult to generalize the findings.

The preschool compensatory programs in Canada and the United States provided enriched environments for children and supports for their families that were designed to compensate for environmental disadvantage. They were part of a social and political context that was striving to ensure an equality of opportunity for all children.

activities are organized to provide specific key experiences in use of language, representation of children's own ideas and experiences, classification, seriation, number concepts, spatial relationships, and time concepts.

Montessori curriculum originates with the work of Italy's first female physician, Maria Montessori, in Italy more than 100 years ago. Montesorri curriculum includes sequences of prescribed tasks, using didactic, self-correcting Montessori materials, which are presented to children in a designated order. The Montessori curriculum includes introducing children to varieties of practical life skills, such as washing dishes, sweeping floors, and watering plants. The curriculum also includes sensorial components, which involve providing materials to help children broaden and refine their sensory perceptions and conceptual components, which means using concrete academic materials to introduce children to reading, writing, mathematics, and social studies.

In countries emphasizing children's holistic development, national curricula for early childhood programs tend to be expressions of principles and values, such as democracy and respect for diversity, with broad goals and guidelines for optimal pedagogical practice (Bennett, 2004). This emphasis puts the onus on early childhood educators to understand and reflect on the underlying intent of the curriculum and to base their practice on this. It is the base for **reflective practice** in early childhood education.

A planned curriculum with goals for children's learning and development impacts on the quality of early childhood settings (Cleveland et al., 2006; Sylva et al., 2004; National Research Council, 2001; Bennett, 2004; OECD, 2006). It begins with an informed understanding of what children are capable of learning and how they learn effectively. It has specific goals for children that support self-regulation (behaviour, emotion, and attention), identity, social inclusion, health and well-being, language and thinking skills, and physical skills, as well as the foundation knowledge and concepts needed for literacy and numeracy. It provides structure and direction for early childhood practitioners who support the development of capacities and skills while respecting a child's interests and choices (Bennett, 2004).

Many factors contribute to children's early learning and development, so it is difficult for researchers to isolate the impact of any one curriculum (e.g., Reggio Emilia, emergent, High Scope, or Montessori). The effect of an individual teacher, early childhood educator, or family worker can outweigh the effect of a particular curricular approach. Curriculum should be applied in the context of how well it enables

Beyond Our Borders

TE WHARIKI

New Zealand's Te Whariki curriculum is mandatory across all early childhood programs for children from birth to the age of entry into compulsory schooling. Te Whariki is a Maori word that means "woven mat." The curriculum is viewed as strands of principles and goals that are woven together. Te Whariki's principles are:

- the curriculum will empower the child to learn and grow;
- the curriculum will reflect the holistic way children learn and grow;
- the wider world of the family and the community is an integral part of the curriculum; and
- young children learn through responsive and reciprocal relationships with people, places and things.

Te Whariki has five broad goals:

1. the health and well-being of the child is protected and nurtured;
2. children and families feel that they belong in the program;
3. opportunities for learning are equitable and each child's contribution is valued;
4. the languages and symbols of children's cultures are promoted and protected; and
5. the child learns through active involvement in and exploration of the environment.

The guidelines for the fifth goal are that:

- play is valued as meaningful learning and spontaneous play is important;
- confidence and control of one's own body is developed;
- children learn strategies for active exploration; and
- children develop working theories for making sense of their world.

Reflecting on Te Whariki's implementation, early childhood educator Ann Smith (2005) notes that it requires "thought, interpretation, reflection, careful planning and observation" (p. 7). She cautions that "because the goals are so broad it is too easy for early childhood staff to say 'We are doing this already' without a deeper understanding of the meaning and implications of the curriculum. . . . Teachers need a strong theoretical foundation on which to reflect critically about the application of [Te Whariki] in their practice" (p. 8).

Source: Dickinson, 2005; Smith, 2005; Carr & May, 2000.

children's full participation (Bernhard et al., 2006b; Bernhard et al., 1997). What is clear is that having a planned curriculum with specific goals for children's holistic development and families' participation benefits children's enjoyment, development, and learning.

A broad research base on early learning and development informs the development and selection of curriculum approaches (National Research Council, 2001; Galinsky, 2006; Bennett, 2004; Siraj-Blatchfield et al., 2002; OECD, 2006). Learning is fundamentally social and takes place within children's cultural contexts. During the early years, children learn through active engagement, activity, observations, experimentation, and social interactions with others. As they develop an understanding about themselves and others, they learn to regulate their emotions, attend to what is important, and to make plans—all based on the cultural values and practices embedded in their social and physical environments. A planned curriculum can support children's interactions with other children and adults and respect those values and practices.

During early childhood, children learn how to learn. Children construct knowledge through physical activity, social interactions with others, and their own active thinking. Children practise the tools of learning: how to plan, monitor, revise, reflect, investigate, and solve problems, and to see and exchange points of view with others. Through observation and action, children form their own hypotheses, try them out, find out what happens, and formulate their own answers. Children develop learning strategies from first-hand actions with objects in their world, and from exchanging points of view with peers and adults.

Children build new understandings from existing ideas and concepts. Starting from what children know and want to know motivates engagement and excitement about overcoming challenges and solving problems. First-hand, concrete experiences shape ideas that can be expressed symbolically in drawings, paintings, dramatic play, and in verbal and written forms (Greenspan & Shanker, 2004). Learning proceeds from the concrete to the abstract.

Information and skills become knowledge when facts are combined with concepts (Keating, 1998; National Research Council, 2001). For example, literacy emerges when children mimic the reading and writing process. Children derive meaning from text by combining a growing sense of story and the structure of language with the idea that print represents spoken language and thoughts. Children's ability to derive meaning from print text is further enhanced with greater understanding of letter–sound relationships and word recognition (Neuman & Dickinson, 2001; Bennett, 2004).

Longitudinal research in both the United States (Schweinhart & Weikart, 1993) and the United Kingdom (Sylva & Wiltshire, 1993) illustrates that linear, didactic, directive teaching in preschool has a negative effect on children's well-being and later academic success. Young children's development is better supported when programming is active and play-based and encourages children to be self-directed participants by enabling them to take initiative and to make decisions. Providing this type of programming requires practitioners who are knowledgeable about child development and able to use this knowledge to encourage and assist children to explore, question, solve problems, and make decisions.

PARENTING

Families need "just in time" access to **parenting** and child development information and guidance from trusted sources. Informal conversations, family events, and structured sessions provide venues for accessing resources. Early childhood programs can provide a range of parenting activities and supports. They can be linked to home visiting and home-care satellites to extend their reach into the community.

The parent–child relationship is the most powerful influence on children's early development, particularly in the first two years. Learning to respond to and stimulate children from birth builds core competency and coping abilities. Parents learn by doing alongside other parents and early childhood staff. Participation experiences strengthen the involvement and engagement of parents in their own child's early learning and development.

Parent Engagement

Parent engagement refers to the level of direct involvement that parents have in their children's daily lives. Children whose parents have more direct involvement tend to have better social and academic outcomes (Ho & Willms, 1996). While much of the evidence is tied to studies of school-age children, research points to similar patterns in early child development. The amount of time that parents are directly connected with their children is related to child outcomes (Cook & Willms, 2002). Employed parents in Canada seem to be increasing the amount of contact and direct care time spent with their young children (Turcotte, 2007).

The National Longitudinal Survey of Children and Youth has collected data about how often parents read to their children (see Figure 1.1).

At age two, parents read or tell stories to their children an average of 12 times a week and at age five it drops to five times a week. These averages are about the same whether or not the child's mother is working full-time.

Reading aloud daily to young children pays off. Parents who read frequently with their children contribute to their development, particularly their language and reading skills. Studies also show a link between early and frequent reading and social development. Daily reading seems to reduce the likelihood of behaviour problems.

The web of family and community anchors a child's early development. Families are the first and most powerful influence on children's early learning and development. Families live in, and belong to, multiple communities that may support or thwart their ability to support young children's optimal development. Relationships between early childhood settings and families and their communities benefit children when those relationships are respectful of family structure, culture, values, language, and knowledge (Weiss et al., 2006).

Increasing families' participation in their children's early learning and development benefits everyone (Mustard, 2006; Greenspan & Shanker, 2004). The learning and care a child receives from family members is the most powerful influence on development. *Learning* begins as infants seek patterns and begin to recognize the familiar voices and faces of family members; in turn, responses to infant cues set in motion a dynamic learning system. Contingent and sensitive responsiveness to children's signals is a natural form of teaching and learning. As children grow, families can offer learning opportunities that are based on the deep knowledge they have of their children. This

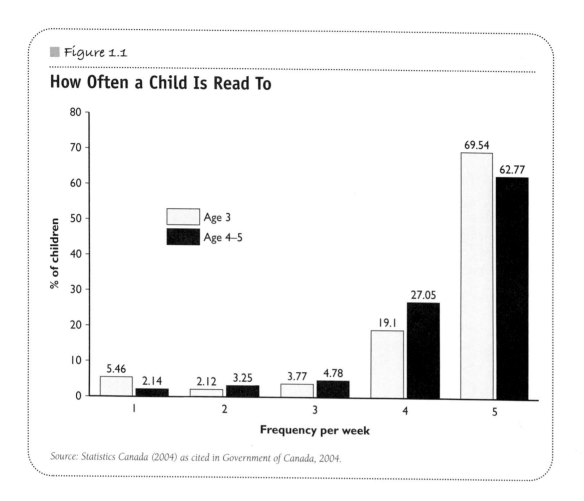

Figure 1.1

How Often a Child Is Read To

Age 3
Age 4–5

% of children

Frequency per week

Frequency	Age 3	Age 4–5
1	5.46	2.14
2	2.12	3.25
3	3.77	4.78
4	19.1	27.05
5	69.54	62.77

Source: Statistics Canada (2004) as cited in Government of Canada, 2004.

can take the form of conversations in the home, shared reading, outings, recreational activities, and other meaningful moment-by-moment experiences. *Care* begins prior to birth and continues throughout life through feeding, sheltering, nurturing, stimulating, and protecting. Care and learning cannot really be separated, since high-quality care includes learning and high-quality learning is dependent on care.

Family involvement in early childhood settings benefits children (Weiss et al., 2006) and multiplies children's opportunities for learning. Parents and other caregivers who are involved in early childhood settings are more likely to actively support children's learning, and their children tend to have positive outcomes in the primary grades (Cleveland et al., 2006; Sylva et al., 2004). Early childhood settings can reinforce the interrelationship of care and learning and the benefits of direct family participation in children's early learning and development.

Family involvement practice in early childhood programs needs to go beyond *whether* parents are involved and focus on *how* they are involved and what happens as a result (Corter & Pelletier, 2004; Epstein, 1995). Parents want to understand how their children develop and learn. They benefit from observations and information about how to support learning and recognize how their children are doing. Parents also benefit from having a say in what is offered in the program and what goes into the curriculum.

Innovation

WHAT DO PARENTS THINK ABOUT PARENTING?

Invest in Kids is a national, charitable organization dedicated to ensuring the healthy social, emotional, and intellectual development of children from birth to age five by strengthening the parenting knowledge, skills, and confidence of all those who touch the lives of Canada's youngest children.

In 1999, Invest in Kids commissioned a national survey of 1643 parents to better understand the context in which young children are being raised in Canada (Oldershaw, 2002). The survey's key findings provide a core understanding of how parents behave toward their children, what they know about child development and parenting, their confidence in their parenting skills, their emotional well-being, and the differences across key subgroups of parents:

- Eighty-four percent strongly agreed that the influence of parents during a child's early years is absolutely critical to the way a child turns out, but less than one in four were knowledgeable about child development.
- Twenty-five percent of parents reported that they were not confident about their knowledge of social, emotional, and intellectual development, and the majority of parents want to know more about child development.
- More than 50 percent did not believe that Canada values its young children or the roles of parents.

What does this mean for early childhood educators?

Source: Oldershaw, 2002.

Early childhood settings provide daily opportunities to connect families with each other. Families have strengths, experiences, and skills that they can share with one another (Gordon, 2005; Wilson, 2005). Families who are newcomers to Canada and far away from relatives and friends who share similar cultural traditions or those who speak languages other than English or French gain from meeting each other. Families also benefit when they learn about childrearing practices from families that have different backgrounds. Informal social networks among families with young children can become valuable resources that promote children's health and well-being (McCain & Mustard, 1999; Weiss et al., 2006).

Family and community involvement is a focus for educational improvement in Canada and internationally. Family involvement in schools is associated with academic success across all socioeconomic groups. Families who are involved are more likely to establish peer networks with other families and to have more information about their children's school. This kind of involvement in school settings includes parenting, communicating, volunteering, learning at home, decision making, and collaborating with the community. These strategies can be useful in organizing family involvement in early childhood settings (Epstein, 1995; Epstein & Sanders, 2002; Epstein, 2005; Corter & Pelletier, 2005).

Family involvement studies in early childhood settings illustrate an array of different program types (see Cleveland et al., 2006). They include home- and centre-based programs and activities. They aim to support families and parents to improve children's early environments and outcomes. Because they are so varied, finding out what really works is difficult. The clearest effects seem to be when programming for parents and other caregivers is combined with programming for their young children (Cleveland et al., 2006; McCain et al., 2007). Engaging parents and other family members in children's activities connects them to their children's early development and ignites the child's learning (Gordon, 2005).

NONPARENTAL CARE

Families require a range of nonparental care arrangements including part-time, full-time, occasional, and respite options. Centres offer full-day (standard school hours) and extended-hour programs (such as those now provided by licensed child care centres) to accommodate parents' work schedules. Figure 1.2 illustrates the use of different types of child care in 2004 and 1994.

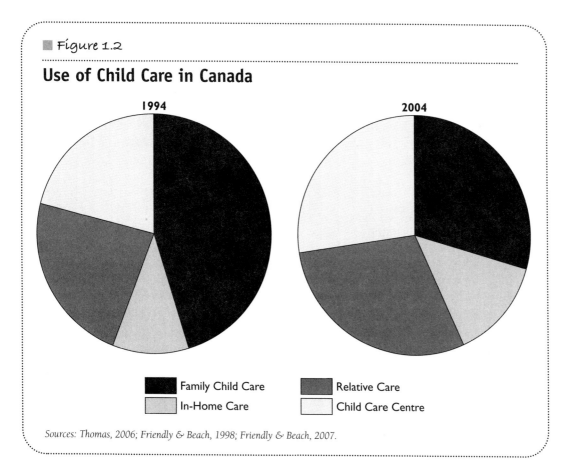

Figure 1.2

Use of Child Care in Canada

1994   2004

Legend:
- Family Child Care
- In-Home Care
- Relative Care
- Child Care Centre

Sources: Thomas, 2006; Friendly & Beach, 1998; Friendly & Beach, 2007.

In the 1950s and '60s, the majority of Canadian families consisted of a wage-earner father and a stay-at-home mother. Since then, there has been a sharp increase in the number of women, and particularly women with young children, in the paid labour force. Today, the majority of families are double-income earners with both parents working outside the home. Over 70 percent of Canadian children have a lone parent or two parents who are in the paid labour force. Only a minority of families with young children fit the profile of that earlier era. The dominant family form in Canada is the dual-earner family with both parents working.

In 1965, less than 30 percent of mothers with children under age six were in the labour force (i.e., working for pay or profit); by 1976 about 33 percent of these mothers were working (Statistics Canada, 2006). By 2006, 64 percent of women with children under age three and close to 70 percent of women whose youngest child was aged three to five years worked for pay or profit. Overall, in 2006, 66 percent of mothers with children under age six years and 78 percent of those whose youngest child was aged six to 15 were employed.

The differences between the employment rates of mothers who are lone parents and those in two-parent families are interesting. In the late 1970s, female lone parents were more likely to work than mothers in two-parent families. Since that time, the employment rate of mothers in two-parent families has surpassed that of mothers who are lone parents. But in recent years, the greatest increase has been found among lone-parent mothers with children under age three. The recent increase in labour participation of lone-parent mothers is, in part, due to changes in welfare policy in some provinces that require mothers of young children to seek employment or engage in training (Beach et al., 2004; Statistics Canada, 2006).

In a generation, the percentage of employed mothers has more than doubled. The entry of the majority of women into the paid work force is the most dramatic social change within families in the past generation. The roles of men and women have shifted, but women still carry the primary responsibility for caregiving (whether for children, the elderly, or other family dependents) and for household tasks.

SOCIAL CAPITAL

Early child development projects can build **social capital**—the collective value of social networks or connections between people and the ways in which people do things for each other (Putnam, 2000). They become universal touch points in the community that are common gathering places and sharing places for young children and their families.

Early childhood programs respect the daily realities of the lives of young children and their families when learning about community life is included in the activities. Community field visits, community experts, and relevant artifacts from home and community bring the local environment into the daily activities of children. It also builds links or social networks within communities. Children benefit from respectful interactions with a variety of community members and the social capital within communities increases. Early childhood programs increase who people know in their own community (McCain et al., 2007).

A Place for Everyone

Strong social capital is only possible when everyone feels a sense of belonging. Early childhood programs recognize that all children have a right to live and learn in an equitable society. They provide an opportunity for getting a place at the table for everyone—making sure that everyone belongs. Demonstration of respect for **diversity, equity,** and **inclusion** are prerequisites for optimal development and learning. They can take into account the differences each child and family brings to an early childhood setting, including appearance, age, culture, ethnicity, race, language, gender, sexual orientation, religion, family environment, and developmental abilities.

Canada is a country of many cultures, religions, and languages, particularly in its urban centres. English or French may be unfamiliar to many children and they need support to maintain and expand their home language as well as learn a new one. For many children, mainstream Canadian culture is different from their home environments. All children gain when they learn early to live together comfortably with others who look and talk differently from themselves (McCain & Mustard, 1999; Shonkoff & Phillips, 2000). Children with developmental difficulties, particularly those who have special needs, can benefit from participation in quality early childhood settings with other children. But despite the good intentions of inclusion, mere exposure to age-appropriate activities and peers is no guarantee that children with special needs will

 ## Beyond Our Borders

COMPENSATORY EARLY CHILDHOOD PROGRAMS

In the United Kingdom the National Childcare Strategy and Sure Start initiatives are expanding early years' programming particularly in low-income communities (OECD, 2001; Rolfe et al., 2003). Local partnerships plan and monitor early years and child care services, including human resource recruitment strategies. Extensive research and evaluation include the review of human resource issues and pedagogical practices. Recent publications and presentations indicate a shift from child care to "early childhood services," with an emphasis on the developmental or educative goals of programs, particularly for children living in socially and economically disadvantaged environments.

The United States continues to support a large-scale compensatory preschool program, Head Start, which is a comprehensive approach intended to reduce the negative impact of poverty on children's early learning and development. In the past decade, awareness about the importance of early child development and learning has motivated considerable expansion of pre-kindergarten programs delivered within the public education system (Barnett, 2003; Burton et al., 2002). Many are offered to children considered to be "**at risk**" and living in low-income communities.

experience positive interactions with their peers or acquire new skills (Frankel, 2004; Irwin et al., 2004). Some children need different balances of child- and adult-directed activity. Special programming strategies may be necessary to support more positive interactions with peers, greater involvement in play opportunities, and social skill development.

Children who are vulnerable (i.e., those experiencing developmental difficulties) may have more difficulties with the social and emotional demands of early childhood settings (Lero et al., 2006). They may need additional attention in supporting their abilities to build relationships, use language, and develop trust.

Early childhood settings can check their curriculum and pedagogy against program standards that reflect inclusion (e.g., see Irwin, 2005). Additional early childhood educators with specific expertise, who can build and support capacity, may be needed to support inclusion. Programs may require technical support and special consultancy or special equipment and materials.

Compensatory, comprehensive early childhood programs are sometimes promoted to ameliorate the impact of social and economic disadvantage. The Beyond Our Borders box on page 27 describes two such large-scale initiatives in the United Kingdom and the United States. These initiatives aim to have a positive impact on the child's home and community life as well as providing an enriched early childhood program. They are trying to increase the social capital of the child's community as well as enhance the quality of the child's home environment.

HEALTH AND WELL-BEING

Early childhood programs, particularly those directed to expecting and new parents, often are designed to support healthy pregnancies, births, and newborns. Expecting and new parents benefit from childbirth and child development information, group discussions, and workshops offered in environments that will connect them to their neighbourhood and community resources. Optimal early child development begins with adequate nutrition from conception onward. Prenatal programs can provide nutritional information and supplements (as necessary) to pregnant women and new parents.

Food and cooking programs provide nutritious meals to children attending centres and demonstrate practices to take home. They are often a draw to engaging families who may be isolated from others in their neighbourhoods and communities.

Resources

Early childhood settings provide information that families can use to enhance children's health and well-being, as well as early interventions that can help children experiencing developmental difficulties and delays. The challenge is often linking young children and their families to needed resources. Early childhood settings can communicate with, and connect families to, other community resources, including public health, primary health care, housing, and specialized services. Early childhood programs can also provide a platform for the delivery of early identification and intervention services, making these resources more accessible to families.

The recommendations of the *Report of the Expert Panel on the 18-Month Well Baby Visit* (Ontario Children's Health Network & Ontario College of Family Physicians, 2005) identify the role of the primary health-care system as pivotal in reaching all young children and their families. The panel recommended an enhanced 18-month well baby visit with a primary care practitioner (family physician, primary care pediatrician, nurse practitioner). This visit is coupled to the last of the immunization visits for several years and includes a developmental review, discussion about healthy child development, information about parenting and community early childhood settings, and referrals to early childhood settings and other specialized services as needed (Williams et al., unpublished).

EARLY CHILDHOOD EDUCATORS AND THE PURPOSE OF EARLY CHILDHOOD PROGRAMS

Early childhood educators understand the benefits of early child development programs, and these benefits are now well documented through research and economic analysis. Such programs make sense in the context of today's Canadian families with young children, from both an investment and a rights perspective. But if the agenda is to move forward in the twenty-first century, early childhood educators are needed to speak up about the benefits and values that will emerge from forging a system that responds to Canadian society, prepares the future work force, and offers every child the right to a nurturing and stimulating early environment.

KEY TERMS

at risk
cognition
compensatory program
curriculum
custodial care
diversity
early child development
early childhood programs
early literacy
emergent curriculum
emergent literacy
emotional maturity
equity
family support programs
Head Start
High Scope
inclusion
inquiry

kindergarten
literacy
Montessori
numeracy
parenting
pathologization
pedagogy
play
pretend play
reflective practice
Reggio Emilia
responsive
school readiness
schoolification
self-regulation
social capital
social competence
symbolic thinking

REFLECTION QUESTIONS

1. How does Te Whariki view young children?
2. What do you view as the primary purpose of early childhood programs?
3. How does the role of early childhood educators reflect the primary purpose of early childhood programs?
4. "Traditional skills associated with school readiness, such as letter–sound awareness, letter recognition, and counting, are byproducts of purposeful play." What does this statement mean?

FOR MORE INFORMATION

1. *Lessons in Learning* is published every two weeks by the Canadian Council on Learning. Each publication is approximately 2000 words and focuses on a specific topic, including those related to early learning. The articles follow a consistent format and provide links to sources of data and related research. To date, the publication has included articles about family literacy, quality child care, and play.

   www.ccl-cca.ca/CCL/Reports/LessonsInLearning/?Language=EN

2. *Our Children, Our Ways: Early Childhood Education in First Nations and Inuit Communities* consists of six videos, with accompanying guides, based on early childhood curriculum areas in diverse First Nations and Inuit communities. This series is a valuable tool for early childhood education training and can be beneficial for any individual or group involved with young Aboriginal children and their families.

   www.rrc.mb.ca/index.php?pid=3262

3. The *Thomson Nelson ECE Resource Centre* is intended to enhance the teaching and learning experience for both instructors and students. The website provides extensive and helpful resources in many different criteria related to early childhood education.

   www.ece.nelson.com

EARLY CHILDHOOD PUBLIC POLICY

CHAPTER

2

CHAPTER OUTLINE

Martha Friendly

The current social policy environment is exciting for early learning and child care and frustrating in Canada as social issues and spending on social programs have returned to the national agenda. In the spring of 2005, the federal government began to sign bilateral agreements with provinces to begin to put the ELCC [early learning and child care] program in place, the March federal budget committed to $5 billion over five years, and work began in the provinces to enhance their child care programs. However, a change in government in early 2006 quickly reversed this decision as the new government broke these agreements, effective March 2007, and replaced new federal spending on child care to an income support program for families.

The international arena has had an important role in shaping the current Canadian ELCC policy environment. Motivating the current context has been the keen interest in ELCC internationally. This interest has taken a number of forms and has been generated by the capacity of early learning and child care programs to contribute to achieving a wide variety of societal goals, such as lifelong learning, women's equality, social integration, amelioration of poverty, and economic prosperity.

The recent reports from the Organisation for Economic Co-operation and Development (OECD) highlighted early childhood education and care programs in 20 countries, including Canada. How did Canada measure up? In spite of our ranking as the fourth wealthiest country, we ranked dead last in the amount of the GDP that we allocate to early childhood programs.

Early childhood programs are defined by the policies of governments. Governments in Canada and internationally have recognized the public's growing awareness of the importance of the early years and desire for programs that respond to the needs of children and families. Generally Canadian governments have not put such programs in place. Instead, program fragmentation continues. While Canadian public investment in early childhood programs is increasing, the rate of increase is not enough. Both a coherent policy framework and substantial public funding are fundamental for putting early childhood programs in place.

Source: Interview with Martha Friendly, Childcare Resource and Research Unit.

chapter Objectives

This chapter will:

1. Define and discuss early childhood public policy
2. Review the history of early childhood program policy in Canada
3. Outline current public policies supporting early childhood programs and related family income benefits in Canada
4. Describe public policy challenges facing early childhood programs

CANADIAN EARLY CHILDHOOD PUBLIC POLICY

Since the late 1990s, Canada's **public policy** landscape has maintained a focus on early child development. The government of Canada expanded its role and commitment to investments in early child development over the decade. Recent joint federal/provincial/territorial agreements and commitments have moved the focus from targeted programs that support children, families, and communities at-risk to policies and funding intended to build a system of benefits and programs for young children and their families.

New public policies that increased families' resources—time and money—include the Canada Child Tax Benefit for children in lower-income families, the Universal Child Care Benefit, and a one-year parental leave for new parents. Spending for and the supply of regulated child care are increasing. The education sector is recognizing the importance of children's early development in setting the foundation for later school learning and academic achievement. Public policies and investments for family support initiatives—from newborn home visiting to expanded family resource centres—have proliferated in every province and territory.

What Is Public Policy?

Public policies are statements of principles underlying governmental action; they can be expressed as local, provincial, or national governmental action such as legislation, resolutions, programs, regulations, appropriations, administrative practices, and/or court

Young children and their families benefit from strong community early childhood programs.

decisions; and they are solutions to public issues. A government's public policy is the set of policies (laws, plans, actions, behaviours) that it chooses. Since governments claim authority and responsibility (to varying degrees) over a large group of individuals, they see fit to establish plans and methods of action that will govern that society.

In any society, governmental entities enact laws, make policies, and allocate resources. This is true at all levels of government. Public policy can be defined as a system of laws, regulatory measures, courses of action, and funding priorities concerning a given topic promulgated by a governmental entity or its representatives.

Individuals and groups often attempt to shape public policy through education, advocacy, or mobilization of interest groups. Shaping public policy is obviously different in Western-style democracies than in other forms of government. But it is reasonable to assume that the process always involves efforts by competing interest groups to influence policymakers in their favour.

A major aspect of public policy is law. In a general sense, the law includes specific and more broadly defined provisions of constitutional or international law. There are many ways that the law can influence how survivors of violence against women are treated and the types of services they receive. Likewise, legislation identifies areas in which research grants can be funded and often determines the amount of funding allocated. Thus, it is not surprising that public policy debates occur over proposed legislation and funding.

Local, Provincial, Territorial, and Federal Governments in Canada

Policymaking in Canada, whether it occurs at the municipal, provincial, or federal level of government, follows an established process, or at least it is intended that it follow an established process. Generally, the bigger the government, the more complex the process is. Each follows a system involving elected officials, committees, staff research and preparation, and public input that varies with the level of government and the particular jurisdiction.

Canada is a federation of ten provinces and three territories, one of which, Nunavut, was created in 1999. The federal government is responsible for matters considered necessary for the development and maintenance of a national community (e.g., foreign policy, defence, citizenship, First Nations people living on reserves, currency, trade and commerce, the postal service, and criminal law). The provinces and territories are responsible for education, social services, health services, labour standards, property and civil rights, language rights, and the administration of the criminal justice system. Control over natural resources is divided between federal and provincial/territorial governments. The provinces and territories frequently delegate certain powers to local governments. Local governments include municipalities and school boards and are often involved in the delivery of social service and education programs. They are also responsible for zoning bylaws, roads, libraries, recreation, policing, and public health programs.

The federal government, the 13 provincial/territorial governments, municipal governments, and the voluntary sector/nongovernment organizations all have roles in Canada's early childhood system. Canada is based on responsible government, meaning that government is made up of elected representatives who have to report to

From the Past

WOMEN, POLITICS, AND THE LAW

In 1918 women won the right to vote in federal elections. In 1919, Agnes McPhail from Ontario became the first woman elected to the federal government.

In the 1920s, Emily Murphy became the first woman appointed as a judge in Canada. Male lawyers and defendants refused to accept her rulings because Murphy was not a legal "person" under the Canadian constitution, and Canada's Supreme Court agreed. Murphy and her supporters fought to have the ruling overturned by the British Privy Council. In 1929, they won the "Persons Case," which declared that women were persons too. Now Canadian law applied to both men and women.

In 2000, the "Famous Five" (Emily Murphy, Irene Marryat Parlby, Nellie Mooney McClung, Louise Crummy McKinney, and Henrietta Muir Edwards, the five women who advocated successfully to have women declared persons in 1929) became the first Canadian women to be honoured with a statue on Parliament Hill in Ottawa.

Source: Heinick, 2004; Friendly & Beach, 2005.

the people in their area. Government decisions have to have the approval of a majority of the elected representatives.

The Federal Government

The federal government is the highest level of government in Canada. It makes laws that apply across Canada. Today there are 308 seats for elected representatives or Members of Parliament from across Canada (see Table 2.1 for a breakdown of representation by province).

The federal government does not have direct responsibility for most early childhood programs. Under Canadian constitutional conventions, social and educational programs like early child development are the responsibility of individual provincial/territorial governments, except for those targeted at specific populations for whom the federal government has responsibility. Exceptions are programs for Aboriginal people, military families, newcomers, and community-based initiatives such as Community Action Program for Children (CAPC), Canadian Prenatal Nutrition Program (CNCP), and Understanding Early Years (UEY).

The federal government supports the development of other early childhood programs through agreements with, and fiscal transfers to, the provinces and territories. Intergovernmental agreements and federal transfer of funds to provincial and territorial governments contribute to early childhood and other programs.

■ Table 2.1

Federal Government Seats

Province/Territory	Federal Government Seats
Ontario	106
Quebec	75
British Columbia	36
Alberta	28
Manitoba	14
Saskatchewan	14
Nova Scotia	11
New Brunswick	10
Newfoundland and Labrador	7
Prince Edward Island	4
Northwest Territories	1
Nunavut	1
Yukon Territory	1
Total	308

Source: Government of Canada, 2007.

The federal government is responsible for a number of family income support programs, including parental leave benefits through Employment Insurance, the Canadian Child Tax Benefit, Child Care, the Child Care Expense Deduction, and the Universal Child Care Benefit.

Provincial and Territorial Governments

Early childhood programs—child care, family support programs, and kindergarten—are the responsibility of provincial and territorial governments. Each province and territory has a program for child care that includes a system of regulation, child care policies, procedures for fee subsidization for certain families, and in most cases, a mechanism to provide regulated settings with some operating funds through a system of grants. Each jurisdiction (with the exception of Prince Edward Island, where child care and kindergarten are part of the same program) also has a separate program of public kindergarten. Provinces and territories are also responsible for income-support programs for low-income families, health care, employment legislation that sets the terms for maternity and parental leave, and post-secondary institutions that train early childhood educators and kindergarten teachers.

Young children across Canada attend early childhood programs.

Local Governments

In the education system, the governing body of the school board/division for a given geographic area operates under powers delegated to it by the province or territory. These elected bodies have a role to play in early child development through their responsibility for the operation of elementary schools and the kindergarten programs within them. In New Brunswick, Manitoba, and Saskatchewan, local governments levy taxes specifically to partly fund the local school system (OECD, 2004). In the territories and the other provinces, schools are funded solely through provincial or territorial general revenues. School boards in Quebec have a mandate to operate child care for school-age children (5 to 12 years) attending kindergarten or elementary school.

Local governments in Ontario have mandated roles in child care services, which include funding, managing services, and policy setting. In addition to these functions, Ontario municipalities operate an estimated 10 percent of regulated child care services in the province. Outside Ontario, local governments do not have a mandated role in child care. However, Vancouver's municipal government has generated revenue for child care through collecting levies from land developers to enable the expansion of spaces. Two municipalities in Alberta operate child care programs and a number in that province also set standards and provide fee subsidies for school-age care.

The History of Early Childhood Program Policy in Canada

To understand the present, it helps to go back to the past and set current events in their historical context. The roots of today's early child development public policy are found

Innovations

FROM TORONTO FIRST DUTY TO TORONTO'S BEST START

Toronto First Duty (TFD) began as a partnership between the City of Toronto and the Toronto District School Board, with support from the Atkinson Charitable Foundation. The TFD partnership tested early childhood service integration but the prime goal was to influence public policy; to bridge the disconnect between child care, education, and family support programs; and to demonstrate the advantages of comprehensive, universal service provision to policymakers, families, and communities.

The TFD concept was tested at five representative sites. Neighbourhood schools partnered with community organizations to demonstrate the core features of service integration—integrated governance, seamless access, parent participation, and an integrated early learning environment planned and delivered by a staff team. Over a four-year period, the sites documented and showcased both the successes and challenges.

The project's findings influenced the Ontario government and are reflected in its "Best Start" strategy. The core elements of the TFD model are incorporated into the Toronto Vision for Children: Best Start Plan. Now, the Toronto District School Board and the city are joined by the Toronto District Catholic School Board, the French language school boards, community agencies, Toronto Public Health, and family support programs in expanding service integration and moving forward on systems change. The goals and objectives of TFD are now contained within Toronto Best Start. The training and assessment tools developed for TFD are now part of the tools available for Toronto Best Start. Learning from TFD continues to inform the ongoing implementation of Toronto Best Start. In short, TFD has fulfilled its goal of making integrated service provision public policy.

The original TFD project sites are now rolled under Toronto's Best Start. They are a demonstration of the TFD vision along the continuum from coordination and collaboration to integration, and are joined by other sites that are demonstrating collaborative efforts through staff teams and high-quality early learning environments.

Sources: Corter et al., 2006; Corter et al., 2007; Bertrand, 2007.

in Canada's earliest crèches, public schools, well-baby clinics, and parent education groups.

The early child care programs of the latter half of the nineteenth century and early twentieth century were established to provide "care" to children of poor mothers who had to work to support their families, and were funded primarily by religious and other charitable organizations. Nursery schools, which began in the 1920s, offered developmental and social experience for preschool age children of middle-class families and

From the Past

CANADA'S FIRST EARLY CHILDHOOD PROGRAMS

FIRST KINDERGARTENS

The provision of care for young children while mothers worked was one of the motivations for Toronto's first kindergarten classes in the public school system in the 1880s. Dr. J.L. Hughes, then director of the Toronto School Board, stated that kindergarten programs for preschool children would ensure that children in elementary school would no longer have to bring their younger siblings along to class with them while their mothers worked (Young, 1994). In 1887, Ontario became the first province to officially recognize kindergartens as part of the public school system, and in 1887 the province began to provide grants to schools to establish kindergarten programs for children three to seven years old (Corbett, 1989).

FIRST "REGULATED" EARLY CHILDHOOD PROGRAM

In 1910, the Infants Hospital in Vancouver opened a crèche for infants and preschool children of working mothers and the Associated Charities and the City of Vancouver jointly organized another crèche. In 1916, both programs were placed under the jurisdiction of the Health Department of British Columbia. In Vancouver the development of early centres to care for children of working mothers was the first instance of government participation in early child development programs (Schulz, 1978).

FIRST PUBLIC HEALTH BOARD

In 1882, Ontario established the first board of health, and public health boards in other provinces followed shortly thereafter. The emerging public health movement in Canada built upon the achievements of nineteenth-century improvements in sanitation and on the dramatic bacteriological discoveries of the 1880s and 1890s (Sutherland, 1976). Public health initiatives brought prenatal and well-baby clinics, milk depots, and home visiting to communities throughout Ontario (Arnup, 1994; Sutherland, 1976). These measures reduced infant deaths and improved maternal health.

were funded primarily by parent fees. The Toronto Board of Education introduced the first Canadian public kindergarten program in 1883 (Prochner, 2000).

During World War II, the federal government introduced emergency legislation, the *Dominion-Provincial War-Time Agreement*, to establish **day nurseries** for children of working women, with provisions for federal–provincial cost-sharing. Both Ontario and Quebec entered into agreements and established preschool and school-age programs (Schulz, 1978).

After the war ended, the federal government stopped the cost-shared program and the Quebec government shut down all the wartime day nursery programs (Schulz, 1978). Attempts to do the same in Ontario were met with strong resistance and a few programs survived. However, rather than merging with the school system, they remained separate programs, with some funding provisions from the province and municipalities operated under the authority of the 1946 Day Nurseries Act.

Changing Families, Changing Public Policy

During the 1960s and 1970s the push for women's equality and increasing numbers of mothers in the paid labour force prompted the federal government to introduce new public policies. These policies have shaped the foundations of child care programs in Canada.

In 1966, the federal government introduced the Canada Assistance Plan (CAP), which enabled federal–provincial cost-sharing of a range of social assistance programs. CAP was a conditional shared-cost program for social assistance programs that prevented poverty and dependence on welfare payments. A significant feature of the Canada Assistance Plan was open-ended funding. Cost-sharing for eligible costs of child care services was introduced in 1972 with changes to the CAP regulations, and the number of child care programs rapidly increased (Schultz, 1978). The changes in the Canada Assistance Plan increased provincial and federal spending on fee subsidies for regulated child care programs. Between July 1971 (when data about the number of child care spaces were first collected) and March 1973, there was a 54.2 percent increase in spaces and a 42.4 percent increase in the number of centres (Health and Welfare Canada, 1973). Unless there were developmental or family problems, the central criterion for eligibility was parental labour force participation.

In 1971 the federal government introduced the Child Care Expense Deduction to the Income Tax Act for parents who choose nonparental care arrangements for their children (Beauvais & Jenson, 2002). To be eligible for the deduction, both parents in two-parent families and lone parents in single-parent families had to be earning an income.

In 1971, the federal government amended Unemployment Insurance (UI) to include a paid maternity leave of up to 15 weeks, providing that new mothers met the eligibility criteria for UI (Beauvais & Jenson). The criteria required that eligible recipients must have paid into the fund for a minimum of 20 weeks. Provincial governments amended labour standards to guarantee maternity leave and ensure working women had access to the UI maternity leave benefits.

In the late 1970s and 1980s, public policies established early childhood programs for parents who were not employed outside of the home and for home-based caregivers. Toy-lending libraries and parent–child drop-in centres developed as programs separate from nursery schools, daycare centres, and kindergarten programs (Kyle & Kellerman, 1998).

A Patchwork of Programs Grows

Throughout the 1970s and 1980s the rules of the Canada Assistance Plan and the Child Care Tax Deduction set the structure for a proliferation of regulated child care programs. Funding for child care programs (through subsidies or tax deductions) was targeted to working parents. Separate funding promoted the development of separate child and family/parenting initiatives and compensatory programs for children and families at risk. Across Canada a patchwork of programs emerged mostly operated by small not-for-profit organizations, although commercial operations dominated in a few provinces (Alberta, Newfoundland, and New Brunswick). Other early child development programs also emerged, but quite separate from the growing numbers of regulated child care programs. The majority of children with working families were cared for in informal arrangements outside of regulated programs.

From Day Care to Child Care: Calls for a National System

Throughout the 1970s, 1980s, and 1990s, governments and advocates danced around proposals calling for a system for the education and care of Canada's young children. Day care became child care. The educative role of child care was recognized along with its role in ensuring equitable opportunities for mothers.

In 1970, the Royal Commission on the Status of Women called for a National Day Care Program (Mahon, 2001) that was both affordable and accessible. The Commission's report stated that all women needed access to publicly supported quality day care in order to allow a real choice between staying at home with young children and entering the paid work force. The report recognized that the responsibility for young children should be shared among the mother, the father, and society. It recommended a national daycare act that would remove daycare from the Canada Assistance Plan with its orientation to families in need. Federal daycare legislation would support provincial legislation that would provide a framework for local delivery (Mahon, 2001). This Royal Commission laid the foundation for a strong advocacy movement for universally accessible child care (Prentice, 2001).

A series of studies and panels recommended universal early childhood programs in Ontario:

- In 1979 the Report of the Commission of Inquiry into the Education of the Young Child recommended that Ontario "should create Centres for the Family and the Education of the Young to serve as the essential instruments for the care of education of children from conception to age eight" (Lapierre & Sherman, 1979, p. 85).
- In 1985, the Report of the Early Primary Education Project of the Ontario Ministry of Education recommended that "the Minister of Education and school boards adjust existing policies related to school closures and use of school space in order to facilitate the provision of educational support services for families and young children in neighbourhood schools" (Ontario Ministry of Education, 1985, p. 116).
- In 1990, *Children First*, the Report of the Advisory Committee on Children's Services, recommended that the "Ontario government, in partnership with parents, service providers and others whose lives touch children, must develop a public agenda to ensure that the entitlements of children are met. The agenda will guide future legislative, planning and policy development in all ministries that have a direct or indirect influence on supports and services to children" (Ontario Ministry of Community and Social Services, 1990, p. 147).
- In 1994, the Ontario Premier's Council on Health, Social Justice and Well-Being recommended in *Yours, Mine and Ours* that "to ensure a balance in work and family

life that allows parents some flexibility when they need it, particularly when children are in their early years, there should be family-friendly policies in the workplace" (Premier's Council on Health, Well-Being and Social Justice, 1994, p. 49).

- Later in 1994, in *For the Love of Learning,* the Royal Commission on Learning recommended that "Early Childhood Education (ECE) be provided by all school boards to all children from three to five years of age whose parents/guardians choose to enrol them. ECE would gradually replace existing junior and senior kindergarten programs, and become a part of the public education system" (Royal Commission on Learning, 1994, p. 67).

In 1996, the federal government eliminated CAP altogether and replaced it with a block transfer—the Canada Health and Social Transfer (CHST). At the same time, federal funds were reduced considerably. Thus, the conditions of CAP were no longer available to apply to child care funding, while the federal government's spending power diminished with its dwindling share of funding. Federal–provincial cost-sharing for child care as a social service ended with the end of Canada's national welfare program. However, the conditions of CAP continued to shape how provinces and territories fund child care fee programs through fee subsidies that are conditional on parental employment status.

The Early Child Development Agenda

During the late 1990s and into the early 2000s, public policy discussions shifted from a focus on daycare and child care to a focus on early child development. The recognition of early childhood as a determinant of health and well-being fuelled a call for a comprehensive approach to early childhood programs. Child care programs were intended to be part of that vision but sometimes were left out of specific policy proposals and initiatives. The early child development vision was articulated in the landmark Ontario Early Years Study (McCain & Mustard, 1999), which is summarized in the Innovations box on page 43.

National Children's Agenda

In 1997 the federal government announced the National Children's Agenda (NCA) as a major initiative to address children's health and well-being. It launched a federal/provincial/territorial dialogue to work together to develop a comprehensive strategy to improve the well-being of children. The NCA set out a shared vision for ensuring that children in Canada have the best possible start in life and the necessary opportunities to realize their full potential. Its goal was to ensure that Canada's children are:

- healthy and safe emotionally;
- safe and secure;
- successful at learning; and
- socially engaged and responsible.

The NCA led to new public policies, including the National Child Benefit, the Early Childhood Development (ECD) Agreement, and the Multilateral Framework on

Innovations

ONTARIO EARLY YEARS STUDY

The 1999 *Early Years Study* (McCain & Mustard, 1999) provided a new frame of understanding about early child development that has galvanized isolated pockets of people, activity, and programs across Canada; opened up political space at all levels of government; and helped to move the early childhood agenda into a prominent place on the public's radar screen.

The central recommendation of the report called for "a first 'tier' program for early child development, as important as the elementary and secondary school system and the post-secondary education system. The system should consist of community-based centres operating at the local level within a provincial framework" (McCain & Mustard, 1999, p. 20).

The report and its recommendations have influenced early childhood policies across Canada. Eight years after the study popularized the findings, interest and investments in early child development in general, and early learning and child care in particular, have expanded.

The *Early Years Study* has also had a significant impact on policies in other parts of the world, including Jamaica, Colombia, Brazil, Chile, Pakistan, Eastern Europe, Australia, and China (Young, 2007).

Early Learning and Child Care, as well as short-lived bilateral federal/provincial early learning and child care agreements in 2005 through 2007. Under the NCA, the federal government expanded supports and services provided to young children and their families.

Early Child Development Agreement

On September 11, 2000, the prime minister and premiers (with the exception of the premier of Quebec) signed the Early Child Development (ECD) Agreement intended to build on existing services and supports, to make them more coordinated and widely available. The objectives of this initiative are "to promote early child development so that, to their fullest potential, children will be physically and emotionally healthy, safe and secure, ready to learn, and socially engaged and responsible, and to help children reach their potential and to help families support their children within strong communities" (Canadian Intergovernmental Conference Secretariat, 2000, p. 2).

The prime minister and premiers agreed on four key areas for action:

- Prenatal, birth, and infancy programs and information, and infant screening programs.
- Parenting and family supports, including family resource centres, parent information, and home visiting.

- Early childhood development, learning, and care, including preschools, child care, and targeted developmental programs for young children.
- Community supports, including community-based planning and service integration.

The federal government continues to transfer $500 million annually to the provinces and territories for programs under the ECD Agreement.

The ECD Agreement announcement did not herald an era of European-like support of early childhood programs for all children in Canada, but it did inject additional dollars in to early child development programs and signalled the arrival of early child development on the public policy agenda. In the context of the fractious federal/provincial/territorial relations on health care and other programs, the agreement on early child development was strong evidence that the issue of early child development continues to have political currency and public support in the twenty-first century. For many, the federal/provincial/territorial agreement was a down payment on an early childhood system in Canada.

ABC Policy (Anything but Child Care)

The mandate was broad and ensured that provinces or territories could sidestep the issue of child care provision (clearly the most expensive and usually least available component of early child development programs). A number of policymakers seemed to set up an artificial distinction between "child-care" and "child development," leading to policies that seem to be ABC—"anything but child-care" (McCuaig, 2004). Care is viewed as a parental responsibility and government involvement is only necessary to support the labour force participation of low-income women. Developmental programs are viewed as stimulation, enrichment, and school readiness programs for young children and families. Much emphasis is placed on information and resources to parents.

In fact, little was spent on regulated child care through this agreement, but six provinces (the four Atlantic provinces, Manitoba, and Saskatchewan) did commit a portion of the funding to child care. British Columbia, Ontario, and Alberta allocated nothing to regulated child care. In 2001, a total of 8 percent of early childhood development funds were spent on regulated child care (Friendly et al., 2002).

The agreement did not contain any specific measures to ensure that provincial/territorial governments would use the federal dollars within even the very wide parameters that are stipulated. Nor did the agreement commit the provincial/territorial governments to increased spending on early child development programs. It did commit the participating governments to monitor and report back to Canadians using 11 indicators on five domains of development.

Parental Leave and Benefits

In 2000 the federal government more than tripled the amount of time an eligible mother or father could receive parental benefits through Employment Insurance after the birth or adoption of a baby. The amended Employment Insurance Act increased the maximum length of parental and adoption benefits for eligible parents from 10 to 35 weeks. The maternity benefits remained at 15 weeks. Effectively, new parents could access up to one year of maternity and parental leave after the birth or adoption of a baby.

Regulated child care programs across Canada are central to an early childhood system.

Multilateral Framework on Early Learning and Child Care

In March 2003, building on the ECD Agreement, the federal, provincial, and territorial ministers responsible for social services agreed to a framework to improve access to affordable, quality, and provincially and territorially regulated early learning and child care programs and services. The objective of the Multilateral Framework Agreement on Early Learning and Child Care is to further promote early childhood development, and to support the participation of parents in employment or training by improving access to affordable, quality early learning and child care programs and services.

The federal government allocated a budget of $900 million over five years to this new agreement. An additional $150 million over two years was announced in the 2004 budget, for a total of $1.05 billion. Unlike the ECD Agreement, these funds had to be spent on regulated child care, and unlike Canada Assistance Plan spending, they were solely federal, not cost-shared. The dollars are transferred to the provinces and territories for regulated early learning and child care programs for children under six, primarily for direct care and early learning for children in settings such as child care centres, family child care homes, preschools, and nursery schools.

QUAD—Quality, Universality, Accessibility, and Developmental

In the 2004 federal election campaign, the Liberal Party included in its election platform a five-year, $5-billion "Foundations" program to accelerate the establishment of a Canada-wide early learning and child care system. Child care, or early learning and child care (ELCC), figured prominently in the 2004 federal election, the October 2004 Speech from the Throne, and the February 2005 federal budget, and the federal government committed an additional $5 billion over five years to an ELCC system based on the four principles.

Moving Forward, Moving Backwards: Early Learning and Child Care Agreements

On April 29, 2005, the governments of Canada and Manitoba struck a historic agreement-in-principle on early learning and child care. This was followed by a similar agreement between the federal government and the other nine provinces. The agreements built on a meeting of the federal, provincial, and territorial ministers responsible for social services in November 2004 and a subsequent meeting in February 2005. These ministers (except the one for Quebec) agreed to shared principles to guide the development of a new national system of early learning and child care.

A series of preliminary bilateral agreements for ELCC were signed with each of the provinces. Ontario, Quebec, and Manitoba signed funding agreements with the federal government. A subsequent election of a Conservative government in 2006, however, has negated these agreements. In spite of considerable opposition, the federal government terminated the signed agreements in March 2007. The Universal Child Care Benefit (UCCB) was instituted in 2006 to replace the federal/provincial child care agreements and the annual $249 Young Child Benefit paid for children under seven years old. The UCCB is an income benefit policy that is paid directly to families regardless of their use of child care programs. It is not funding for early childhood programs.

EARLY CHILDHOOD PROGRAMS AND FAMILY INCOME BENEFITS

The first part of this chapter outlined the history of early childhood programs, ending with the broad federal/provincial/territorial agreements that are constructing the current context for early child development programs. Public policies related to early childhood programs range from public health regulations that monitor the hygiene in child care centre kitchens to provincial policies about the age children can start public school kindergarten programs and policies that transfer financial dollars from the federal government to provincial and territorial governments for specific early childhood programs.

In Canada there are approximately 2 million children aged five and under. These children and their families may participate in a variety of early child development programs scattered across the country. Each of Canada's 14 jurisdictions (ten provinces, three territories, and the federal jurisdiction) has it own approach to early childhood, including a number of programs for "care" and "education" as well as family support programs that address poverty issues or support parents' abilities to nurture their children. Early childhood programs are complemented by maternity and parental leave and benefits, the Child Care Tax Deduction, the National Child Benefit, and the Universal Child Care Benefit.

Regulated Child Care Programs

Child care centres and most nursery schools and preschools operate as regulated (or licensed) programs under provincial or territorial child care legislation, with limited public funding. Provinces and territories have regulated child care that includes part-time or half-day programs (such as nursery school or preschool), full-time centres, and

Beyond Our Borders

EARLY CHILDHOOD AND FAMILY POLICY IN FINLAND AND SWEDEN

Families in Finland enjoy one of the most comprehensive parental leave and home child care support systems in the world. Parents have approximately 43 weeks of parental leave, followed by a period until the child is three that they can opt for either (a) caring for the child at home on care leave and receiving child home care allowance, (b) having the child cared for in a private daycare with the private child care allowance, or (c) having the child cared for in a municipal daycare. As of 1996, the parents of all children under school age are guaranteed the right to a space in a daycare provided by their local authority.

Children enter formal schooling in Finland at age seven. Until 2000, children aged three to six were cared for in child care/nursery school settings. In August 2000, preschool reform initiated a preschool education (administered by the Ministry of Education), which provides 700 hours of preschool education during the academic year. This free voluntary program is comparable to full-day kindergarten, although it is provided for six-year-olds (rather than five-year-olds, as is typical in many countries) and can be provided either in daycare or school settings.

Sweden has extensive social, family, and health benefits that ease the responsibility for child care faced by families in many developed countries in the world. Such entitlements include house and child benefit allowances, parental leave for maternity and sickness, and full-coverage health care. In addition, families have access to preschool for children up to age six. These programs are called "preschool" because of a long-time philosophy in Sweden that care and education should be linked. There is now a preschool *class* (similar to our kindergartens) provided for all six-year-olds on a half-time basis. Although there are no national statutory regulations for staff-to-child ratios, monitoring is compulsory and ongoing, and ratios average 1:5/6 in preschools and 1:13 in preschool classes. Mandatory full-time school attendance begins at age seven, as in Finland. The government guarantees all children whose parents work or who are in school full-time a space in preschool from age one onwards (paid maternity leave benefits for 15 months ensure that all infants are cared for by their parents). This policy has resulted in a ten-fold increase in child care spaces in the past two decades. During that time, the parental fee component has increased from 10 percent to 16.5 percent of the total cost.

Sources: Ministry of Social Affairs and Health, 2004; OECD, 2001, 2006.

home-based family child care. Provincial or territorial legislation stipulates requirements for service operations and funding arrangements, usually within a social or community services ministry. These requirements are discussed in more detail in Chapter 5. The government of Canada is also responsible for on-reserve regulated child care in First Nations communities.

Provincial and territorial jurisdictions subsidize some or all of the costs for regulated child care for low-income parents. Eligibility requirements include parental employment or at-risk social conditions and low family income. In most jurisdictions, the number of eligible parents exceeds the limitations on numbers of subsidies. The subsidy often does not cover the full parent fee, and the gap can be significant. Child care fee subsidies were shaped by federal–provincial cost-sharing legislation (the Canada Assistance Plan, which was introduced in 1966 and eliminated in 1995), which accounts for the common elements across provincial and territorial subsidy systems. However, there are also significant differences in the types of child care programs that parents can access with fee subsidies, in financial eligibility levels, in maximum and minimum user fees, and in conditions and limitations on eligibility.

Provincial and territorial governments also provide a range of one-time and recurring grants to regulated child care centres and family child care programs. The amounts and types of funding vary widely across jurisdictions. Many of the grants come in the

Innovations

CENTRES DE LA PETITE ENFANCE IN QUEBEC

In 1997, Quebec began the overhaul of its child care and kindergarten system with the introduction of a new family policy. The massive reorganization of the child care system transformed it into the early childhood care and education component of the new family policy. The reform was indeed substantial and ambitious. Quebec revised its family policy away from sizeable payments to parents on the birth of children to a multi-pronged approach: maternity/parental leave for employed and self-employed parents that covered up to 75 percent of salary, a progressive child allowance, and low-cost child care.

Children up to age four are the responsibility of the Ministry of the Family. Children in this age group are served by Centres de la petite enfance, or CPEs. Each CPE provides both group and family child care for 300 families. The majority of programs (80 percent) are operated by parent boards (at least two-thirds must be parent users). CPEs began by joining up existing neighbourhood child care centres and family child care programs. (At age five children begin school full-time. When 12 or more parents request child care, the Ministry of Education requires school boards to establish before- and after-school programs. The main focus for school-age children is to provide recreation and assistance with school assignments.)

CPEs now receive 87 percent of their funding from government, and parents pay a flat fee of $7 per day (the amount increased from $5 in 2003). Children of parents on social assistance are entitled to free enrollment for 22.5 hours a week. The policy objectives facilitate work–family balance, encourage the labour force participation of parents on social assistance, and provide children—no matter the financial status of their parents—with high-quality early childhood education and care that fosters their social, emotional, and cognitive development, as well as readiness for school.

The system, fuelled by high demand, grew rapidly to serve nearly 235 000 children, in 178 000 spaces, by 2004. Another 35 000 children are waiting for spots to open up. The goal is 200 000 spaces by 2008. About 63.4 percent of young children were in CPEs in 2003–04. Recent analysis of data about enrollment in CPEs indicates that children from all socioeconomic groups are equitably represented. In other words, children from poorer families are as likely to be enrolled in a CPE as children from more affluent families (Cleveland, 2007).

Quebec took steps to improve quality in CPEs by establishing curriculum expectations, raising staff qualifications, and improving salaries and benefits. Previously, only one in three staff members required a diploma; now two-thirds of staff in CPEs must have a college diploma or university degree in early childhood education. A series of labour actions in 2000 led to the establishment of a province-wide wage scale negotiated between the government and the CPE association. Program supervisors now average $30 per hour, trained staff members earn about $19 per hour, and a pension plan has been established.

The new government that took office in 2003 was determined to restructure the system. Parent fees were raised by $2 a day, $40 million was cut from the $1.3-billion budget, centres were not allowed to build up reserve funds, and a preference was shown for commercial centres and family child care.

The original vision for CPEs included plans to forge links with CLSCs (community health and social service centres) in local neighbourhoods. CLSCs provide direct health care, pre- and postnatal supports, family supports, and early identification and intervention programs. However, their funding is now being curtailed and, except for a few isolated situations, these links are not happening.

A recent study (Japel & Tremblay, 2005) shows that only a quarter of programs are meeting quality objectives. Quality is most problematic in for-profit centres, 27 percent of which were graded inadequate (compared to 7 percent of CPEs).

Children from poorer families are more likely to be in for-profit child care settings that are of inferior quality (20 percent versus 9 percent of children from well-off families). This problem is exacerbated by the service design. It is difficult to establish and maintain parent-run programs in low-income and transient communities; therefore, for-profit operators are filling the gap.

Sources: Friendly & Beach, 2007; Tougas, 2004; Japel & Tremblay, 2005; Cleveland, 2007.

Child care settings provide opportunities for early learning while parents are working.

form of wage grants to raise staff salaries. Apart from Quebec, overall the proportion of provincial/territorial child care funding that is allocated to fees varies from 21 percent in Nunavut to 76 percent in Alberta (Friendly & Beach, 2005).

Quebec no longer uses fee subsidies to fund child care services. It has established Centres de la petit enfance (CPEs) to provide educational child care in centres and family child care homes for children aged four and under. CPEs receive capital and operating grants and parents pay $7 per day. Low-income parents may have the fee waived. See the Innovations box on page 48 for more about Quebec's CPEs.

As noted in Chapter 1, regulated child care services are viewed primarily as a labour force support or an early intervention by provincial or territorial governments. Child care fee subsidies are tied to parental paid employment or to ameliorate at-risk conditions. Only Quebec has recognized and allocated funding to child care based on its value in promoting optimal child development and learning.

In the past few years, the overall spending and supply of child care programs has increased. Major policy differences continue in the way child care is organized and managed across provinces and territories. Quebec has seen significant gains in funding, regulations demanding higher program standards, and a tripling in capacity. Manitoba is increasing its direct funding to child care settings, while British Columbia has withdrawn direct operating funding (effective March 2007).

Kindergarten and Pre-Kindergarten

Kindergarten

Provincial and territorial governments have responsibility for the delivery of kindergarten programs within the public education system for five-year-old children (and sometimes four-year-old children) under ministries of education. Kindergarten programs that are publicly funded are offered to all five-year-old children and some four-year-old children in the school system under the authority of provincial/territorial education legislation, usually on a part-time basis.

Approximately 335 000 five-year-old children and another 128 000 children under age five attend public kindergarten programs in Canada. Except for Prince Edward Island, public kindergarten is part of the public education system and is the responsibility of ministries or departments of education. In Prince Edward Island, kindergarten is delivered by regulated child care programs. Kindergarten is mandatory in New Brunswick, while attendance is optional in other jurisdictions.

Kindergarten programs offered within the public education system are usually part-time (2.5 hours per day) but are offered for the full school day in New Brunswick, Quebec, and Nova Scotia. Full school-day kindergarten is also offered by some school boards in other jurisdictions. In many instances, kindergarten is delivered on alternative full days rather than for half a day, five days a week.

All teachers in kindergarten programs operated by the public education system are required to have a degree and a recognized teaching credential, but no early childhood education (ECE) specialization. In Prince Edward Island, where kindergarten is part of regulated child care programs, a two-year ECE diploma is the required teacher qualification. The numbers of children per class and teaching assistants varies across jurisdictions.

Kindergarten curriculum is guided by school board and provincial/territorial education ministries or departments. Some must meet province-wide guidelines and assess children's progress in meeting specified learning expectations. Generally, kindergarten curriculum is described as play-based and developmentally appropriate.

Kindergarten is a publicly funded **entitlement** and there are few instances of parent fees. The costs of kindergarten programs are rolled into elementary school budgets and are thus difficult to disaggregate to calculate actual costs per kindergarten child.

Pre-Kindergarten

In Ontario **Junior Kindergarten** is available in almost all school boards and more than 90 percent of all four-years-olds attend. Other provinces offer kindergarten programs for some four- or three-year-olds. These programs are targeted to children or communities deemed to be at risk, but are not province-wide. In Quebec, kindergarten for four-year-olds is offered in inner-city neighbourhoods as an extension of the school system. Nova Scotia offers **pre-kindergarten** to four-year-olds within public schools as part of a pilot project. There is limited kindergarten for four-year-olds through the public education system available in Winnipeg. Saskatchewan has introduced more than 100 pre-kindergarten classes for three- and four-year-old children living through designated community schools that are located in high-need areas.

Table 2.2 provides information about kindergarten for younger children in those provinces that provide this service.

Early Identification and Intervention

Early identification and **early intervention** are more of a concept than a specific early childhood program category (Shonkoff & Meisels, 2000). Early identification and

■ Table 2.2

Kindergarten for Younger Children

Newfoundland and Labrador	Kinderstart is a short-term school readiness program operated by school boards.
Nova Scotia	Pre-primary pilot program for four-year-olds.
Quebec	Two programs are available for some four-year olds: *pré-maternelle,* a part-day program initially established for inner-city children (enrollment of 6932 in 2001) and *passe-partout,* a short-term program, originally developed for low-income children in rural areas.
Ontario	Most school boards offer Junior Kindergarten for children who are age four by December 31. Enrollment was 114 669 in 2001.
Manitoba	Two school divisions offer a nursery school program for four-year-olds. Enrollment figures are not available. Early Child Development Initiative offers school readiness programs to preschool children.
Saskatchewan	Pre-kindergarten may be provided part-day for four-year-olds deemed to be at risk and living in targeted communities that meet specific criteria.
Alberta	Children with special needs may attend early childhood services (kindergarten) at age two-and-a-half if they have a severe disability or at age three-and-a-half if they have a moderate disability.
British Columbia	Strong Start, a family resource program with a specific child development focus, is offered in 16 schools in 2007 and is expected to expand across the province. Ready Set Go is a short-term school readiness program.

Sources: Friendly & Beach, 2005; OECD, 2006; McCain et al., 2007.

intervention range from screening and other approaches to identify the early signs or symptoms of a problem with health or child development to the services provided to intervene or treat the problem. Developmental problems that are identified and addressed early are less likely to have a long-term impact on a child's development.

Early intervention target groups vary (Shonkoff & Phillips, 2000). Broad-based health promotion initiatives, including early identification of possible developmental problems, are usually aimed at the general public. Compensatory early childhood programs are targeted to at-risk young children, families, and communities, and specific treatment services are aimed at young children with developmental disabilities.

In spite of the diversity within early identification and intervention initiatives, research findings show that effective initiatives share common characteristics (Irwin, 2005; McCain et al., 2007; Shonkoff & Phillips, 2000):

- Strategies of early intervention are grounded in an understanding about the typical sequence of early human development and the typical variation in its timing.
- All developmental domains are based on an interaction between genetic predisposition and early experience. Nothing is shaped only by genetic inheritance or elements of the environment.
- Early brain development underlies development in all domains and is a product of the interaction of genetic expression and experiences from conception onward.

- The relationships young children have with family members and other primary caregivers have a major impact on their social, emotional, language, cognitive, and physical development. Responsive, reciprocal, and nurturing relationships promote optimal growth and development, regardless of disabilities, risk factors, or illness.
- The ability of families and other caregivers to meet the individual needs of young children is influenced by their own emotional, financial, and social resources.
- Early identification is not an end goal. Identifying problems without having supports and resources in place may have a negative impact on children's early development.
- Early intervention programs may be set up to affect children directly through structured experiences in compensatory early childhood programs or prescribed therapies. Other early intervention programs are set up to indirectly have an impact on children through the caregiving environment. Interventions that focus on children's primary caregivers include information, instruction, support, and assistance in accessing resources and services.

Examples of Canadian early identification and intervention programs include British Columbia's Infant Development Program; Manitoba's Baby First and Early Start; and Ontario's Healthy Babies, Healthy Children, the 18-month Well Baby Check, the Preschool Speech and Language, the Infant Hearing Program, and the Pre-school Intervention Program for Children with Autism.

Out-of-School Programs

Several types of out-of-school programs are offered across Canada. Regulated child care programs for school-age children (ages six to ten or twelve years old) provide programming for children outside of school hours and on school holidays. Except for Quebec, regulations for school-age child care programs are included in provincial child care legislation and may stipulate specific requirements (e.g., staff-to-child ratios) for school-age centres and regulated family child care. Most provincial child care regulations do not address the specific developmental needs of this age group in requirements for staff qualifications, regulations, and physical environment (CCCF, 2006). While most jurisdictions offer some level of fee subsidies to parents below a minimum income level, this funding is often not extended into the school years.

Quebec has integrated out-of-school programs into its overall family policy. School-age child care centres are operated through the education system in school spaces. Staff are employees of the local school board and report to the school principal. They are not covered by provincial child care regulations and there are no specific training requirements. Maximum parent fees are $7 per day.

Recreation programs operated by municipal governments or local school boards also provide a range of programming for children. However, these programs are generally for limited time periods and do not cover the child care needs of families with working parents and school-age children.

Out-of-school programs are essential programs to support optimal development in the middle years (Child and Youth Health Network for Eastern Ontario, 2005). Public policy for out-of-school programs helps parents earn a living to support their children. Out-of-school programs offer children opportunities to develop stable friendships and can encourage a sense of belonging to their school and community. Programs can provide children with opportunities to develop competencies as they begin to define their identities. Out-of-school programs provide physical and arts activities that are not part of the school day.

Family Support Programs

Family resource and parenting support programs typically do not have regulatory requirements but are shaped by the requirements of a plethora of public and nongovernment funding sources. Provincial and territorial governments provide and/or support a range home visiting programs, family resource programs, and parenting programs. **Family support programs** that are primarily intended to support parenting capacity supplement kindergarten and child care programs in promoting children's early learning and development. Program activities may be primarily parent education—that is, they are directed at parents or other primary caregivers. Other family support programs are two-generational and offer programming to parents (or primary caregivers) and their children.

Compared to the relatively universal social script of kindergarten and the more complex but finite forms of child care, family support programming is very diverse and often occurs in combination with programming or interventions for the child. A Canadian definition that is generally accepted is "Family support programs are community-based organizations working with children, families and caregivers to enhance strengths, to build capacities and to promote healthy development" (Malcolmson, 2002).

In Canada all levels of government, including federal, provincial/territorial, and local (municipal, school board, and public health authorities), may be involved in the funding, planning, and delivery of family support programs. There are an estimated 2500 family resource programs (FRPs) across Canada, serving approximately 40 percent of families with a child under age six (Malcolmson, 2004). While some FRPs target specific populations—usually children deemed to be at risk—the majority provide support to families across the socioeconomic spectrum. FRPs deliver a range of services, including information about community resources, toy and equipment lending, parent/child play groups, adult educational upgrading, and assistance to families seeking affordable housing. They are known by names such as family place, neighbourhood house, *maison de la famille,* military family resource centre, parenting and family literacy centre, Community Action Program for Children, Early Years Centre, and parent–child resource centre.

Military family resource centres, located on Armed Forces bases and stations, serve military families. The federal government provides core funding for each centre through a formal agreement and requires that each provide specific core services, including information about local resources, referrals, parenting education, and emergency child care. The centres are operated by a community-based elected board of directors. Individual centres may provide other child and family services, such as regular child care, and may also receive funding from other sources. Whether or not parents are required to pay a membership fee or are charged for a service depends upon the individual centre and sometimes upon the specific service being provided. The federal government directly funds military family resource centres (approximately $4 million annually).

Family support programs provide an opportunity for parents and other family caregivers to connect with other families and to become more actively involved in their child's early learning and development.

Aboriginal Early Child Development Programs

The federal government supports **Aboriginal** early child development and early learning/child care through several initiatives. Aboriginal early child development programs include Health Canada's Aboriginal Head Start on Reserve and Urban and Northern programs, Human Resource Development Canada's First Nations and Inuit Child Care Initiative, and Health Canada's Fetal Alcohol Spectrum Disorder program in First Nations and Inuit communities. The federal government also supports a broad range of other federal programs, including Health Canada's Community Action Program for Children, Canada Prenatal Nutrition Program, Brighter Futures, and Indian Affairs Canada's First Nations Child and Family Services, National Child Benefit Reinvestments, Special Education Program, and Parental Engagement Programs.

Aboriginal child care programs are delivered on-reserve through different provincial/territorial arrangements.

The 2004 Organisation for Economic Co-operation and Development (OECD) review of Canadian early childhood programs concluded that Canada should draw on expertise and experience in other countries with significant indigenous populations, particularly Finland, Norway, and New Zealand:

- Norway's indigenous population, the Sami, constitute 1.7 percent of the population. Sami-language early childhood programs are funded generously wherever there is a concentration of Sami families (OECD, 2001).
- Three different Sami languages are spoken in Finland. Early childhood programs support the Sami language and make Sami culture a part of daily activities and

experiences in cooperation with children's parents and other representatives of the Sami culture (OECD, 2001).

- The early childhood education and care curriculum for all children in New Zealand is Te Whariki, which is described in Chapter 1. It was developed in collaboration

 Beyond Our Borders

INTERNATIONAL ABORIGINAL EARLY CHILDHOOD PROGRAMS

Drawing on international experiences and studies, several critical success factors emerge for Aboriginal early childhood programs (Bernard van Leer Foundation, 2000; OECD, 2000, 2001). The following recommendations for practice are endorsed by the United Nations:

- *Direct support to indigenous people.* Supports are needed to ensure that indigenous people (global term frequently used for "Aboriginal") have the resources needed to develop early child development programs that are consistent with their own vision and values.
- *Appropriate curricula.* The curriculum and pedagogy offered in early child development programs should be consistent with children's lived experience, cultural and linguistic background, and emerging skills and abilities. In some instances it is necessary that early childhood curricula for indigenous children be constructed in a way that finds a common ground between an indigenous perspective of appropriate early child development programs and pre-existing program frameworks.
- *Teachers/early childhood educators.* Early childhood educators should come from indigenous communities. If this is not possible, non-indigenous staff will probably need special training to understand the children's culture.
- *Bilingual teaching and language acquisition in the mother tongue.* Children's language development is best supported by preschool and primary school programs that combine the child's mother tongue with the mainstream language.
- *Involvement and participation of parents and other family members.* Early child development programs that involve parents and other family members are able to amplify opportunities for learning.
- *Community-based structures.* Infrastructures that are decentralized create more opportunities for local input in developing early child development programs that accommodate parents and families in indigenous communities.
- *Viability.* Successful indigenous early child development programs need available resources and a supportive political climate.

with Maori groups and incorporates Maori concepts of belonging and contribution. New Zealand preschool and kindergarten programs are based in a biculturalism that respects and celebrates the language and values of its indigenous people.

Integrated Early Childhood Programs

Increasing interest in **seamless** early childhood programs that integrate kindergarten, child care, and family support programs has led to community experimentation and considerations of new public policies. Some jurisdictions are reorganizing the delivery of early childhood programs to reflect the new research and international developments pointing towards increased integration and delivery of comprehensive and integrated early childhood programs (OECD, 2006).

In Chapter 10, we will review specific strategies related to integrating existing programs. Here we will consider a few of the public policy innovations in Canada that establish the policy framework to accommodate integrated early childhood programs. Five of these are outlined in the Innovations box below.

Innovations

NEW POLICY DIRECTIONS FOR INTEGRATED EARLY CHILDHOOD PROGRAMS

Provincial governments have taken steps towards the kinds of public policy infrastructures that would be necessary for a comprehensive early childhood system. Five examples are outlined here:

- *Healthy Child Manitoba Act.* Established in 1999, Manitoba's Healthy Child Committee of Cabinet is a standing committee comprising eight ministers and remains the only standing cabinet committee in Canada dedicated to the well-being of children and youth. It has established a budget process designed to allocate provincial expenditures to evidence-based investments in early childhood development. In 2001, Manitoba began funding parent–child coalitions across the province to anchor government policies in communities through partnerships. Equally important are the advocacy efforts on behalf of children. In 2006 the government tabled legislation to entrench the healthy child structures within government and the community.

  www.gov.mb.ca/healthychild/index.html

- *Saskatchewan Early Learning.* Saskatchewan has amalgamated responsibility for child care, pre-kindergarten, and kindergarten under its education

(continued)

ministry. Despite the cancellation of the federal–provincial child care agreements, the province is proceeding with plans to expand half-day pre-kindergarten to all four-year-olds. The programs are operated by school divisions and enhanced by partnerships with child care and other human service agencies. They are capped at 16 children, staffed by schoolteachers, and designed to support child development and parenting capacity.

 www.earlychilddevelopment.ca/

- *Ontario's Best Start.* This program is a ten-year strategy to expand child care and parenting supports in convenient locations for parents. In partnership with school boards, public health units, municipalities, and child care and children's services providers, the plan is to:
  - Integrate preschool, junior kindergarten, senior kindergarten, quality child care, public health, and parenting programs into a seamless system that supports families and children.
  - Provide early and ongoing screening of Ontario's children to identify potential issues, needs, and risks.

Following the elimination of federal ELCC funding after 2006–07, Ontario spread its final federal payment over four years. To date, the program has funded 15 000 new child care spaces (mainly in schools), streamlined subsidy eligibility, established panels to develop an infant screening mechanism, enhanced professional recruitment and retention, and developed an integrated early learning curriculum.

 www.children.gov.on.ca/CS/en/programs/BestStart/default.htm

- *Prince Edward Island's Children's Secretariat.* A broad, inter-sectoral group, which includes community representatives and government representatives from seven provincial government departments, that focuses on key areas of action for healthy child development. The Children's Secretariat is a "network of networks" and links with other existing networks and coalitions that are working on behalf of young children and their families. The province has made early child development a standing item of cabinet.

 www.gov.pe.ca/hss/hcd/index.php3?number=1005282&lang=E

- *British Columbia's Neighbourhood Hub Initiative.* British Columbia's provincial government announced new funding to integrate and expand existing early childhood programs in 22 communities. Neighbourhood hubs are centres that locate early childhood development, child care, and family strengthening programs under one roof. Projects can involve partnerships with school districts, local governments, health authorities, Aboriginal communities, or delegated and community agencies.

Provincial funding for neighbourhood hubs is aimed at:
- increasing child care spaces;
- offering convenience for families by co-locating programs;
- improving cost effectiveness for service providers;
- enhancing programs that are tailored to meet the needs of individual communities; and
- increasing the use of public buildings whenever possible.

www.mcf.gov.bc.ca/early_childhood/pdf/bg_Hub%20Grants_Provincial_revised.pdf

Source: Adapted from McCain et al., 2007 with permission.

Family Income Benefits

Three family income benefits impact on early childhood programs, and influence what families need and how they access early child development programs:

- Maternity and parental leave benefits through Employment Insurance now offer up to one year of benefits to eligible mothers and fathers. The demand for family support programs during the first year after birth appears to be increasing and demand for full-time infant child care before 12 months is likely to decrease over time.
- The Child Care Tax Deduction continues to recognize regulated and unregulated child care options and benefits higher-income families more than those with lower incomes.
- The Universal Child Care Benefit, introduced in 2006, provides a universal benefit to families for children under seven years old.

Parental Leave

The federal, provincial, and territorial governments support maternity and parental leave and benefit programs through Employment Insurance and provincial/territorial labour legislation. Provincial/territorial employment legislation determines the length of the leaves except in federally regulated workplaces, where this is done by the federal government.

Parental benefits are available to both biological and adoptive parents and can be shared by the parents, and now only one parent must serve the two-week waiting period when parents share parental benefits. For biological parents, the combined maternity and parental benefits are now paid for one year. Federal benefits provide eligible employees with salary replacement of 55 percent of earnings, up to a maximum of $413 per week. All provinces and territories have revised their employment standards legislation to reflect this extended benefit period, but there is some variation across jurisdictions in the details of the leave provision.

Benefits for the maternity leave portion are available only to a birth mother, while benefits for parental leave are available to either a birth parent or an adoptive parent. Provincial/territorial leave provisions provide job protection for at least as long as the period covered by federal benefits, although specific rules and requirements vary by province/territory. The combined effect of the federal and provincial/territorial programs generally means that almost a full year of partially paid leave is available to eligible families that take maternity leave followed immediately by parental leave.

Since January 2001, the majority of new parents are eligible for a one-year parental leave and benefits. Reports indicate that parents (mothers and an increasing number of fathers) are taking longer parental leaves and are more likely to return to work at the end of the benefit period. There has been a dramatic increase in both the numbers of claimants and the duration of the benefit. Early results suggest that eligible parents are taking a significantly longer period at home following the birth or adoption of a child; however, in 2001 61 percent of women received benefits, compared with 54 percent in 2000 and 52 percent in 1995. Employment Insurance benefits for maternity and parental leave have more than doubled from $1.2 billion in 1995 to $2.8 billion in 2004 (Social Development Canada, Public Health Agency of Canada and Indian & Northern Affairs Canada, 2005).

 Beyond Our Borders

THE INTERNATIONAL EARLY CHILDHOOD SECTOR

The field of "early childhood" goes by different names among different countries and among different stakeholders within the same region (UNESCO, 2002):

- According to the Consultative Group on Early Childhood Care and Development, *early childhood care and development* (ECCD) "includes all the supports necessary for every child to realize his/her right to survival, to protection, and to care that will ensure optimal development from birth to age eight" (Evans et al., 2000).
- The World Bank defines early child development (ECD) programs as comprehensive programs that address children's basic needs—health, nutrition, emotional, and intellectual—to foster the development of capable and productive adults (Young, 2002).
- According to the Organisation for Economic Co-operation and Development, early childhood education and care (ECEC) "includes all arrangements providing care and education for children under compulsory school age, regardless of setting, funding, opening hours, or program content" (OECD, 2001).
- The Canadian International Development Agency (CIDA) uses the term early childhood education (ECE) to define a range of home-based and centre-based programs and initiatives that are intended to support children's early learning and development before entry into primary schooling. ECE is viewed as an integral component of health, nutrition, safety, social cohesion, and income security initiatives that support early development. ECE programs may be delivered within broader ECD policies and programs.

Child Care Expense Deduction

The federal government's Child Care Expense Deduction (CCED) relieves eligible parents of part of their tax liability on earned income. The amount that can be claimed is limited to the actual child care costs or two-thirds of the eligible parent's income up to a maximum of $7000 a year. The type of care being used to claim the deduction may be unregulated or regulated, but parents have to be able to produce a receipt if asked.

Universal Child Care Benefit

The Universal Child Care Benefit (UCCB) was instituted in 2006 to replace the federal/provincial child care agreements and the annual $249 Young Child Benefit paid for children under seven years old. The UCCB is a taxable allowance paying $100 a month for each child up to six years of age. The program costs $2.4 billion. It has been criticized on a number of fronts. Notably, it's misnamed—the voucher is not enough to offset actual child care costs. Because it is a taxable benefit based on the income of the lowest-earning parent, it disproportionately rewards high-income and single-earner two-parent families to the detriment of single-parent and low-income families (Battle et al., 2006).

EARLY CHILDHOOD POLICY CHALLENGES

Canada's public policies for early childhood programs are evolving in each province and territory and in local communities. As described earlier in this chapter, Quebec introduced an ambitious new family policy that includes increased child tax benefits, expanded parental leave, full-day kindergarten, universal out-of-school programming, and the framework for a universal educational child care system. The federal government's initiatives in the past decade have brought significant new financial resources into the sector, but have not maintained the momentum started at the beginning of the decade. During the first round of early child development funding in 2000, provincial and territorial governments introduced new public policies that established and expanded family support programs, and a few expanded their provision of regulated child care. The second round of federal funding nudged provincial and territorial governments to update their child care policies and, in some instances, used the increased resources as an opportunity to redesign child care and other early childhood program delivery. Much of this activity was stalled by the federal government's switch from program funding to an income support policy in 2006.

A coherent system for all young children and their families remains a vision, not a reality. There are pockets of innovation and some increased levels of investment but no overall cohesive approach.

There are a number of outstanding issues that need to be resolved before it will be possible to re-engineer and expand existing programs into an early childhood system that can accommodate the majority of young children and their families.

Access

The majority of children under age six do not have access to early child development programs. There are too few programs or services to meet the needs of Canadian families who want to use them. Apart from kindergarten for five-year-olds, early childhood programs are available to only a minority of families with young children. For example, four times as many children between age three and six have access to early learning and child care programs in European countries as in Canada (OECD, 2006).

The level of access is not equitable from community to community or family to family. Some children and families have programs in their communities but others do not. Choice and equality of opportunity vary, particularly for lower-income Canadian families. Rules for eligibility for child care subsidies vary from one province to the next, meaning that families with the same income levels but living in different communities may have very different choices available to them.

The increase in programs and initiatives in local communities over the past decade is often disorganized with overlaps and duplications in some areas and gaps in others. For families, it is often a confusing maze to find programming that suits a family's particular needs (see Figure 2.1).

Quality

Provincial/territorial education and child care legislation set *minimum* requirements for early childhood settings, but high-quality programs strive to do more.

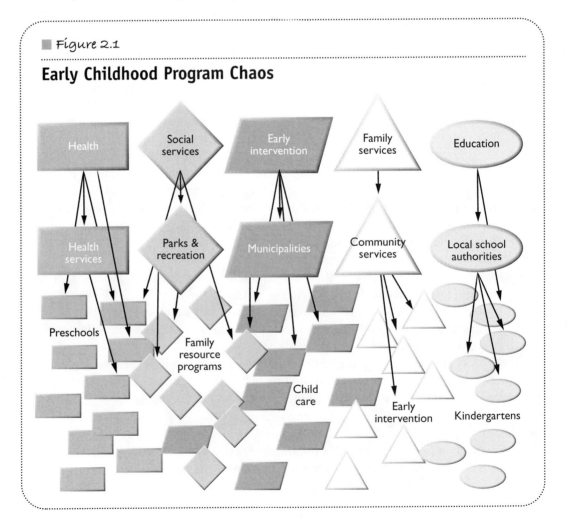

■ Figure 2.1

Early Childhood Program Chaos

The current regulatory environment is fragmented. Licensed child care programs are regulated under provincial/territorial legislation, while kindergarten programs are regulated under the provincial education legislation. Family support programs are not covered by any regulatory system. Policies and regulations are not harmonized. Different requirements and funding approaches make it difficult for early childhood programs to integrate with each other.

The current regulatory environment has not kept pace with new knowledge, and does not reflect recent research on early childhood development. Each regulatory system has specific weaknesses that must be addressed. Child care legislation focuses primarily on ensuring compliance with health and safety requirements rather than on the quality of early childhood programs. Provincial and territorial child care legislation seems to be able to protect children's physical safety, but does not go as far as it could to influence the quality of their early learning experiences (Goelman, 2006).

Education requirements for practitioners do not reflect current knowledge about the importance of post-secondary education in early childhood development. Teachers in kindergarten programs are not required to have any specific courses in early childhood development or how young children learn, or any practice teaching in a program for young children.

Education requirements for supervisors, directors, and other leaders have not kept pace with the demands of their responsibilities, such as increasing numbers of children with special needs, more diversity, families under greater pressure, the need to manage and mentor staff, and the capacity to plan and deliver integrated programs.

Funding

Funding is key to quality and accessibility. Kindergarten programs and many family support programs are 100 percent publicly funded and accessible to all children and families. The same, however, is not true for regulated child care. According to the 2006 OECD review, weak public funding for services for children under age five is a "fundamental flaw in the early education and care system in Canada." In fact Canada spends less than 0.25 percent of its gross domestic product (GDP) on early childhood programs, while Denmark spends a full 2 percent of GDP (OECD, 2006).

The division between child care services and the range of other early child development programs and initiatives remains. Child care programs are the only government-supported programs for children that are based on a user-pay system rather than government direct or block funding for the program. Most government funding for child care programs is used to subsidize low-income, working parents rather than directly funding child care programs. Quebec is the exception—child care programs are funded through government program grants and parents pay a flat fee that represents about 15 to 20 percent of the actual costs.

A comprehensive early childhood system requires the same kind of investment that is now made for children in the public education system. Even taking into account kindergarten programs (that are universal for all five-year-olds and available to almost half of all four-year-olds), overall public spending is less than 40 percent of what is spent on children once they reach age six (McCain et al., 2007). Figures 2.2 and 2.3 illustrate Canada's overall spending on early childhood programs for children under age six compared to spending in the education sector for children aged six to twelve.

Figure 2.2

Investments in ECD Programs, 2005

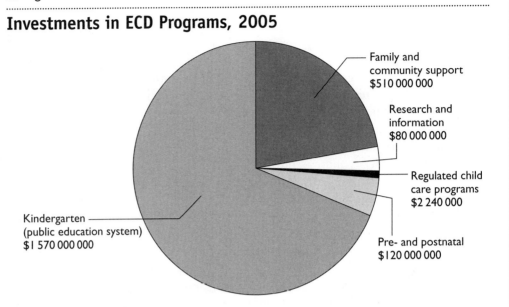

Family and
community support
$510 000 000

Research and
information
$80 000 000

Regulated child
care programs
$2 240 000

Pre- and postnatal
$120 000 000

Kindergarten
(public education system)
$1 570 000 000

The estimate of total federal, provincial, and territorial investment in early childhood programs has increased with new federal contributions.

Source: Adapted from McCain et al., 2007.

Figure 2.3

Investment per Child, ECD Program and Public Education

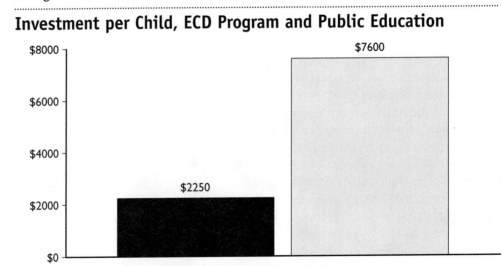

Despite Canada's increased investment in early childhood programs, expenditures are much lower for children under age six.

Source: Adapted from McCain et al., 2007.

Care and Education

The recent context of the distance between child care programs and the public education system was captured in the Canadian OECD review, completed in 2004, that summarizes the policy context and delivery of child care (and other early childhood) programs in Canada. The review points out the problems created by the two solitudes: education and child care. It identifies the need to heal the rift between kindergarten programs and child care, emphasizing the need to "build bridges between child care and kindergarten education, with the aim of integrating ECEC both at ground level and at policy and management levels" (OECD, 2004 p. 7).

At present, there is little integration between kindergarten and other early learning and care programs—even when both are located in a school. The two programs tend to coexist and do not complement or build on one another, or work together to meet each child's needs. Many families with five-year-olds make complex arrangements for their children who attend kindergarten and require some other form of early learning and care before and after school hours. This leads to a fragmented day for children and parents, and lost opportunities for learning to be reinforced and extended through a planned, seamless program.

Integrated learning environments and building early learning and care teams can present several challenges (Corter et al., 2006; Doherty, 2007; Sammons et al., 2005; OECD, 2006):

- Governance issues between programs run by school boards and those operated by child care agencies or municipalities.
- Disparity in wages and working conditions between teachers and early childhood educators.
- Different expectations of kindergarten (e.g., offered at a set period of time, focused on preparation for school, teacher with children for a relatively short period of time) and child care (e.g., offered throughout the day to meet families' needs, focused on early learning and care with activities scheduled to meet the child's needs, practitioners expected to be with children consistently throughout the day).
- A different ratio of children to *qualified* practitioners in child care centres and kindergartens.
- The space and environmental changes required to meet young children's whole needs, including a kitchen, an area for health care for mildly ill children, suitable washrooms close to program areas and rest areas, and appropriate indoor and outdoor space for active play.
- Schools are closed during the summer and other holidays, school custodial staff may only be available certain times of the day, and child care programs may not have easy access to facilities such as the library or gym.
- There is a possibility of developing a two-tier system of early learning and care where parents feel that only school-based programs provide early learning.

Middle Years

Since the late 1990s, early childhood program initiatives, funding, and policies have focused on children prior to entry to Grade 1. The major reports (e.g., McCain & Mustard, 1999) and federal initiatives (e.g., the National Children's Agenda and Early

Beyond Our Borders

BRINGING CHILD CARE INTO EDUCATION

New Zealand was the first country in the world to integrate responsibility for all early childhood services within the education system. Changes toward an integrated system of care and education began in the late 1970s, and in 1986 the administration of ECE (birth to age five) was brought under the Ministry of Education. The Ministry of Education funds approximately 85 percent of basic operating costs of ECE, with parent fees and fund-raising making up the additional 15 percent (almost the opposite of funding realities for most families in Canada). Sixty-four percent of the children from birth to age four have access to early childhood programs, with close to 100 percent having participated in at least one kind of licensed early childhood setting in their first five years. In addition, about 30.6 percent of Maori preschool children attend readiness/language-immersion programs (known as Kohanga Reo) for six hours each day.

In Sweden child care programs (for one- to five-year-olds) and the preschool class (for six-year-olds) were taken over in 1996 by the Ministry of Education and Science from the Ministry of Social and Family Affairs. Long before that, the educational functions of both child care and preschool classes were recognized along with key notions of interaction, communication, and dialogue, and professionals working in daycare and preschool classes were expected to have similar training and work on similar content for children of all ages. At the same time the national curriculum for elementary and secondary students has become more clearly formulated, child care and preschool have become more decentralized and deregulated. Decisions about program operations are meant to be made at the municipal or local government level, and many decisions about curriculum and programming are made by staff and children in the centres.

Sources: Goelman, 2004; OECD, 2006; McCain et al., 2007.

Child Development Agreement) focused on children under six years. Out-of-school programs seem to fall outside of early childhood programs and yet are often tied to child care and facilitated by child care legislation.

Many children may spend almost as much time in out-of-school programs if they attend before-school, lunch, and after-school hours as well as full days on non-school days (summer, professional development days, and school breaks). The developmental needs of middle years children (from six to twelve years) differ from younger children in early childhood programs (Shaffer et al., 2005), but there is less awareness about what those needs are. The early years from birth to age six may form a foundation for later development, but later development in the middle years and adolescence continues and can expand or undermine that development. Many of the expectations and practices in the delivery of school-age programs are out of step with what we know about development during middle childhood (CCCF, 2006). School boards ensure children are given learning opportunities during school hours, but often do not collaborate with school-age child care programs in terms of offering gymnasium, library, and art-room facilities to these same children during out-of-school hours. Parents may expect that school-age care should take the form of a "homework" club, which is at odds with the aim of many school-age care programs to provide children with time away from their desks and opportunities to pursue recreational and leisure interests.

Funding issues are evident. Affordability of quality school-age programs is an issue for many families. Recent federal funding is only available to programs for children up to six years. Fee subsidies are less available and dedicated to programs serving children in the early years.

The scarcity of programs experienced broadly across the early childhood sector is exacerbated in school-age child care. Mothers of children in their middle years are in the work force in greater numbers (Statistics Canada, 2006), and there are fewer programs available. Those that do exist often don't meet the needs of working families, as they don't cover school holidays—such as professional development/parent-teacher interview days, Christmas, spring break, and summer.

An Early Childhood Work Force

Canada is not able to support and maintain a skilled and knowledgeable work force that is fairly remunerated for all early childhood programs (Beach & Flanagon-Rochon, 2007). The requirements for kindergarten teachers across the country are similar—a university undergraduate degree and professional teacher education. The requirements for early childhood educators in other types of early childhood programs vary from one- or two-year certificates or diplomas or less. Compensation for early childhood educators varies across the country and between programs but is generally low.

Provincial governments are responding to the challenges involved in recruiting early childhood educators to positions within regulated child care programs (Friendly & Beach, 2007; Friendly & Beach, 2005). Here are some examples:

- Ontario established the Expert Panel on Quality and Human Resources in 2005. Its mandate includes a review of strategies to improve the recruitment and retention of qualified early childhood educators in early learning and care programs. Its final report and recommendations were expected to be released in 2007.
- Manitoba instituted a training requirement for family child care providers licensed after January 2003. Providers must complete an approved 40-hour course in family child care or early childhood education within their first year of being licensed. A training grant of up to $250 per provider is available upon successful completion of the course. This grant is also available to child care assistants working in centres who must also complete 40 hours of training. Manitoba has established a forgiven loan program for ECE students and has the ECE Recruitment Grant to attract early

childhood educators who are not currently employed in child care programs to return to child care positions for a minimum of two years.

- In Saskatchewan, the 2001 amendment to the Child Care Regulations introduced a three-tiered system for staff in child care centres and increased hours of required training for family child care providers and includes a $70 per class tuition reimbursement for those upgrading ECE training levels, including family child care providers.
- Nova Scotia has an Early Childhood Education Training Initiative that includes a bursary program for full- and part-time students, additional support to training institutions, development of online courses, and use of Prior Learning Assessment and Recognition.
- In Alberta, the Child Care Accreditation Program includes a pre-accreditation phase introduced in January 2003. As part of this program, family child care agencies receive $200 per provider to develop training to meet the provincial safety standards training requirement (meeting key learning outcomes in areas of child development, behaviour management, family dynamics, individual needs, serious incidents, culturally sensitive strategies, children with disabilities, community resources, working with parents, and adoption issues). Professional development funding is available to allow child care staff to pursue training opportunities. In 2007 the Alberta government announced a $5000 grant to attract early childhood educators back to child care positions for a minimum of two years, and professional development grants of

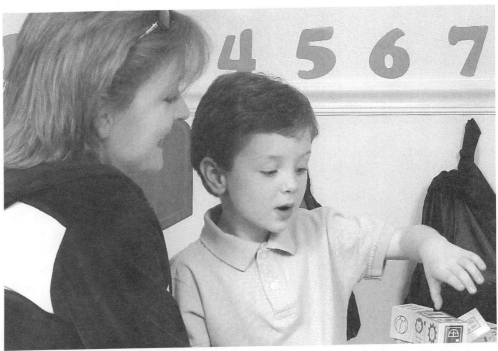

A skilled and knowledgeable early childhood educator is essential to quality early environments for young children.

up to $1000 for staff of child care centres. The province also is funding bursaries to senior child care staff to improve their leadership skills.

- The British Columbia Early Childhood Education Bursary established in 2005 offers up to $200 for each eligible course at a recognized training institution.
- Several jurisdictions have increased funding for child care wages. New Brunswick put an additional $3 million into wage enhancement that is tied to early childhood educational credentials. In 2007, Alberta allocated an additional $8 million to wage grants that are tied to program accreditation. A 2006 pay equity agreement in Quebec provides an increase of almost 9 percent for staff working in CPEs. Newfoundland introduced an income supplement program for low-income early childhood educators in 2007.

OECD Policy Lessons

The *Starting Strong* report (OECD, 2001) identifies eight key elements of policy that are likely to promote equitable access to quality early childhood education and care. The elements are broad and inclusive so that they can be considered in many different country contexts.

1. A systematic and integrated approach to policy development and implementation.
2. A strong and equal partnership with the education system.
3. A universal approach to access, with particular attention to children in need of special support.
4. Substantial public investment in services and infrastructure.
5. A participatory approach to quality improvement and assurance.
6. Appropriate training and working conditions for staff in all forms of provision.
7. Systematic attention to monitoring and data collection.
8. A stable framework and long-term agenda for research and evaluation.

EARLY CHILDHOOD EDUCATORS AND PUBLIC POLICY

The spotlight on early child development and the recent influx of public funding enhances the prospects for early childhood educators who are launching careers in this sector. While the actual numbers of children from birth to age six years is not increasing over the next few years, the numbers of programs are expanding. So, too, the demand grows for early childhood educators now and in the years ahead.

Canada's fragmented delivery of early childhood programs is the product of overlapping and sometimes contradictory public policies. The current public attention and increased public investment presents a period of greater opportunity and vulnerability for early childhood programs and for early childhood educators.

How public policy addresses these issues will shape working environments for early childhood educators in the years and decades ahead. Early childhood educators are entering a sector that is a central component of the public policy framework that supports Canadians, and the options are wide open.

KEY TERMS

Aboriginal

day nurseries

early identification

early intervention

entitlement

family support program

junior kindergarten

pre-kindergarten

public policy

seamless

REFLECTION QUESTIONS

1. What personal experience have you had with an early childhood setting? Did you attend a nonparental care or early education setting before beginning formal schooling? Do you have children who are attending or who have attended an early childhood program? What are the possible strengths and challenges of different types of early childhood programs?

2. How is Quebec's approach to early childhood program policy different from that in the rest of Canada?

3. What does the phrase "early childhood program fragmentation" mean?

4. What are the benefits and challenges of federal, provincial/territorial, and local government involvement in early childhood programs?

FOR MORE INFORMATION

1. *Family Resource Programs* is a video series produced by Red River College in Winnipeg, Manitoba, that celebrates the diversity, scope, and value of family resource programs across Canada. The series includes:

   - *Supporting Communities* (17 min)
   - *Supporting Babies* (19 min)
   - *Supporting Early Years* (22 min)
   - *Supporting Families* (24 min)

   www.rrc.mb.ca/index.php?pid=3264

2. *Early Childhood Education and Care in Canada, 2006* is Canada's most complete database about early childhood programs and policies.

   www.childcarecanada.org

3. The Child Care Advocacy Association of Canada (CCAAC) is sponsoring *Child Care Policy: Making the Connections* to build the capacity of the child care community, provincial and territorial governments, and other interested community

members to better understand and comment on early learning and child care policy and investments.

www.childcareadvocacy.ca

4. *Thomson Nelson ECE Resource Centre* is intended to enhance the teaching and learning experience for both instructors and students. The website provides extensive and helpful resources in many different criteria related to early childhood education.

www.ece.nelson.com

ABOUT QUALITY

CHAPTER OUTLINE

Clyde Hertzman

Three broad domains define the scope of early child development: language and cognitive, social-emotional, and physical development, from zero to school age. Life course research teaches us that each of these domains can influence health, well-being, and learning skills for the rest of our lives. The course that development will take in each person depends, critically, on the quality of stimulation, support, and nurturance that the child experiences in his or her family, neighbourhood, and care environments. Just as the developing lungs respond to the airborne environment, the developing brain responds to the qualities of the environments where the child grows up, lives, and learns. Thus, child development is about the ecology of early childhood environments.

In Canada the nurturant qualities of many of the environments where children spend their early lives are not as strong as we would like. Our National Longitudinal Survey of Children and Youth shows that by kindergarten age, a "gradient" in development has emerged across the socioeconomic spectrum, such that the proportion of children who are vulnerable in their development gradually increases as one goes from the most to the least affluent families in Canada. Although the change is gradual from income strata to income strata, the overall differences are large, five-fold or more, from one end of the socioeconomic spectrum to the other. Although income *per se* plays an important role, these differences are due to a full range of influences in the family, neighbourhood, and care environments. In other words, Canada has a long way to go to provide an ecosystem that is supportive of early child development.

In British Columbia, we have assessed and mapped child development, neighbourhood by neighbourhood, and school district by school district, for the province's kindergarten children. Our maps show that there is a six-fold difference (from 14 percent to over 70 percent) in the proportion of children who are vulnerable from the most to the least vulnerable neighbourhoods. We are also able to map many neighbourhood characteristics that show us how the differences in children's development relates to differences in their environments.

Source: Interview with Clyde Hertzman. Hertzman is the Director of Human Early Learning Partnership in British Columbia. He is an epidemiologist who studies community early child development.

Chapter Objectives

The chapter will:

1. Describe how early childhood programs are evaluated.
2. Explore child assessments.
3. Explore community early child development reporting.
4. Review what early childhood educators need to know about understanding and using early child development research.

Quality early childhood settings use ongoing **assessments** and systematic **program evaluations** to gather information on children's learning and development and the quality of the program. Results benefit children by informing decisions about pedagogy and curriculum. The assessments and evaluations should support conversations with parents and be sensitive to the cultural and community context of children's lives. **Monitoring** early child development at the community level helps early childhood educators understand how well the community environment is meeting the needs of families with young children.

The terms *assessment, evaluation,* and *monitoring* are often interchanged with each other. In this chapter, *evaluation* will refer to early childhood settings and the implementation of the framework, *assessment* will be used when focusing on individual children, and *monitoring* will be mainly associated with identifying and measuring the community-level early child development.

Assessment, evaluation, and monitoring are conducted in early childhood settings for the following reasons (Bertrand & Corter, 2007; Kagan, 1998; National Research Council, 2001):

- Child assessment to observe, document, and support children's development.
- Child assessment to identify possible developmental problems.
- Evaluation of program quality.
- Community monitoring of program impact.
- Provincial monitoring of program impact for public policy analysis and accountability.

When considering ways to assess children's development, it is impossible to see a child as separate from his or her family and community. It is also unlikely to evaluate a program productively without considering the impact, role, and expectations of the surrounding community or the overall context of Canada's early childhood sector. Early childhood settings can change the daily lives of children and their families and, given enough resources, can transform whole communities.

EVALUATING EARLY CHILDHOOD PROGRAMS

Evaluating an early childhood setting is a multifaceted affair; it must include consideration of structural characteristics such as ratios, educational requirements, and compensation. Additional program guidelines can be used in addition to health, safety, and nutrition requirements.

As the public spotlight and investments increase, early childhood programs face closer scrutiny. Early childhood educators need to better understand the tools that are available to monitor the quality of environments for young children and research findings that study the impact of early childhood programs on children and families.

How Can Program Quality Be Improved?

In the past two decades, there has been considerable discussion about high-quality child care in North America. As a result, there is a large amount of **peer-reviewed** research literature and many empirical studies of characteristics, correlates, assessment, and measurement of quality. Whereas the European literature has focused primarily on the ideas that underpin the concept of quality and the kinds of policy initiatives needed to achieve high-quality programs, the empirical research has mainly been carried out in jurisdictions where child care is more a collection of individual programs than a system. This research has generally been concerned with quality at the level of the individual program.

Policymakers, researchers, and early childhood educators do agree that quality in early childhood programs needs to improve (Beach et al., 2004; OECD, 2004; Goelman et al., 2000). Less is known about the quality of kindergarten programs or family support programs but there is agreement that quality should be high in all early childhood programs.

The Organisation for Economic Co-operation and Development (OECD) in its *Thematic Review Report* called for a national quality framework for early childhood programs across all sectors and jurisdictions, and provincial infrastructure to implement the framework. It noted that such a framework is a key contributor to quality in many countries. The framework is intended to focus on broad national aims and children's holistic development, rather than on detailed curricular objectives. The framework would include:

- A statement of values and goals to guide early childhood programs.
- A summary of **program standards** (e.g., child/staff ratios and staff qualifications).
- An outline of knowledge, skills, dispositions, and values across broad developmental areas that children at different ages could be expected to achieve.
- Pedagogical guidelines outlining how children achieve these goals and how early childhood educators can support them.

The OECD report echoes Canadian reports (Beach et al., 2004; Doherty et al., 2000; Cleveland & Krashinsky, 2003) that identify the need for adequate and regular funding of services and high-quality management to ensure the provision of quality programs.

Work carried out by the Education and Training Division of the OECD exemplifies the international interest. Its review of Canadian early childhood programs was the 17th in a multi-country thematic review conducted by the Paris-based economic organization between 1998 and 2005. One of the project's key summary documents noted that "policy makers have recognized that equitable access to quality early childhood education and care can strengthen the foundations of lifelong learning for all children and support the broad educational and social needs of families" (OECD, 2001, p. 7).

Accreditation

Accreditation is a process by which a recognized independent body establishes standards for services and evaluates programs based on those standards (Doherty, 2000). It is typically based on standards, detailed operating criteria, and indicators or benchmarks of what is considered effective practice (based on research findings, professional judgment, and community values).

Early childhood program accreditation is the process by which a program volunteers, or is required, to demonstrate its high quality to an authorized, external agency of professional peers through an assessment of its program of services, personnel,

Beyond Our Borders

QUALITY TARGETS IN SERVICES FOR YOUNG CHILDREN

In Western Europe, the European Union has had a strong interest in early learning and child care since the 1980s. In the 1990s, the European Commission's Childcare Network carried out extensive exploration of the dimensions and features of quality in child care (see www.childcarequality.ca/wdocs/QbD_QualityTargets.pdf). This paper, together with two others that were part of the network's work on child care quality, was republished (with permission from the European Commission) by the Childcare Resource and Research Unit in 2004.

Source: European Commission Network on Childcare and Other Measures to Reconcile the Employment Responsibilities of Men and Women, 1996.

facility, administration, governance, and community relations. Licensed programs meet minimum standards and provide programs that support the basic health, safety, and well-being of children. Accreditation is perceived to offer a higher quality by (Doherty, 2000):

• fostering the continuous development and improvement in the quality of services;
• providing a system of evaluation in relation to organizational objectives and established service standards; and
• providing families with an assurance of a high standard of service, beyond the basic minimum licensing requirements.

The National Association for the Education of Young Children (NAEYC), which is based in the United States, established an accreditation system to set professional standards for early childhood programs and to help families identify high-quality programs. NAEYC accreditation is a voluntary system by which programs measure themselves against a national set of standards. From only a few hundred accredited programs in 1988, there are now more than 10 000 NAEYC-accredited programs, including a few programs in Canada.

To date, large-scale accreditation processes have not been linked with improvements in quality (Whitebook et al., 1997; Doherty, 2000) independent of the infrastructure in place to support early childhood programs. In other words, if an accreditation process does not have the kinds of supports that are known to be related to program quality, the act of accreditation is not likely to make much of a contribution to program quality.

The province of Alberta has embarked on a province-wide voluntary accreditation of regulated centre-based and family child care programs (Alberta Association for Accreditation, 2006) as one strategy that aims to address staff recruitment and retention issues (see Chapter 2). The Alberta Child Care Accreditation Program (ACCAP) aims to raise the quality of care beyond the basic regulatory requirements. Program standards, known as ACCAP Quality Standards (AQS), and related criteria and indicators are used to review the program. The process includes a self-study review, staff and family surveys, and a site visit by an external reviewer. These standards build upon, but do not replace, the standards for licensing. To be accredited, therefore, programs must provide evidence of consistent compliance with the AQS and consistently meet the licensing requirements that apply to their service.

The accreditation process in Alberta includes resources, supports, and financial incentives for child care programs. The Alberta Resource Centre for Quality Enhancement supports child care centres and family child care agencies in the process of accreditation through workshops, mentoring, written guides, and technical assistance in completing the process.

Manitoba is also considering an accreditation program for its child care programs. The Manitoba Child Care Association and the Canadian Child Care Federation formed an advisory committee to provide advice and insights to a feasibility study on the accreditation of licensed child care centres and family child care programs in Manitoba (MCCA & CCCF, 2006). The study developed an accreditation framework that includes four parts:

- *Components*—broad categories such as relationships, health and safety, learning, and development.
- *Standards*—a statement of what is desirable in each component. Usually there are several standards for each component.
- *Criteria*—descriptions of what is required to meet a standard. Criteria are checkable through observation, documents review, and/or interviews with user-parents, staff, or members of the board of directors.
- *Indicators*—description of what to look for when trying to determine compliance with a criterion. Each criterion has several indicators.

In May 2007 the draft of standards, criteria, and indicators were made available to the child care community as a tool to help improve the quality of services. The next step is to finalize the standards and to set up a regulatory body to be responsible for the accreditation process.

Early Childhood Environmental Rating Scale—Revised

The Early Childhood Environmental Rating Scale—Revised (ECERS-R) is the most commonly used standard program evaluation tool. It measures quality in diverse early childhood programs. ECERS-R provides a scale with which to review the quality of preschool environments. The scale focuses on the physical environment and looks at the use of space, play materials, and learning experiences, as well as at adult–child interactions. There are 37 items on the scale, with a continuum of possible performance.

ECERS-R is used as a measure of quality for research studies and is useful as a tool to assist individual program development. In addition to the scale for preschool ECERS

Innovations

MADE-IN-CANADA TOOLS FOR EVALUATING PROGRAM QUALITY

RAISING THE BAR ON QUALITY

Raising the Bar on Quality is a tool to enhance quality in licensed child care centres that was developed in Hamilton, Ontario, and is now in place in several regions across the province (see www.ascy.ca). It is a voluntary, annual community accreditation program that assesses levels of quality achieved in three categories: quality assurance, best practices, and staff professional development. Bronze-level programs follow fundamental quality indicators and are in full compliance with provincial child care legislation, notably, the Ontario Day Nurseries Act. Silver-level programs have additional strategies to enhance quality, and Gold-level programs demonstrate a long-term commitment to high-quality early childhood environments. Raising the Bar on Quality builds on the strengths of local child care communities, is sustainable without additional financial resources, and works in combination with other program evaluation tools. Participating communities can adapt or modify the standards to ensure the program will be achievable and sustainable in their regions.

SPECIALINK CHILD CARE INCLUSION PRACTICES PROFILE AND PRINCIPLES SCALE

The SpeciaLink Inclusion Child Care Practices Profile and the SpeciaLink Child Care Inclusion Principles Scale (see www.specialinkcanada.org/project/index.html) are tools that assess the quality of inclusion of children with special needs in child care centres. They provide a picture of sustainable and evolving inclusion quality. They include 247 indicators that are organized into a rating scale format.

settings, there are comparable tools for infant and toddler settings, school-age settings, and family child care settings.

ECERS-R is used to measure quality in a variety of environments that offer programs to preschool children including child care centres, family resource and parenting programs, and kindergarten classrooms. It has become the standard measure of quality for family support programs, child care, and kindergarten in North American research. Some Canadian examples of studies that have used the ECERS-R include the following:

- The 1998 "You Bet I Care!" Canadian study of child care staff and quality in child care centres used ECERS-R to measure the quality of preschool programs located in full-time child care centres.
- Parent–child readiness programs have used ECERS-R to collect information about the quality of the child's environment in adult–child programs (Pelletier & Brent, 2002).

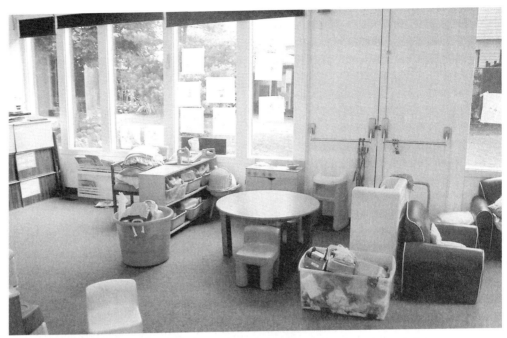

High-quality early childhood settings organize the physical environment to accommodate young children's active play and involvement with learning materials and each other.

- A Canadian study of child care and kindergarten environments in four provinces applied ECERS to assess and compare the quality of the environment in several child care rooms and kindergarten classes (Johnson & Mathien, 1998).

The ECERS-R is a standardized measure. Since its development in the early 1980s, the tool has been validated. Researchers have carefully measured children's outcomes, controlling for other factors such as family characteristics, and compared changes in outcomes to differences in the ECERS-R assessments of early childhood environments. Repeatedly, researchers report that higher ECERS-R scores are related to better child outcome measures.

Researchers have tested the tool's reliability to determine if two different observers are likely to arrive at the same score for the same environments. The findings indicate that if observers receive training and follow the directions, they are likely to arrive at similar scores for the same early childhood environments.

The use of a standardized rating scale (such as ECERS) allows quality comparisons between preschool rooms in a program and among programs. Programs can use ECERS to evaluate changes in quality as staff teams work together to improve their programs.

ECERS-R does *not* measure the quality of parenting programming and activities, but it does measure the quality of the children's environment in those programs. Nor does it measure the quality of the work environment for school programs, such as kindergarten. It is a snapshot of the quality of the early learning environment in family support programs and in kindergarten classrooms. Staff may not be able to change limitations in the daily schedule or physical setting. ECERS-R can point to changes in practice and ways to work around permanent limitations, resulting in enhanced early learning environments for young children.

ASSESSING CHILDREN

Early childhood educators are responsible for assessing children's development as an ongoing aspect of their daily professional practice. Assessment is a systematic process for obtaining information from observation, interviews, portfolios, projects, tests, and other sources that can be used to make judgments about characteristics of children. In early childhood programs, assessment can serve different purposes, including:

- To provide information for curriculum planning for individual children and groups.
- To communicate with parents and families about children's progress.
- To identify children with special needs who may need additional supports or interventions.
- To evaluate if the program is meeting its goals (NAEYC & NAESP, 1990).

The assessment of child outcomes measures aspects of child development. *What* is measured about child development is influenced by what is valued about children and beliefs about how children learn. It begins with the understanding of childhood, as discussed in Chapter 1.

Measures of child outcomes typically focus on aspects of the traditional developmental domains of cognitive, linguistic, social, emotional, and physical development. Additional domains and dimensions (e.g., spiritual, creative, learning styles) may be included, and specific areas within the broad domains may be emphasized (e.g., gross and fine motor skills listening and speaking, gender and ethnic identity). Assessment of the cognitive-language realms sometimes includes pre-academic skills and knowledge in reading, writing, numeracy, and science. Some assessments take into account the child's context including gender, family demographics and characteristics, number of children, ethnicity, citizenship status, and caregiving arrangements.

Early childhood educators have a long tradition of coming to know the child through direct observation in order to understand and support individual development. In more recent times, this practice has been challenged by standardized tools for measurement and, most recently, by postmodern views that shun objectifying the child (Pence, 2006). Currently, no single view predominates, but there are major developments on the Canadian and international scene that may affect policy and the everyday lives of early childhood educators and children. Some of these developments relate to "new functions" of early assessment such as determining whether children are on the right track to succeed in "standards-based" education or whether they are "ready" for school. Closely related is the more traditional function of "early identification" for children who have special clinical or educational needs. In this era of evidence-based services, child outcomes are more and more a focus for studies of program efficacy or quality.

In early childhood settings where the central perspective is that the child is an active learner with rights and skills, assessment is *primarily* based on observation and documentation of what children's experiences are and how they illustrate emerging developmental skills. The primary purpose is to support curriculum planning that is based on where the child is at and what interests the child. Early childhood educators document individual levels of knowledge and abilities as a basis for planning curriculum, and they record the progress of development and learning over time, in order to ensure that the child is benefiting from the early childhood setting. Early childhood educators use information from continuous assessments about individual children to plan curriculum and to tailor interactions that respond to their strengths and needs. This information ensures that the program meets its goals for children's learning and developmental progress and can inform what improvements are needed to improve the program. Further, systematic assessment helps to identify children who may be experiencing developmental difficulties and may need additional developmental assessment and specific interventions.

Observation and Documentation

Continuous assessment through observation and documentation of each child's development is an essential part of the professional practice in early childhood settings. This is the child's right and it is crucial to delivery of programs that promote child

Children's art shows emerging abilities to represent their world.

Beyond Our Borders

LEARNING STORIES IN NEW ZEALAND

New Zealand has introduced learning stories from early childhood programs to offer snapshots of children's learning and development in action by describing actual, unique experiences (Carr, 2001; Dickinson, 2005). They document children's activities. Early childhood educators assess what learning and development are taking place and plan for the next steps.

The observation, documentation, and analysis of learning stories create a sample of children's learning that is rich in context, articulate, and complete in terms of the situation, the actions, and the conclusion. Learning stories are narrations that document children's engagement in learning experiences, including the analysis or assessment of that learning and the child's emerging developmental skills. The stories and assessments can be presented in children's portfolios for children, families, and practitioners to read and reread.

Learning stories from early childhood settings offer snapshots of children's learning and development in action by describing actual, unique experiences. They depict early childhood practice and the active involvement of adults and children in learning. Learning stories show how development and learning are integrated in programs and how content is meaningful to children. They reflect the community and cultural and linguistic diversity.

Learning stories stay close to the children's real experiences and provide an alternative to mechanistic and fragmented approaches. Learning stories allow early childhood practitioners to assess complex outcomes in early childhood. Other assessments may exclude skills that are difficult to measure using a checklist or testing that uses simple and low-level outcomes.

development. A compilation of individual profiles of learning and development (e.g., observations, learning stories, children's creations and work) can create a holistic picture of the child's experiences and learning. Assessments are intended to identify, document, support, and promote children's learning and development.

Families and other caregivers can contribute to assessments that are based on observation and documentation. They can bring forward what is meaningful to the child and expand practitioners' understanding about where the child is at and what the child can do. Assessments that are organized into portfolios are conversation starters among practitioners and families that build everyone's understanding of child development.

Tests and Learning Standards

A test is one or more questions, problems, or tasks that are designed to estimate a child's knowledge, understanding, ability, skill, and/or attitudes in a consistent fashion across individuals. Information from a test or tests may contribute to judgments made as a part of an assessment process. A standardized test is a testing instrument that is administered, scored, and interpreted in a standard manner, such as the NLSCY measures that are described in Chapter 1. Standardized test questions are useful for large-scale surveys, but are not very useful for early childhood programs.

From the Past

CHILD ASSESSMENT

Arnold Gesell (1880–1961) studied developmental changes in motor behaviour, language, visual capabilities, adaptive functions, and personal and social relations of children from birth to age ten. He studied about 50 children, using moving picture photography to record their behaviour in natural settings. These children came from American middle-class families who lived in the New England states. Gesell and his colleagues used these observations to create tests, measuring procedures and techniques of observation relating to children's development.

Gesell and his co-workers developed the Gesell Developmental Assessment, which became a standard procedure for the direct observation and evaluation of a child's behaviour throughout most of the twentieth century. The purpose of the assessment was to do the following:

1. Observe a child's overall behaviour in order to compare the child's developmental level in relation to his or her chronological age. This helps in understanding the child's overall growth pattern.
2. Monitor a child's growth over time. Comparison of initial responses with subsequent behaviours provides an understanding of that particular child's growth pattern.
3. Identify a child's developmental age in relationship to placement in early childhood programs. This assessment assists in matching the child with his or her developmental peers. It is intended to be combined with other information from teacher observations, parents, and other pertinent records to provide a more complete picture of the child.
4. Identify children whose behaviour reveals atypical patterns, indicating the need for further evaluation.

Here are some examples of items on the Gesell assessment:
- *Cubes.* Children are asked to reproduce a picture of a cube structure using small coloured cube blocks. This test provides information about visual perception, fine motor skills, coordination, attention span, and perception of form, as well as the ability to follow directions and to function in a structured task. The child's visual motor integration skills relate to handwriting, colouring, and cutting. The short-term memory skills in the task relate to reading comprehension, spelling, and math.

- *Copy forms.* Children are asked to copy seven geometric designs. The size, shape, and organization of the products indicate maturity in fine motor ability, organizational skills, awareness of detail, visual perceptions, ability to execute angles, and overall eye–hand coordination. These skills relate more to comprehension of materials and cognitive maturity than to rote memory of academic skills (e.g., reciting the alphabet or counting).
- *Incomplete man.* Children are asked to complete a drawing of a man. The task gives information about a child's eye–hand coordination, awareness of detail, and social-emotional expression. The overall completion was used to determine age-appropriate peer groups.

Gesell's assessment test has been used throughout much of Canada and the United States to determine children's readiness to enter kindergarten or Grade 1 classrooms.

Sources: Osburn, 1991; Braun & Edwards, 1972; Weber, 1984.

Sometimes early childhood educators use **early learning standards** that describe expectations for the learning and development of young children across the domains of health and physical well-being; social and emotional well-being; approaches to learning, language development, and symbol systems; and general knowledge about the world around them to guide their assessments of children's development.

Developmental Screening

Developmental screening is a procedure designed to identify children who should receive more intensive assessment or diagnosis for potential delay or disability. The prime reason for developmental screening is to ensure that children with behavioural or developmental challenges and their families have the earliest possible opportunities for intervention. Earlier detection of delays leads to improved child health and well-being for identified children and for their families. Screening generally involves the use of a brief procedure or instrument designed to identify children who may need further assessment to verify developmental and/or health risks. Routine screening involves regular and scheduled screenings at intervals throughout a child's life, ideally commencing prenatally. Ongoing records are kept to enable comparisons of development over time. Subtle developmental problems, which can point to the probability of more serious problems later, may only emerge as a pattern over time.

Early childhood educators can use screening tools to identify special needs or delays in development that would indicate the need for intervention and referral to specialized services. In the early years, development is rapid, and it is crucial that early intervention occurs in a timely manner in order to be preventative in nature. Identification of concerns or delays depends on knowledgeable and observant parents and professionals recognizing when the continuum of development is delayed or significantly atypical. Screening tools are valuable for both parents and professionals as a means of sharing observations and discussing any concerns that may indicate the need for referral of additional support.

Innovations

NIPISSING DISTRICT DEVELOPMENTAL SCREEN™

The Nipissing District Developmental Screen (NDDS) is a screening tool designed to identify problem areas in a child's development. The tool examines 13 key developmental stages: 1 and 2 months, 4 months, 6 months, 9 months, 12 months, 15 months, 18 months, 2 years, 30 months, 3 years, 4 years, 5 years, and 6 years. A child's vision, hearing, speech, language, communication, gross motor, fine motor, cognitive, social/emotional, and self-help skills are included.

The screen forms for each of the developmental stages include "Activities for Your Baby/Child." These suggestions are intended to provide parents and other caregivers with some information and activities to enhance their child's development. Thus, the NDDS becomes a useful conversation starter with parents.

The NDDS is used and recognized as a general developmental screening tool. In Ontario, family support programs, early identification and intervention programs, and many regulated child care programs use the NDDS with parents, and the report of the Expert Panel on the 18-Month Well Baby Visit recommends NDDS as part of the primary health-care developmental review. The NDDS is also becoming more common in regulated child care programs and in junior kindergarten registration.

Functional Assessment

Early childhood researchers and practitioners have proposed another way to assess early development. Rather than using single tools that measure isolated abilities and achievements, some are suggesting that we assess the processes of social and emotional development and underlying functional capabilities that lead to cognition and communication skills (Shonkoff & Phillips, 2000; Greenspan & Shanker, 2004). **Functional capabilities** include self-regulation skills such as regulating emotional responses, paying attention, and managing sensory stimulation. Other functional capabilities include interpersonal skills, abilities to establish relationships, problem-solving strategies, and the ability to generalize learning from one situation to another.

Rather than "test" a child, information-gathering can be ongoing and often best collected while observing children at play and asking simple questions of parents and other primary caregivers (Greenspan & Shanker, 2004). For example, "Does your baby look toward you when you are talking?" or "Does your preschooler use a number of ideas in a row that make sense to you?"

Guidelines for Child Assessment

Concerns about assessing children's development, and the use of the information that an assessment can provide, are legitimate. Standardized assessments carried out in early childhood have limited validity for comparative or predictive purposes

Early childhood educators regularly observe and document children's play.

(Kagan, 1998). However, if properly carried out, assessment has an important role to play in planning and supporting children's learning, and for documenting and communicating this to parents and other professionals as relevant. It can also contribute to the identification of developmental difficulties.

The following principles apply to the assessment of children in early childhood settings (NAEYC, 2005; Ministry of Child and Youth Services, 2005):

- Observing and documenting the progress of young children is central to the practice of early childhood practitioners.
- Documentation of young children's learning must incorporate information from a variety of means, including observation in comfortable and natural settings, learning stories, samples of children's work, and parental input, in addition to well-researched tools.
- Children should be assessed as individuals with unique patterns of development and learning, not assessed in comparison to others.
- Formal and informal assessment tools must be developmentally, culturally, and linguistically appropriate.
- Assessments should be administered by professionals appropriately trained for the purpose and tools utilized, and results of assessments should be used only for the purposes for which they were designed. It is extremely important to differentiate between screening, documentation of current development and in-depth assessment, and how the resulting information should be communicated and used.
- Results of assessments should not be used as a barrier to access to early childhood settings.
- The child must be the primary beneficiary of any assessment; individual assessments should not be aggregated for the purposes of evaluation of early childhood programs.
- The value of observations, learning stories, and screening tools (such as the Nipissing District Developmental Screen) for beginning the conversations with parents about their children's development should be recognized as a prime factor in the use of assessment results.

- When assessing the development of children who are new to Canada and/or have a first language other than French or English, it is essential to take these realities into account, particularly when assessing skills against a screen or standardized benchmarks.

Vulnerable Children

Most Canadian children between birth and age 12 years are healthy, cope with daily challenges and demands, get along with others, and are ready for school learning.

One-quarter of children in Canada are vulnerable when they enter Grade 1—that is, they have learning, health, or behaviour problems that are likely to interfere with their academic achievement and ability to get along with others (Willms, 2002; Kershaw et al., 2006; Janus, 2006). In some communities, the percentage of vulnerable children is much higher. Families and communities facing poverty, employment demands, transient living conditions, health problems, minority racial or linguistic status, and limited time and/or resources are more likely to have difficulties, but vulnerable children are present across the socioeconomic spectrum (McCain et al., 2007). In fact, the majority of vulnerable children live in middle-class, two-parent families. Early identification of learning and other developmental difficulties combined with additional support to families can lead to interventions that reduce difficulties and set children on more optimal developmental pathways.

Lower-income children may be more likely to have difficulties, but most make a successful transition to school (Willms, 2002). The majority of children who have trouble come from the large demographic of moderate-income families with two parents (Barnett et al., 2004; Hertzman, 2002; Willms, 2002). Targeting early intervention programs only at disadvantaged children, families, or communities fails to reach the majority of children who are experiencing difficulties (Barnett et al., 2004; Hertzman, 2002; Willms, 2002).

The more economic, social, and psychological pressures and problems that are in a child's daily life, the greater the likelihood of social, emotional, or learning difficulties (Boyce & Keating, 2004; Burchinal et al., 2000; Rutter & Rutter, 1993). These stressors are known as "risks." While the majority of children who have risks do not have difficulties, alleviating risk factors is important, particularly for children who face multiple and chronic risks.

Vulnerable young children (i.e., those experiencing social, emotional, or learning difficulties) and children who are at risk benefit from regular, consistent participation in quality early learning programs rather than targeted, time-limited compensatory initiatives, particularly if they attend programs that include a mixed group of children from different social and economic backgrounds (Brooks-Gunn, 2003; Doherty, 2001; Sylva et al., 2003).

COMMUNITY EARLY CHILD DEVELOPMENT

Early childhood educators gain useful insights about children and their families when they are aware of children's development within the context of their community environment. Communities influence child outcomes. The family within the community is the primary place where children grow and learn. Being able to describe and understand the community is essential to curriculum development, individual program and service planning, and assessing development. Understanding of the community is not limited to knowledge and understanding of children and families enrolled in an early childhood setting. Inclusive programs strive to know, understand, and involve those families that do not (from choice or otherwise) participate. Although the community context cannot be just reduced to maps, charts, and statistics, knowing information about families, including family income, education and occupation, immigration, languages spoken, and available community resources, helps to better understand the developmental opportunities that children need to thrive.

The **Early Development Instrument (EDI)** is an accepted community-level measure of early development at the time of entry to Grade 1 (Janus & Offord, 2000; Kershaw et al., 2006; Mustard, 2006). The EDI assesses domains that are closely aligned to the social/emotional, cognitive, and physical domains of development. Early childhood settings can use community data, including EDI data, in a context of other information about income, parental education, and home languages, to plan programs for young children and their families. Communities may choose to use community-level EDI to establish specific targets and develop corresponding planning and monitoring mechanisms.

Innovations

EARLY DEVELOPMENT INSTRUMENT

The Early Development Instrument (EDI) is a Canadian measure of early development that allows communities to measure children's early development before they enter Grade 1. The EDI was developed by Dr. Magdalena Janus and Dr. Dan Offord and released in 2000. It assesses community outcomes in child development in respect to health, learning, and behaviour. The EDI is a 100-item questionnaire filled out by kindergarten teachers on all the children in their class. Information collected using the EDI is analyzed at a group level (e.g., school catchment area or a neighbourhood).

The EDI has the following characteristics (Goelman & Hertzman, n.d.):

- It is completed by kindergarten teachers based on several months of observation.
- While reliable at an individual level, the EDI does not provide a diagnosis of a child's developmental problems.
- It provides a population level measure—results can be interpreted for groups of children.
- The results may be used to identify the weak and the strong sectors of a community.
- The results can be used by communities to mobilize for improved child outcomes.

(continued)

The Early Development Instrument assesses five child developmental domains:

1. Physical health and well-being.
   - Above the 90th percentile, a child is physically ready to tackle a new day at school, is generally independent, and has excellent motor skills.
   - Below the 10th percentile, a child has inadequate fine and gross motor skills, is sometimes tired or hungry, is usually clumsy, and may have flagging energy levels.

2. Social competence.
   - Above the 90th percentile, a child never has a problem getting along, working, or playing with other children; is respectful to adults, is self-confident, has no difficulty following class routines, and is capable of pro-social behaviour.
   - Below the 10th percentile, a child has poor overall social skills and exhibits regular serious problems in more than one area: getting along with other children; accepting responsibility for their own actions; following rules and class routines; showing respect for adults, children, and others' property; lack of self-confidence and self-control; difficulty adjusting to change; frequent inability to work independently.

3. Emotional maturity.
   - Above the 90th percentile, a child almost never shows aggressive, anxious, or impulsive behaviour, has good ability to concentrate, and is often helpful to other children.
   - Below the 10th percentile, a child has regular problems managing aggressive behaviour; is prone to disobedience; is easily distractible, inattentive, or impulsive; is usually unable to show helping behaviour towards other children; and is sometimes upset when left by the caregiver.

4. Language and cognitive development.
   - Above the 90th percentile, a child is interested in books, reading and writing, and rudimentary math; is capable of reading and writing simple sentences and complex words; and is able to count and recognize numbers and geometric shapes.
   - Below the 10th percentile, a child has problems in both reading/writing and numeracy; is unable to read and write simple words; is uninterested in trying; is often unable to attach sounds to letters; has difficulty remembering things, counting to 20, recognizing, and comparing numbers; and is usually not interested in numbers.

5. Communication skills and general knowledge.
- Above the 90th percentile, a child has excellent communication skills, can tell a story and communicate with both children and adults, and has no problems with articulation.
- Below the 10th percentile, a child has poor communication skills and articulation and limited command of English; has difficulties in talking to others, understanding, and being understood; and has poor general knowledge.

The EDI gives us average scores for groups of children and in this way can help to determine the number of developmentally "vulnerable children" in a city, community, or neighbourhood, and the types of vulnerability they may be showing. Vulnerable children are those children in the bottom 10 percent of scores on any one of the five EDI subscales. This means that they are likely to have a developmental, social-emotional, cognitive, or physical problem that will interfere with their success in school (Janus, 2006).

The EDI data are collected for individual children, and EDI scores correlate reliably with other similar measures of child development. They predict later outcomes, including academic achievement in primary school. However, the EDI is not designed to be a tool to diagnose individual delays or developmental problems. The EDI's strength is allowing the aggregation of individual data to the group or community level, which makes it possible to integrate child development outcomes with other sources of data about children, families, and communities (Janus, 2006).

The EDI has now been applied widely across Canada. The Canadian EDI database includes over 400 000 five-year-old kindergarten children and another 50 000 four-year-old kindergarten children (Janus, 2006). Approximately 50 percent of all Canadian children are now assessed on the EDI measurement before entry to Grade 1.

The Offord Centre for Child Studies (OCCS), at McMaster University, is the national repository of the EDI in Canada and where the majority of the data are stored. Once data are collected and analyzed, each site receives a report of demographics, descriptions in perspective with other sites, behavioural profiles of children with the highest and lowest scores, and school-level reports.

Source: www.offordcentre.com/readiness/index.html.

Measuring early child development at the community level is both a research approach and a community development strategy:

- *A research approach.* Across Canada, researchers and communities are working together to better understand patterns of early development within communities. Communities are monitoring how children are doing and what kinds of environments they are living in during their early years. Information about developmental outcomes, community resources, and socioeconomic characteristics can be combined to illustrate child development within different community contexts.

- *A community development strategy.* Canada is investing public funding and efforts in community-based early child development reporting to forge collaborations among initiatives and services for young children and families at the local level. Community early child development reporting is viewed as a way to plan locally for more effective early child and family programs. To date, the emphasis has been on providing information and support while relying on community initiative and direction to build the early child development system. Reporting on community-level child development indicators and outcomes is thought to build synergy across communities and allow a more integrated, holistic service delivery system to emerge.

Community reporting of early child development has highlighted information about the distribution of vulnerable children in regions across Canada. In most communities, the neighbourhoods that have the highest percentage of vulnerable children are usually not the neighbourhoods that have the highest numbers of vulnerable children. While the highest risk for vulnerability is often found in the poorest neighbourhoods, most of the total number of vulnerable children are spread more thinly across more affluent neighbourhoods (Hertzman, 2002; Janus, 2006).

Early childhood educators are valuable participants in initiatives that are using community early child development reporting. Right now, it is unknown if these efforts will be effective in creating an early childhood system and/or improving early childhood learning and development outcomes. Continued efforts in numerous communities across Canada are an opportunity to monitor the impact of community early child development reporting on programs, children, and families. Early childhood educators bring an understanding of early development and knowledge about the kinds of environments to support that development. Community-based opportunities that draw together child and family programs can open up opportunities for new program delivery and new opportunities for early childhood educators.

The Understanding Early Years initiative is community-level research, now in over 50 communities across Canada, that involves teachers, parents, and community organizations (including early childhood programs) in exploring the associations between community factors and children's developmental outcomes. Community early child development reporting is emerging as an innovative approach to tracking child development in local context.

Community mapping uses geographic information systems (GIS) that are computer applications that map and analyze information for a specific geographic location. The central value of mapping is that it quickly tells a story of what has happened or is happening in neighbourhoods or larger communities.

Neighbourhoods across Canada are now mapped in terms of child development outcomes, community assets, and socioeconomic characteristics. This technique provides an accurate and accessible means of looking at population data regarding child vulnerability and well-being on a neighbourhood basis. It is fascinating to look at maps of elements as diverse as child literacy rates, cost of a nutritious food basket as

Innovations

THE EARLY CHILD DEVELOPMENT MAPPING PROJECT

HELP (Human Early Learning Partnership) is a network of biological, medical, and social science researchers from British Columbia universities who work together to "research, understand, and enhance the quality of children's early years." HELP hosts the Early Child Development Mapping Project that brings together academic, government, and community partners to better understand early childhood development in B.C. neighbourhoods. Academic, government, and community partners cooperate to develop neighbourhood-based maps related to EDI data, socioeconomic factors, and community assets and resources. To date, HELP has mapped child development measures, socioeconomic circumstances, and community assets and resources in partnership with local coalitions in 491 B.C. neighbourhoods.

The Early Child Development Mapping Project has produced the *British Columbia Atlas of Child Development* (Kershaw et al., 2006), which charts the geography of opportunity for young children in Canada. The atlas is a visual summary of early child development trends across neighbourhood, school districts, and provincial geographies in B.C. Colour maps depict information about the many intersecting environments in which B.C. families live and young children grow, including the socioeconomic, community, and policy environments.

The project has set up a Mapping Portal (see http://ecdportal.help.ubc.ca/) on the Internet that houses a wide collection of maps, datasets, and other useful tools related to early child development in British Columbia. This includes ongoing results from the EDI, asset mapping, and socioeconomic and demographic data. It is the primary portal for geographic data related to early child development planning.

The site is set up for local "ECD coalitions" that are taking the lead in planning and coordinating programs for young children in British Columbia's communities. The site is also a portal for the general public to have access to information about their communities. It is a good illustration of what kinds of information and reporting can be made available to the early childhood sector and to local communities.

The ECD Mapping Project in British Columbia is reported to have influenced over 110 projects in 41 school districts (Mort, 2004) and increased programming, partnerships, and linkages among early childhood professionals. Early childhood educators are taking active roles in community coalitions that are using the results to improve programming quality and increase coordination of early childhood and family programs.

HELP is using community mapping of early child development as a strategy to support integrated early childhood planning. EDI results are a baseline and

(continued)

communities can set targets to reduce inequalities in children's development at the local, regional, and/or provincial level (HELP, 2005). For instance, in Vancouver (Hertzman, 2002) the inequality ranged from 6 percent to 38 percent. A goal for neighbourhoods might be to work together to improve early environments and reduce that range.

HELP's community early child development reporting seems to be influencing policy directions for child care and related programming. The Child and Youth Office for British Columbia (2005) has recommended a neighbourhood hub approach that will encourage local child care, family support, family health, and early intervention programs to coordinate efforts, possibly co-locating in primary school space. The report stipulates that regulated child care should be a central component of the hubs and that a funding envelope with appropriate accountability mechanisms should be given to community tables for planning and program delivery. In 2007, Strong Start centres (parenting centres) were introduced into 80 elementary schools, and 22 communities received grants to support child care capacity as part of emerging neighbourhood hubs.

Source: www.earlylearning.ubc.ca/mapping

percentage of total income, crime rates, and percentage of parents for whom English is a second language. Gradually, one gets a clear picture of the realities of living in specific neighbourhoods—a good basis for action.

USING RESEARCH TO SUPPORT QUALITY PRACTICE

Understanding early child development is based on multiple sources of information. Information from theoretical models and empirical studies joins program evaluation and professional experience (Shonkoff & Phillips, 2000).

Early childhood educators need to differentiate between established knowledge, reasonable hypotheses, and unwarranted assertions (Shonkoff, 2000). Scientific research findings with rules of evidence and rigorous peer review in academic journals determine what is established knowledge. Reasonable hypotheses are really educated guesses that are based in established knowledge but extend beyond the boundaries of what is proven by scientific research. Reasonable hypotheses tap into the wisdom and experience of early childhood professionals who are working with young children and their families to extend what we know from science. Future scientific investigations may prove or disprove reasonable hypotheses. In the meantime, reasonable hypotheses make up much of the knowledge base that guides daily practice and policymaking. Unwarranted assertions misrepresent current knowledge and often misuse science to advance commercial or ideological interests. Informed early childhood educators need to understand the knowledge base, use reasonable hypotheses to guide their practice, avoid misuse of science, and keep current with new, credible information.

EARLY CHILDHOOD EDUCATORS AND QUALITY

Knowledgeable, skilled, and caring early childhood educators are central to quality programs that benefit children, families, and communities. Using tools to evaluate programs and assess children's development contributes to the quality of the environments in settings for young children.

The most important first step to take is the ongoing observation and documentation of children's development as they interact with adults and other children in early childhood settings.

KEY TERMS

accreditation

assessment

Early Development Instrument (EDI)

early learning standards

functional capabilities

monitoring

peer-reviewed

program evaluations

program standards

REFLECTION QUESTIONS

1. *Skills Challenges:* What are the optimal educational levels for an effective early childhood work force? How can the effectiveness of content and delivery of post-secondary ECE programs be assessed? What is the most effective preparation program for early child development program managers and directors? How can professional development opportunities be planned and delivered to be effective in increasing the skill level of staff and caregivers and the overall quality of child care programs?

2. *Working Environment Challenge:* Is it possible to organize the work in a full-time, full-year child care centre to ensure a more pedagogical approach without compromising the quality of care and protection?

3. *Recognition Challenge:* Is it possible to leverage public awareness and interest in early development to support increased public investment in child care?

FOR MORE INFORMATION

1. *Preschool Program Quality Assessment Instrument* (PQA) is an up-to-date and comprehensive rating instrument for evaluating early childhood program quality and identifying staff training needs. The PQA can be used in all centre-based early childhood settings, including (but not limited to) those using the High/Scope educational approach.

   www.highscope.org/Assessment/pqa.htm

2. *Quality in Early Learning and Care in Ontario: Measuring Up?* intends to increase knowledge and public policy dialogue about age-appropriate outcomes for children's development and about the tools and approaches available both in Canada and abroad to measure and enhance them. The Ontario Coalition for Better Child Care is hosting the project.

www.childcareontario.org/measureup/index.html

3. *Alberta Child Care Accreditation Program* is offered by the Alberta Association for the Accreditation of Early Learning and Care Services. It provides resources and guidance to child care programs seeking accreditation.

www.abccaccred.ca/

4. The *Thomson Nelson ECE Resource Centre* is intended to enhance the teaching and learning experience for both instructors and students. The website provides extensive and helpful resources in many different criteria related to early childhood education.

www.ece.nelson.com

Managing Early Childhood Programs

Managing early childhood programs is the coordination of tasks and the setting up of systems to carry out the goals of the program. The management of an early childhood program provides infrastructure that determines how decisions are made, the arrangement of physical space, hours of operation and program schedules, staffing arrangements, and financial administration.

Managing early childhood programs is essential to quality experiences for young children and their families. Overall, management practices make a difference to the quality of all early child development programs. Research has consistently found that when management systems are not in place and at work, high-quality interactions and early learning environments cannot be sustained (Talan & Bloom, 2004). Effective decision-making and administrative practices are necessary to ensure positive outcomes for children and families.

If the management of an early childhood program works well—that is, the program is well organized and administered—the infrastructure is often invisible to staff working in the program. However, when there are problems that are not managed well, inadequate infrastructure becomes very visible. Think about a leaky roof or broken toilet, indecision about fee increases, delayed paycheques, or late lunches. The management of an early childhood program has an impact on what children and their families experience. And it has a direct impact on the quality of the work environment.

Effective management begins with decision making that is based on the program's governance. The operations of an early childhood program include the health and safety of the physical space, risk-management plans, enrollment procedures, child development profiles, program planning and evaluation, record-keeping, and technological resources. Human resource management includes recruitment and retention strategies, wages and working conditions, and performance review. Fiscal management (vital to the survival of early child development programs) consists of planning and record-keeping.

The focus in the next four chapters is on the management of full-day child care centres and part-day nursery schools/preschools, as they have defined space requirements, other health and safety measures, staffing requirements, and designated funding that are contained in provincial/territorial regulations. However, the operational guidelines and examples included in this section are often applicable to other quality early childhood programs, even if these programs do not require a licence and may not be required to meet these standards. Many of the strategies, suggestions, and examples are based on those found in *The Child Care Management Guide* (Bertrand, 1990; OCBCC, 2003; also see www.childcaremanagement. ca/). Specific samples are found in the Appendix.

In some provinces and territories, family child care homes may be purpose-built in nonprofit housing and may have defined space requirements, but usually they are located in the caregiver's home. Regulated family child care settings are required to meet some space, health and safety, and program requirements. Kindergarten programs operate within territorial/provincial education legislation (with the exception of Prince Edward Island) and are part of the administrative structures of local school boards or districts. In some jurisdictions, there are guidelines for family resource programs.

Each of the four chapters in this section begins with a description of a fictitious early childhood program, Downtown Squire Early Childhood Centre. The chapter descriptions illustrate how the program is administered.

GOVERNANCE

CHAPTER

4

CHAPTER OUTLINE

Downtown Squire Early Childhood Centre

Downtown Squire Early Childhood Centre opened January 4, 1990. It is a workplace child care program that came into existence as the result of the initiative of a forward-thinking developer and a determined community. It is located in the Squire Factory building in downtown Quesceville, in southwestern Ontario, along the shores of Lake Ontario.

Squire Factory houses over 120 cultural producers and entrepreneurs. In 1985, architect Sahira Kahal purchased the 90-year-old building and transformed it into a fully leased cultural and commercial centre. A strong supporter of the arts, she wanted to create a work environment that would be affordable and supportive to people who work in arts and culture. This project was not simply a real estate deal but an original way of combining commerce, culture, and community.

The eclectic tenant base at Squire Factory includes visual artists, musicians, filmmakers, talent agencies, social scientists, and a variety of nonprofit organizations. In 1989, understanding her tenants' needs, Ms. Kahal envisioned a centre that would be a key element of a supportive work environment, allowing people to be more productive as well as providing an opportunity to develop learning opportunities for children in an environment greatly enriched by local arts and culture. She hired a child care consultant to investigate the possibility of opening a workplace child care centre.

The consultant conducted an assessment of the community needs related to child care and found that there was a significant demand among tenants for on-site child care, particularly for infants and for school-age children before and after school and on school holidays.

Squire Early Childhood Centre is a true example of a community coming together to make something special. Squire Factory renovated the space and continues to provide the facility rent-free. Local merchants donated close to $10 000 worth of equipment and loaned a staff consultant's time during the months leading up to the opening. Tenants, local businesses, and individuals from the community donated time, money, services, and products, without which the centre could not have opened. This tremendous support from the community is a perfect example of the community values, which form the foundation for Downtown Squire Early Childhood Centre's program philosophy.

Downtown Squire Early Childhood Centre is operated as a nonprofit corporation and overseen by a volunteer board of directors, which includes five to seven parents, a management representative from Squire Factory, and the principal from the local elementary school. The director of the centre is an ex-officio member of the board of directors.

The board meetings usually include a program update from the program's director, a financial status report from the treasurer, and a report on news from the local school.

chapter Objectives

The chapter will:

1. Identify basic responsibilities and types of governing bodies.
2. Discuss not-for-profit board structures and functions.

3. Describe the purpose and functions of meetings to make decisions.

4. Explore opportunities for early childhood educators to have input into the decision-making process.

DECISION MAKING: WHO, WHAT, AND HOW

The term "**governance**" refers to the decision-making structure and processes in the management of an organization. Governance is the structure within an organization that has the final authority and responsibility to make decisions and set policies. The governance structure defines *who* decides. Governance also refers to the process of making decisions—*what* is decided and *how*.

Governance Structures

Governance structures are defined by specific legal requirements for different types of operations. Early childhood programs are governed by five different types of structures:

- individual ownership,
- commercial board of directors,
- not-for-profit board of directors,
- cooperative, or
- government.

If early childhood programs are operated by a structure or organization that has responsibilities broader than early childhood programs, it is common for an advisory committee to be established to provide input and guidance to the program.

The governance structure defines the type or **auspice** of legal organizational structure that operates early childhood programs. In Canada, a public (government) authority, a private **not-for-profit** organization, a **cooperative**, a **commercial** business, or an individual may operate early childhood programs.

Apart from universal access to kindergarten, the majority of early childhood programs are offered by not-for-profit organizations (McCain et al., 2007). Therefore, the focus of this chapter will be on not-for-profit boards of directors, unless otherwise indicated. Many of the practices and policies related to governance can apply in commercial or public programs, particularly if there are advisory committees in place.

Governance Processes

The governing body is responsible for the stewardship—the legal and fiduciary oversight—of the organization. It should understand the organizational mandates, legal documents, and regulatory requirements that established the early childhood program. The governing body is the organization's structure to make decisions, set policies, and be the final authority.

Governing bodies of early childhood programs have a responsibility to represent the communities they serve as well as their responsibility to guide a quality program that effectively serves children and families. Governing bodies represent the people participating in programs, rather than the staff managing the program. Families participating in early childhood programs and the larger community need access to the governing body. Procedures for hearing and resolving complaints should be established and implemented.

Each member of the governing body has a set of responsibilities. Individuals who may be may be owners, board members, cooperative members, or representatives of elected officials must attend meetings, read material that is pertinent to making decisions, and carry out their duties in a reasonable and responsible manner. They are responsible for understanding the organization's policies and how program activities are implemented; staying current with developments that impact the organization; advocating for the organization, as well as informing others about it; suggesting nominees that could contribute to the organization and the governing body; adhering to conflict-of-interest and confidentiality policies; participating in programmatic and fiscal reviews of performance; and serving on committees and taking on special assignments that fit with their expertise.

In *Basic Principles of Policy Governance,* John Carver and Miriam Mayhew Carver (1996) describe four functions of governance. These functions are relevant to both public, not-for-profit, and privately owned early childhood organizations:

- Create a process that leads to defining goals.
- Establish boundaries and limits that describe management's authority and responsibilities for implementing the early childhood program.
- Link with staff and assess staff and/or organizational performance to ensure that management and staff are moving toward program goals.
- Design governance processes to ensure that families taking part in the programs receive quality services and that the organization's policies are being followed.

The governing body must address broad values in these areas to fulfill its mandate.

In *Maximizing Child Care Services: The Roles of Owners and Boards,* Elaine Ferguson and Tammy McCormick (2001) set out a governance framework that describes the roles and responsibilities of public, commercial, or nonprofit governance structures. Owners and boards:

- Set the direction for the provision of a quality service and define what the program intends to achieve and whom the program is intended to serve.
- Hire, monitor, and evaluate the administrator and ensure he or she has resources necessary to provide a quality program.
- Participate in public relations by promoting the program.
- Advocate with the government, the general public, and the business community regarding the inherent value of the program.
- Ensure that legal requirements are met, including employment legislation, licensing regulations, and business and incorporation laws.
- Conduct themselves in an ethical manner and uphold honest, prudent, and best practices in exercising their responsibilities.

Governance Versus Administration

The governing body is responsible for ensuring that the early childhood program operates effectively and responds to issues and concerns in the community. Early childhood organizations must have internal systems to ensure accountability, measure the effectiveness of programs, and determine whether the organization's activities are focused on the needs of the population. It is important not to confuse the oversight or stewardship role of governance with the administrative role of management and staff. Governance refers to general and legal oversight and not to implementing day-to-day operations, which is the responsibility of management and staff.

It is important to clarify governing and administrating responsibilities, to decide who is responsible for what, and to define the activities of the board or advisory committee. An **organizational chart** can show who is accountable to whom and who communicates with whom.

Usually, a voluntary board of directors in the nonprofit sector hires a director or supervisor who is directly accountable to the board for the implementation of the program as determined by the board. The board of directors assumes responsibility for establishing policy and supporting the supervisor or director and other staff in carrying out the policy. In order to find the balance between board and staff roles, it is important to clearly state expectations of the board and of the staff. This information must be provided to the board, staff, parents, and all other members of the organization.

Not-for-Profit Board and Staff Responsibilities

Not-for-profit early childhood organizations should outline the responsibilities of the board of directors and of the lead staff person—usually the director or supervisor, with a background in early childhood education. The following discussion illustrates an example breakdown of not-for-profit board and staff planning, and legal, organizational, program, personnel, financial, and community outreach responsibilities.

Planning

The *board* will ensure programs are delivered to children and their families that fulfill the purpose and philosophy by establishing the board's goals and objectives for each area of responsibility. The board will assess its own performance annually.

The *director* will implement the program in a manner that is consistent with the purpose, philosophy, goals, and objectives. The director will coordinate staff input into the annual board of directors' review, design a program review that considers program goals and objectives, and review program staff performance.

Legal

The *board* will ensure that the centre meets all legal requirements by updating incorporation and reviewing other legal documents such as program licence reports, leases, insurance, and service agreements for funding or subsidies.

The *director* will ensure that the centre meets legal requirements by monitoring compliance with requirements from appropriate federal, provincial, and municipal legislation. All inspection reports will be presented at board meetings. The program staff will be familiar with and follow regulatory requirements.

Organizational

The *board* will provide a governing structure that is able to develop policies and make informed, democratic decisions that support the policies written through effective board communication.

The *director* will enable the board to make informed decisions by presenting a written report to each board meeting; preparing background information for planning board, committee, and general meetings as requested; distributing agenda minutes and reports; taking part in the orientation of new board members; and updating board of directors' handbooks.

Program

The *board* will ensure high-quality early childhood and parenting programs are carried out by establishing program policies that reflect the program's values; promote optimal child development and learning; ensure compliance with policies and practices that protect the health, safety, and well-being of all children; complement parents' childrearing responsibilities by establishing equitable enrollment policies; and encourage parent participation in the ongoing life of the centre.

The *director* will carry out the program policies by developing and managing appropriate procedures for enrollment and parent involvement, providing leadership in establishing curriculum goals and objectives, observing the program regularly, and reviewing weekly program plans. The program staff will plan and implement developmentally appropriate activities and experiences, guide children's behaviour by establishing and maintaining realistic expectations, monitor the environment for hazards, implement parenting sessions, encourage parental participation, and encourage conversation and information-sharing with parents.

Personnel

The *board* will ensure responsible functioning of the program by hiring and monitoring the supervisor, establishing fair personnel policies that are reviewed annually, and delegating staff hiring and supervision to the director.

The *director* will implement personnel policies, maintain open communication with all staff, facilitate staff development, hire program and support staff, and recommend probation, permanent status, or termination of staff to the personnel committee.

Financial

The *board* will ensure the financial viability of the program by developing and approving financial plans, monitoring financial records and reports, establishing fee collection and spending policies, and securing adequate financial resources.

The *director* will prepare accurate financial information for the treasurer, finance committee, and board by monitoring financial records, assisting in financial plans, preparing regular reports, and implementing financial fee collection and spending policies.

Community Outreach

The *board* will ensure favourable external relations for the centre by carrying out a public relations program in the community, establishing partnerships with other community groups, and responding to identified community needs.

The *director* will liaise with local organizations, and inform the board of early childhood initiatives and policies.

AUSPICE

The type or auspice of legal and organizational structure that operates an early childhood program is determined by the type of legal governance structure that is responsible for the operation. The majority of early childhood programs across Canada are operated as small or large not-for-profit organizations (McCain et al., 2007). The majority (almost 70 percent) of regulated child care programs are operated by not-for-profit boards of directors, while about a quarter are commercial operations (Friendly & Beach, 2005). Publicly delivered child care programs account for less than 5 percent (mostly municipally operated child care programs in Ontario). Out-of-school programs that are not licensed child care programs are often operated by municipalities, school boards, or not-for-profit organizations. For example, Quebec's extensive school-age programs are publicly operated by school boards. Family support programs are typically operated by not-for-profit organizations, although parenting centres in British Columbia and Toronto are operated by school boards. Home visiting programs are often operated by public health departments or agencies, which are publicly operated services. Kindergarten programs operated within the school system are also public programs that are operated by local or provincial/territorial governments, while kindergarten programs offered within private schools may be commercial or not-for-profit organizations. In Prince Edward Island, kindergarten programs are operated within child care programs, both not-for-profit and commercial. Early identification and intervention programs are mostly delivered through public health, provincial governments, or not-for-profit organizations.

Not-for-profit early childhood programs are incorporated as not-for-profit corporations or they are part of a not-for-profit corporation that includes a variety of programs and activities. They may also be incorporated as cooperative organizations, which usually means that all parents using a program are general members of the organization. Not-for-profit corporations, sometimes called "non-share capital corporations," are different from for-profit corporations or business corporations in three fundamental ways:

- The not-for-profit corporation is composed of members, whereas the for-profit corporation is owned by shareholders.
- The members of a not-for-profit corporation cannot receive any financial gain during the life of the corporation, whereas a for-profit corporation may distribute profits to its shareholders in the form of dividends.
- The powers of a not-for-profit corporation are limited to what is written into its objects (purposes), whereas, typically, the for-profit corporation has no such limits.

Not-for-Profit Organizations

Boards of directors govern not-for-profit organizations. As discussed earlier, clear governance policies and procedures that outline board and staff responsibilities and how the board will function are key. Board members who understand their role and how decisions are made and implemented are better able to be effective.

Early childhood programs may exist as stand-alone programs or may be a program area within a larger, multi-service organization, such as a multi-purpose community

Early childhood programs are operated by not-for-profit organizations, owners, or governments.

centre or a YMCA. When early childhood programs are operated within multi-service organizations, there may be a parent/community advisory committee that supports and guides the program and provides an avenue for specific parent and community input. The board of directors for the larger organization retains the governance authority, but the advisory committee is able to provide more direct input into the day-to-day operation of the program.

Not-for-profit cooperative early childhood programs often involve parents in the actual delivery of the program as well as in the governance structure. While most tend to offer half-day nursery school programs, some run full-time child care programs. Canada has about 526 cooperative nurseries, 270 of them in Ontario (Rushowy, 2007). Cooperative nursery schools began in 1916 in Chicago, when a group of professors' wives sought a program that would combine education for their children, parenting help, and social networking, as well as some free time for themselves (Rushowy, 2007). The From the Past box on page 107 describes Canada's first cooperative early childhood program.

Commercial Operations

Commercial programs exist among Canada's regulated centre- and home-based child care programs. Sometimes commercial child care is called for-profit child care.

From the Past

PARENT PARTICIPATION AND COOPERATIVES

Cooperative nursery schools first emerged in Canada during the 1930s and exploded in greater numbers in the 1950s. The programs were based on parent participation and shared (children and adult) learning. In 1937 a committee of parents started Toronto's Manor Road Nursery School, which is believed to be the earliest cooperative program in Canada (Stevenson, 1990). Early participants in nursery school cooperatives recognized that as parents and staff worked together, a sense of community evolved over a relatively short period of time.

In the late 1960s and early 1970s, cooperative day care centres began to appear in Canada. Many were located on university campuses and were often supported by the recent changes and expansion of child care fee subsidies and the federal Local Initiatives Projects program. Regular parent participation in the daily program and parent control of decisions were characteristics of the cooperative child care programs. Parents and staff worked together to plan and monitor children's programs that reflected alternative values and beliefs—collective decision making, gender and cultural equity, and more choices about daily routines (Russell & Morrow, 1978). There was a strong sense of building alternative communities and, in fact, for many families the social connections from early day care cooperative experiences were a kind of kinship that provided a valuable web of support.

Commercial child care programs are privately owned businesses. Across Canada, approximately 25 percent of regulated child care programs are owned by individuals or commercial corporations. The majority of regulated child care centres in Alberta, Newfoundland and Labrador, and New Brunswick are commercial, about 22 percent of licensed child care in Ontario is commercial, and Manitoba has no commercial child care programs.

Commercial child care programs, like other commercial operations, are structured and organized to generate a profit for the owners. Small commercial programs are often owned and operated by an early childhood educator who is committed to quality programming, and financial gain is often limited (or nonexistent). Commercial corporations that operate a chain of programs are operating businesses that are intended to generate a profit. They are more common in Australia and the United States.

Family Child Care

Regulated and unregulated family child care is often organized as a small business. The caregiver is self-employed in her or his own home-based business. Two basic models exist for the provision of regulated family child care in Canada: the licensing model and the agency model (Cox, 2005; Friendly & Beach, 2005).

In the licensing model, the family child care provider applies to a governmental department that grants a licence and supervises the family child care provider. The

Beyond Our Borders

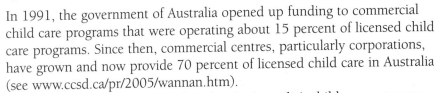

COMMERCIAL CHILD CARE IN AUSTRALIA

In 1991, the government of Australia opened up funding to commercial child care programs that were operating about 15 percent of licensed child care programs. Since then, commercial centres, particularly corporations, have grown and now provide 70 percent of licensed child care in Australia (see www.ccsd.ca/pr/2005/wannan.htm).

In 2006, a national survey of quality in Australia's child care programs reported that, in the view of child care staff, the quality of care provided in chains was markedly lower than that provided in not-for-profit or individually owned for-profit programs. Corporate centres were less likely than not-for-profit and owner-operated centres to always provide nutritious food, less likely to have more than the minimum number of early childhood educators, and less likely to support individual relationships between early childhood educators and children. Staff turnover is considerably higher in the chain commercial programs and salaries are lower.

The study concludes that the lower quality of care in chain corporations is due to the nature of the corporate enterprise. According to Rush (2006, p. 11), "Managers of corporations are legally obliged to act in the best interests of their shareholders. In a market like child care where there is limited scope to raise prices without additional government subsidies, corporate chain providers often have little choice but to adopt a business orientation where humanist concerns are secondary to those regarding efficiency and cost containment."

licensing model is found in British Columbia, Saskatchewan, Manitoba, New Brunswick, Prince Edward Island, the Yukon, and the Northwest Territories. In the agency model, the family child care provider is affiliated with and supervised by a non-profit or commercial agency that in turn is licensed by a government department. Alberta, Ontario, Quebec, and Nova Scotia have adopted the agency model. In Newfoundland and Labrador, there is a dual model based on both the agency model and on direct licensing. In all situations, the family child care provider in regulated child care is considered to be an independent contractor, self-employed, and essentially operating a small business that is entitled to claim business expenses.

Public Programs

Public programs are run by government, and are ultimately the responsibility of elected officials. Kindergarten delivered within the school system is the largest early childhood program in Canada. Such programs are governed either by a provincial education department or a local school board that is elected. Often, parents and other community members can have input into decisions through participation on committees or making deputations to elected officials.

Innovations

CITY OF TORONTO

The City of Toronto's Directly Operated Child Care Services operates a licensed home child care agency and 58 public licensed child care centres, serving approximately 4100 children in predominately high-needs neighbourhoods. The directly operated child care centres and home child care agency are publicly operated by the municipal government, and the child care staff are unionized employees of the city, represented by Canadian Union of Public Employees Local 79. Toronto operates the largest number of publicly operated child care programs in North America (apart from those operated within the school system). With more than half a century of experience, the city has a wealth of expertise to share with any jurisdiction considering a public child care system.

Public delivery of child care has its challenges. The culture can be bureaucratic and perhaps less responsive to the immediate needs of families and neighbourhoods. Operational practices and reporting remain centralized. While it is possible to move staff between centres to accommodate staffing needs and provide opportunities to work in different settings, this practice can mean increased "turnover" from the child's perspective. The directly operated centres seem separate from the child care community and their own neighbourhoods.

On the other hand, the city is able to establish and maintain management stability that is often difficult to find in community-based programs. It is also able to implement and follow through on specific curriculum directions or specialized service delivery without losing the central concept in the translation across multiple service providers.

Sources: Beach et al., 2004; Corter et al., 2004; Mahon, 2004.

The Organisation for Economic Co-operation and Development review (OECD, 2004) recommended that early childhood programs should be a publicly managed service. This suggests a public authority should manage functions such as planning, training and professional development, finances, and infrastructure, although services may not necessarily be publicly delivered (Friendly & Beach, 2005).

The Issue of Auspice

In the Canadian child care sector, the debate about commercial and not-for-profit child care continues. For many the issue is related to quality. In a recent studies, University of Toronto economists found that nonprofit child care centres outscore their commercial counterparts in all aspects of early learning and care (Cleveland & Krashinsky, 2003; Cleveland, 2007). The studies found that quality differences between not-for-profit and commercial programs were greatest in the following areas:

- Personal care provided to children, such as diapering, rest, and meals (6.9 percent higher scores in nonprofit centres).
- The use of materials, activities, and teaching interactions that affect language and thought development (nonprofit centres scored 6.5 percent higher).
- The way staff interact with children, including supervision, discipline, encouragement, warmth, and respect (nonprofits centres rated 8.3% higher).
- Issues specific to parents and staff, such as the level of staff communication to parents about their children, and support for the personal and professional needs of staff (nonprofits scored 18.6 percent higher).

Higher-quality care in nonprofit centres held true even when scores were adjusted to consider other factors that could affect quality. For instance, nonprofit centres are better regardless of the province where the centres are located and child population is served. Even when scoring was adjusted to consider variables such as availability of financial resources and the higher education levels of staff in nonprofit centres, the for-profit programs still came out at the bottom.

Not all commercial child care programs are of poor quality, nor are all nonprofit programs high quality. But overall, the research findings point to better-quality environments in nonprofit programs compared to those delivered in commercial operations, and better compensation for staff. The results of a study on quality in Australian child care programs (see the Beyond Our Borders box on page 108) raise serious concerns about widespread corporate chain child care programs. The study also highlights differences between small owner-operated programs that were similar to community-based, not-for-profit child care and that found in the larger commercial chains.

Some advocates and policymakers in the early childhood sector are promoting public delivery of programs to ensure quality, equitable access, and reasonable compensation for staff (Friendly, 2006; McCain et al., 2007). Licensed child care programs are the only early childhood programs that have a significant proportion of services operated by small or large commercial owners. The majority of the other programs operate as not-for-profit programs that receive government funding or they are public programs operated by a school board, municipality, or provincial/territorial government.

NONPROFIT EARLY CHILDHOOD PROGRAMS

In the world of not-for-profit and public agencies, service to the public is not a strategy but an end in itself (Wolf, 1990). This underscores the need to have internal systems that ensure accountability, measure the effectiveness of programs, and determine whether the activities of the organization and its programs are geared toward the people who are eligible for its services.

Boards of directors should understand whom they represent, as well as the roles and responsibilities of the board and how to best represent the interests of its constituencies. This helps to ensure that the governing body remains accountable to the children, families, and communities that the program serves.

Incorporation Legislation

Not-for-profit organizations must become corporations. In law, a corporation is a legal entity that has a distinct existence, separate and independent from that of its members. A corporation continues to exist unless its members take steps to dissolve or end it. Not-for-profit organizations incorporate (i.e., become legally recognized corporations) either as not-for-profit corporations or as cooperative corporations.

The process of incorporation for not-for-profit corporations differs from incorporation from commercial corporations, although the process varies from jurisdiction to jurisdiction. Incorporating a for-profit entity is a routine matter of submitting the correct forms and payments. Incorporating a not-for-profit entity at the federal level and in most provincial/territorial jurisdictions, however, requires government review and approval. For instance, not-for-profit entities incorporating federally under the Canada Corporations Act must apply to the federal minister of industry to issue letters patent to the corporation. The proposed bylaws of the corporation must accompany the application.

In some jurisdictions, additional approvals are required or conditions must be met for the incorporation of certain types of not-for-profit organizations and for those with certain words in their name. For example, a not-for-profit corporation that wants to use the term "Canadian" must receive federal approval, and a corporation that wants to describe itself as an "institute" or "academy" usually has to obtain approval from the appropriate provincial education ministry.

A not-for-profit entity can incorporate either federally or provincially, depending on the scope of its stated purpose and proposed activities. Each jurisdiction has its own legislation for the incorporation of not-for-profit organizations, and its own approval process.

Key Documents

Legal documents and other instruments create nonprofit organizations and provide the tools for their maintenance. Several key documents and materials help boards of directors meet their responsibilities.

For all not-for-profit organizations, these include the annual report (if one is produced), the audit and financial statements, the strategic or long-range plan, organizational charts, and articles of incorporation and bylaws. In addition, periodic reports of program and financial status are typically provided to the board. Other important documents include organizational brochures, newsletters, materials that describe the program and organization, and any published newspaper or journal articles about the programs.

Annual Report

An annual report is a document that is often used as an informational and public relations tool by an organization. It contains the year's program and financial highlights and may be distributed at the annual meeting. Public agencies and not-for-profit organizations that receive public money are usually required to produce annual reports.

Annual reports can become useful documents that highlight a program's strengths and celebrate its successes. Most programs now post their annual reports on their websites, so it is possible to view a number of reports and compare content, style, and format.

Policies and Procedures

The letters patent and bylaws of a nonprofit program and the legislated legal requirements create the broad framework for that organization's actual operation. Policies and procedures describe in more detail the day-to-day practices that bring the group's goals and objectives to life. Policies usually describe what is to be done and procedures describe how it is to be done. In a nonprofit early childhood organization, formulation of policy is the responsibility of the board of directors and execution of policy is the responsibility of the supervisor and other program staff. To work smoothly, this division of responsibility requires a great deal of discussion between the board of directors and staff. In everyday situations, the line between policy and procedure becomes blurred and it can be difficult to make clear distinctions between policy and procedure. For example, policies determine the spending and fee collection practices, personnel, and program procedures. The annual budget is really a major policy statement.

Boards of Directors

Boards of directors for not-for-profit organizations are made up of volunteers who work together to manage the organization. They are geared to change and open to inspection and evaluation. The structure of a board of directors can allow users—in this case, parents—to have power to determine the direction of the centre. A board of directors is selected/elected from the general membership and is accountable to that same group. In a sense, it is the same way government is determined in Canada, except on a much smaller scale. And that smaller scale makes the whole process more accessible to individuals. In fact, boards of directors in a local community offer opportunities, not always available in other institutions, to participate in the democratic process.

The board of directors:

- maintains an overview of the organization's operation on behalf of the general membership;
- sets policies and makes decisions;
- has the powers and responsibilities stated in the centre's letters patent bylaws; and
- must comply with the legal requirements set out in the relevant legislation.

The composition of a board of directors is an important issue embedded in the organization's bylaws. Many nonprofit early childhood organizations elect to have only parents/guardians of children who are currently enrolled or participating in the program as members of the board of directors. Others have few if any parent/guardian members and decide to have community members who are not users of the program act as directors of the board. The composition of the board of directors may be split between parents/guardians and others who bring specific skills (e.g., early child development expertise, financial skills, and legal abilities) or who represent community partners (e.g., community centre staff, school teacher or principal, or public health practitioner).

Parents/Guardians as Directors of the Board

Parents who are directors of the board are actively involved in the decision-making process. In many community-based programs, parents using the program fill the majority of positions on the board of directors. There are several reasons behind this practice: notably, parents have a personal interest in and commitment to managing the program, and parent board members are persuasive advocates in promoting early childhood programs.

There are, however, some drawbacks to having only parent members. In particular, parents do not necessarily bring management, financial, or legal expertise to a board of directors. Not-for-profit early childhood programs have become complex organizations and these skills must be available to boards of directors. Parent boards of directors for not-for-profit early child development programs are a unique kind of volunteer board, particularly when parents make up the majority of members.

Community-based early childhood programs with parent board members are mechanisms for ensuring parent and community involvement in the provision of programs. Their structure allows parents and community members to make decisions about how an early childhood program will operate. Serving on a board of directors provides parents with an opportunity to participate in a democratic process while building a program for themselves and their own children. Parents have the biggest investment in providing the best possible program for their own children. The challenge is to organize the work of boards of directors so that the energy and commitment of parent members is not overwhelmed by the demands and responsibilities.

Program advisory committees in larger not-profit-agencies, community colleges, or municipalities that operate multiple programs can provide opportunities for parent input and involvement to decision making about the early childhood program without the employer or financial responsibilities (discussed later in this chapter) that accompany participation on a not-for-profit board of directors.

Community Representatives as Directors of the Board

The board of directors often includes members of the community who may not be users of the program. For example, individuals who represent other organizations in the community can serve as a liaison between these organizations and the program, which can improve communication and promote the centre's activity in the community. In addition, individuals who have specific skills and are interested in and committed to an early childhood program can make a valuable contribution as members of the board of directors. Sometimes individuals who are not personally involved with the services do not attend to the business of the board of directors as closely.

Staff as Directors of the Board

Including staff as members on the board of directors raises a number of issues. Employees cannot be voting members of the board of directors in nonprofit or cooperative centres that have charitable status. It is, however, possible in these instances to include staff members as ex-officio members who can contribute to discussions but not participate in votes. In cooperative organizations that are not charitable organizations, it is possible to include staff members on the board of directors.

Staff board members have a clear conflict of interest when salary levels are being decided or when a disciplinary issue is being discussed. At such times, it is appropriate for the individual board member or the president to declare the conflict and for the board member to abstain from the discussion or decision. Staff board members who are in a conflict-of-interest situation must abstain from key financial and management discussions and votes, thus placing a greater burden on the other board members.

Early childhood programs usually involve a unique relationship between program staff and parents. Open communication is critical. This communication may be supported through direct staff participation on the board of directors and may help reduce employer–employee tension.

Staff members have a day-to-day understanding of the program, which can be a valuable contribution to the decision-making process. Staff members may be more likely to participate in this process if they have a real say through power to vote at general meetings and board meetings. But one token staff vote may not be as important as maintaining the opportunity for staff members to participate in board meeting discussions.

Officers

Officers who have specific duties may be selected at the first meeting of a new board of directors or may be directly elected to officer positions by the annual general meeting. It is also possible to appoint individuals who are not directors of the board to officer positions. The bylaws specify how many officers there will be, their titles, how they are elected, and their powers and duties.

Choosing the right people to be officers is important. The board will be more effective if the officers can fulfill their duties and provide leadership to the board and to the organization as a whole. Often, officers have been board members in previous years.

The *president* usually acts as chairperson of the meetings of the board and general members. She or he is often the spokesperson for the organization and provides leadership to the board, staff, and parents. In some instances, a chairperson is a separate position from the president. If there is an executive committee, the president is the chairperson. The president's responsibilities include:

- chairing board meetings and general meetings;
- preparing agenda for board meetings and general meetings;
- serving as a member of the personnel committee;
- participating in the hiring and performance review of the supervisor;
- maintaining regular contact with the supervisor between board meetings; and
- representing the centre to the community.

The *vice-president* takes on the president's responsibilities in her or his absence. The vice-president often is the chairperson for one of the important committees of the board, such as personnel or strategic planning. Responsibilities of the vice-president include:

- chairing board meetings and general meetings in the president's absence;
- chairing standing committees, such as the personnel committee; and
- monitoring changes in government early childhood policies and funding.

The *treasurer* is responsible for the books of account and other financial records and for maintaining an overview of the organization's finances. If there is a finance committee, the treasurer is usually the chair. Other responsibilities of the treasurer include:

- preparing a draft of the annual budget with the director or supervisor;
- monitoring payment of fees and cheque disbursement;
- ensuring accurate records of all financial transactions are kept;
- reporting to each board meeting on the financial affairs of the program and making recommendations for adjustments as required;
- meeting regularly with the supervisor or director;
- signing the monthly bank reconciliation; and
- reviewing audits.

The *secretary* is primarily involved with record-keeping and correspondence related to board activity. Responsibilities of the secretary include:

- recording minutes of all board meetings and general meetings;
- keeping a record of attendance at each meeting;
- filing all minutes, once approved, in the minute book;
- keeping a duplicate copy of the minutes;
- updating the motion book on a regular basis;
- updating bylaws and policies regularly for reference; and
- keeping correspondence specific to the board of directors.

Committees

Much of the actual work of a board of directors is done by committee. Smaller groups are able to take on a particular area of responsibility and report back to the full board with specific recommendations or suggestions. In many early childhood programs, as in other organizations, not all of the committee members are members of the board. In many cases, board members and other members of the organization work together on a particular policy issue. This is an effective way to introduce people to the board of directors. It is also a way to use specific areas of expertise on a given project. Often programs look for early childhood educators who are working in other programs to sit on committees because of the expertise and perspective they bring to the discussions.

There are two types of committees:

- *Standing committees.* These committees are permanent and are usually defined in the bylaws. They oversee a general area such as personnel or finance, and monitor the centre's activity in this area and make recommendations to the board of directors. Many nonprofit programs have other standing committees, including an executive committee, advocacy committee, program committee, fund-raising committee, education committee, and a public or community relations committee.
- *Ad hoc committees.* These committees are appointed by the board to complete a specific task and once the task has been carried out, ad hoc committees usually disband. A nominating committee, for instance, would be formed by the board to solicit nominations for new board members. Once the nominations have been presented to the annual general meeting and voted on, the committee would dissolve.

Recruiting Board Members

Finding board members to maintain the organization is a vital task and an important responsibility of the board of directors. The term of office for board members is defined in the bylaws and varies from one year to several years. Some nonprofit organizations find that a three-year term allows for a few members to change each year. New members can work alongside those with more experience. Other organizations prefer to have two-year terms, with half of the board changing each year. Still other groups find that a commitment of more than one year is not realistic for their board members, and they must seek out other ways to ensure administrative stability and consistency.

Many not-for-profit early childhood programs with a balance of parent board members have a one-year term for the board of directors. It may not be realistic to ask for more than a one-year commitment when many children attend the program for a year or two and then move on to other schools and neighbourhoods. Parents can be actively encouraged to sit on the committees that report to the board, which provides an opportunity to learn how the program is operated and to have input into the process before making a commitment to actually be a board member. If board members can be elected to two terms of office, it is likely that each new board of directors will have some seasoned participants. At the same time, there is a limit to how long any one member may stay in office.

Parents can make valuable contributions to early childhood programs by being members of the governing board of directors.

A nominating committee is usually selected by a board of directors to seek out members of the organization who would be willing to be elected to the board at the annual general meeting. The nominating committee is an ad hoc committee made up of board members who are not seeking another term on the board. In small organizations, the nominating committee may be one individual who is responsible for finding new recruits. Responsibilities of the nominating committee include the following:

- Reviewing the membership of the board of directors as defined in the bylaws.
- Finding out which board members would like to serve another term, and on what committees or officer positions.
- Deciding what skills and resources are needed from new members to meet the needs of various committees during the upcoming term of office.
- Soliciting nominees for the board of directors. Sometimes a short article in the monthly newsletter outlining the agenda over the next year and the kinds of skills needed will alert parents who are willing to volunteer.
- Preparing a short outline of the expectations of board members and reviewing these expectations with potential new members.
- Presenting the nominations to the annual general meeting. Nonprofit boards must elect their boards at an annual general meeting. In most organizations, the board recruits nominations in advance but additional nominations may be made at the meeting. A vote either by show of hands or ballot is called. The process for nominations and voting is set out in the bylaws.

An inventory of the skills, qualities, and knowledge that the board will need in order to address the challenges facing the early childhood program in the next few years may help the nominating committee to identify new candidates. The board inventory translates an early childhood program's strategic goals and priorities into a description of the kinds of people who are needed for the board.

Legal Obligations

The specific legal obligations of boards of directors of nonprofit early childhood programs are determined by legislation and regulations governing incorporation, child care operations, children's services, child protection, employment practices, and human rights. Members of boards of directors are obligated to ensure that the operation of the program is in compliance with all of the legal requirements. In order to ensure compliance with all requirements, members of boards of directors must be knowledgeable about what the requirements are.

Regulated child care program board members may be held responsible if they knowingly contravene corporation legislations, child care legislation, or other relevant legislation, or mishandle finances so that the organization is unable to meet its financial obligations. They may also be held responsible for contraventions that they were unaware of through neglect.

Financial Obligations

Not-for-profit board members are expected to act honestly and in the best interests of the organization. The financial affairs of the organization should be managed by the board members in a responsible manner that benefits the children and families who use the service.

Each director must ensure that his or her actions as a board member do not result in personal gain. If an individual board member could profit personally from the result of a decision made by the board, that member must declare a conflict of interest and withdraw from the decision-making process.

Possible conflict-of-interest situations include:

- A staff member who is also a member of the board is discussing the personnel committee's recommendations and voting on the annual staff salary increases. The staff/board member votes on annual salary increases.
- A board member who is a sales representative for a chocolate bar company volunteers to set up a fund-raising event to sell chocolate bars. The board member will receive a commission on the chocolate bars sold.

Obviously, board members who abuse access to the organization's funds and commit **fraud** or embezzle money are not meeting their financial obligations to be honest. These are criminal acts and require the intervention of the police.

Boards of directors are legally responsible to follow basic financial management principles. These include:

- setting up adequate controls requiring regular financial reports;
- establishing spending and fee collection policies;
- reviewing financial reports; and
- seeking professional advice on legal, accounting, or personnel issues.

Financial difficulties may still arise in organizations because they are usually vulnerable to any changes in government policies that affect child care subsidies or changes in licensing requirements. Bankruptcy may occur, but individual board members are not financially responsible if proper financial management principles are followed.

Not-for-profit boards of directors are employers and do have legal and financial obligations to the staff employed in a nonprofit program. Boards of directors are responsible for income tax deductions if the organization has not deducted or remitted the required amounts. Board directors may be liable for wrongful dismissal charges if a staff member is dismissed without just cause and without reasonable notice of termination. Both "just cause" and "reasonable notice of termination" are based on a number of complicated legal factors. Boards of directors should consult a lawyer knowledgeable in this area before taking such actions. For example, the need for staff layoffs brought on by low enrollment is not just cause and thus requires reasonable notice of termination or layoff.

Board members can reduce their liability by knowing what is in the bylaws of the organization, attending meetings regularly, disclosing possible financial interests, getting professional legal and accounting counsel, and reviewing reports and correspondence from licensing and/or regulatory authorities. Insurance for board members can reduce individual board members' liability if they act in a responsible manner without willfully contravening regulations.

Nonprofit organizations usually require legal advice when applying for letters patent and establishing or changing bylaws. Legal advice and legal representation may be advisable when negotiating a collective agreement or contract of employment with staff or dismissing a staff member. Board directors may also want legal counsel if there are allegations of child neglect or abuse by staff or serious occurrences that are reported to authorities.

A board member may be a lawyer and be willing to provide legal advice to the board. Otherwise board members and the supervisor can seek out a lawyer who is knowledgeable about nonprofit corporations.

Orientation

Once new members are recruited to a nonprofit board of directors, it is important to keep them. New board members should have a thorough orientation to their new responsibilities even if they have a good understanding of how the organization works as a whole. Organizations, hopping from one crisis to the next, can overlook this critical process. The result is uninformed board members making crucial decisions.

At the orientation meeting, guest speakers may be invited to speak to board members about the kinds of programs offered and the role of boards of directors. A video presentation of the program activities may be effective particularly if some of the new board members are not familiar with the day-to-day operation. Staff members may be invited to participate, and it may be possible to combine the orientation session with a social event such as a late-afternoon tea or family supper, depending on the schedules and availability of board members.

MEETINGS

General meetings and board meetings are the decision-making vehicles for nonprofit organizations. The rules for the time, place, advance notice of meetings, and quorum are outlined in the organization's bylaws.

The annual general meeting for an incorporated organization includes the election of the board of directors and presentation of the annual report including the president's report and audited financial statement and the supervisor's report. The members approve the appointment of the financial auditor for the upcoming year and any other proposed resolutions to change the bylaws of the organization.

All members may attend the annual general meeting and vote on the business items. Formal notice of the meeting must be given to members. Often other community representatives and advisers are invited to attend the meeting, and after the business portion is concluded there may be a guest speaker or other item of interest such as a video. Many organizations use this opportunity to socialize by providing refreshments and an opportunity to chat informally.

Additional general meetings of the general membership may be called by the board as needed to deal with emergencies or other major situations. Some organizations have additional general meetings as a way of involving a broader spectrum of the membership or to pass a resolution on a difficult issue. Members may themselves call for a general meeting to discuss an issue or pass a resolution or replace directors.

Board of directors' meetings manage and control the ongoing operation. Most of the meeting time should be spent on the major areas of responsibility identified earlier.

All board members are expected to attend board meetings, and most programs encourage staff and parents to attend as well. It is one way for staff to better understand the kind of organization they are working for and what the operational issues and challenges are.

Committee meetings work on a particular piece of business, such as deciding the annual projected budget, drafting new personnel policies, or working out the details of the annual lobby of politicians. Usually, the process is more informal than board or general meetings but it is important to keep attention focused on the matter at hand. Committees do not have the power to actually make policy decisions. Rather, they pull together information, perhaps with specific recommendations, so that the board of directors can make informed decisions.

Organizing for Effective Meetings

The challenge of productive meetings is faced by most organizations and workplaces, and it is no different in decision-making meetings in early childhood programs. Meetings can be planned to accomplish specific tasks, make decisions, and identify what needs to happen next.

An agenda is the order of business to be dealt with at a meeting. It reflects the organization's priorities and concerns and informs participants about what is coming up, and what they should be prepared to discuss, decide, and take action on. It may be accompanied by specific reports, correspondence, or other background items. An agenda also provides practical information about where, when, and for how long the meeting will run.

Usually, the president of the board, in consultation with the supervisor or directors, develops the agenda for board meetings, which is produced and distributed to board members in advance. Staff members may also be asked for items for the agenda discussion.

Low turnout at board meetings is a problem common to many organizations. Regular meeting time may be inappropriate for board directors or the advance notice of times and content of meetings may be inadequate, particularly for parents, who often require care for their children. The group dynamics may be problematic so board directors avoid the meetings. Or perhaps the discussions are viewed as boring or as a monologue from the supervisor rather than a dialogue that requires participation.

Procedures for Meetings

The chairperson (usually the president) chairs or runs board meetings. An effective chairperson:

- is prepared in advance and familiar with the agenda, including background information and what actions have already occurred;
- understands the rules of order;
- makes sure everyone has an opportunity to participate in discussions and debates, and does not "take sides";
- is able to summarize discussions; and
- does not wish to dominate the meeting.

Most nonprofit organizations use some form of *parliamentary procedure* for their board of directors' and general members' meetings. This set of rules helps to ensure a democratic process at meetings, meaning:

- Equal rights for all members.
- The right of the majority to decide.
- The right of the minority to be heard.
- The right of individual members to participate.

Robert's Rules of Order is the standard rulebook describing parliamentary procedures and is used by many different organizations for running meetings. Unfortunately, this is not a quick read, as the book is complex and requires considerable skill and experience to master. Using the book to find the answer to a simple "how to" question can be an intimidating experience. Board members may find a summary of parliamentary procedures helpful.

Another way to make decisions at meetings is *to seek consensus.* Rather than a "majority rules" approach, decisions are built on mutual agreement and compromise. To be effective, all members of a group must participate in the process and, through discussion and a lot of listening, work through issues and problems to find a solution that everyone can agree on.

To solve a problem through consensus, the group can do the following:

- *Identify the issues*. What is the problem? Find a definition everyone can agree on.
- *Check the available information*. What are the facts? Are critical pieces of information all available? What additional information is needed and how can it be obtained?
- *Brainstorm*. What solutions *might* work? Any suggestion is okay at first. List all possible solutions without judging their merit or feasibility. An atmosphere of unconditional acceptance may get the cooperative and creative juices flowing. Try to get some suggestions from every member of the group.
- *Choose a solution*. Consider each solution—is it possible, legal, and financially viable? Eliminate unworkable solutions and examine the remaining solutions. Are there any workable combinations or compromises? Continue to eliminate and combine ideas. Reach agreement on one solution.

Boards of directors and committees can use consensus as a technique to work out solutions and then use the parliamentary procedure to make them official. The solution becomes a motion that can be put to a vote.

Open Communication at Meetings

Communication is a process of sharing ideas and concerns with others and receiving feedback. Good communication keeps people working *with* each other, not *at* each other.

When people communicate with each other, there is a verbal component, a nonverbal component, a situational context, and personal history. This all adds up to a lot of potential for misunderstandings and interference in communication.

The nature of parent/community boards of directors can make communication complex for several reasons:

- The parent–staff dynamic is complex. Most parents did not attend group programs as young children themselves, thus the roles of parents and staff in early childhood programs are new to most participants.
- The employer–employee dynamic is not new but it can be complicated and even confrontational. It becomes more intense when combined with the parent–staff dynamic.
- The scarcity of human and financial resources is both well documented and a challenge in most not-for-profit early childhood programs.

A sound organizational structure and clear meeting procedures go a long way in supporting honest and constructive communication. Below are some other issues to keep in mind.

Conflict

Disagreements between members of the board can be constructive and actually help to ensure that decisions are well thought out. Much depends on how conflict is viewed and handled by individuals and the group as a whole. Here are some suggestions on dealing with conflict in meetings:

- Appreciate the difference between a disagreement, an argument, and open hostility.
- Know how to differ with a point of view and not attack the person holding that view.
- Confront those who confuse arguments and hostility, frank debate, and personal attack. This is often unpleasant, but necessary for the well-being of the group. Basic respect for each other's point of view is essential.
- Try to avoid an overly polite atmosphere in which people back away from expressing differences. The possibility for a few to dominate in such an atmosphere is high.
- Open, reasoned debate between people with differing points of view is a positive element in making good decisions and can allow for a thorough, thoughtful exploration of issues and possible courses of action.
- Know that the commitment to follow-through on decisions reached through open debate is usually greater and more active than the commitment to decisions arrived at by a fear of hurting feelings.
- Provide a democratic forum by keeping a speaker's list to ensure that everyone has the option of sharing his or her ideas. Have people write down their positions briefly so that words are carefully chosen and misunderstandings minimized.

Confidentiality

Confidentiality is often a concern in early childhood program board meetings. Quite often, board members know parents and staff as friends, neighbours, and even relatives. There may be a strong perception that issues discussed at board meetings will become known to a wider audience. Information about personnel performance or parental concerns is often discussed at board meetings as part of the business of a board of directors. This same information should *not* find its way into casual conversation or gossip.

Finding resolutions to differences is central to good decision making.

The board meeting itself must maintain a business-like tone, only raising information that is related to the operation of the program. For example, the marital status of a parent who has written a letter with a concern about health standards should not be up for discussion—it is not relevant. Board members may be cautioned from time to time by the chairperson or the supervisor that a particular topic is confidential and information should not be discussed outside of the meeting. Staff members who are attending board meetings should maintain confidentiality.

Minutes

The minutes of a meeting are the official record of decisions and actions taken by the voting participants at board or general meetings. They also provide a clear record of who agreed to do what.

It is best to use a standard format at each meeting. Beside the text of the minutes, it is noted who agreed to take some sort of action. The minutes then become a planning tool to follow up on who should be carrying out the activity. A full set of minutes from the previous year should be included in a board of directors' handbook.

Minutes should be accurate, stating motions and resolutions as well as the actual decisions made. The secretary of the board takes notes at the meetings and then prepares the minutes. Usually, the supervisor makes sure the minutes are typed and distributed to all board members. At the beginning of the next meeting, they are reviewed by the members present and any corrections are made. The adopted minutes must be signed by the chairperson and secretary. Resolutions must be recorded in the minutes, and minutes can be used to summarize discussion on issues. It is also useful to identify any action or follow-up to be taken and by whom.

The approved minutes are signed and filed with the organization's records. The secretary may keep a copy of the minutes. The record of the minutes is part of the public record of the organization and should be available for viewing by parents or staff members.

A simple format for minutes includes the following information:

- type of meeting;
- names of board members present and absent;
- approval of minutes from the past meeting;
- updates or additions to minutes from last meeting;
- correspondence;
- reports from committees;
- new business or announcements;
- time of adjournment; and
- date, time, and place of next meeting.

EARLY CHILDHOOD EDUCATORS AND GOVERNANCE

Who makes decisions and how they are made shapes the infrastructure and management of early childhood settings. Transparent, clear decision making is related to more productive work environments, and early childhood programs are no exception. Early childhood educators need to be aware of the type of governance that is in place and what it means for decisions about program activities and the work environment.

Apart from early childhood programs, such as kindergarten, that are publicly delivered by local school boards and districts, most early childhood programs in Canada are delivered by not-for-profit organizations. Understanding the governance structure is probably the first step in having some input beyond the day-to-day decisions. Knowing how decisions are made, and who is responsible for what, allows early childhood educators to direct their questions and concerns to the individuals who make those decisions.

KEY TERMS

auspice	governance
commercial	not-for-profit
cooperative	organizational chart
fraud	

REFLECTION QUESTIONS

1. Decisions about daily routines and activities are typically left to front-line early childhood educators. How does the vision influence these day-to-day decisions?

2. Can you see advantages and disadvantages in having parents on boards of directors in not-for-profit early childhood programs? Explain.

3. Hassan is working in a school-age program. Children are required to take part in a "creative" activity before they can play popular sports games in the gym. Hassan finds that he spends most of the first hour after school directing the same children to take part in the daily creative activity. He questions this practice and asks his colleague, Sophia, about it. Sophia replies, "That's the rule." Hassan would like to question the rule but wonders where to start. What is your advice to Hassan?

4. Meredith has worked in the preschool room at Bloomsbury Children's Program for three years. She enjoys the program and is eager to take more responsibility. Her goal is to be a director of a small early childhood program, perhaps in another five years. But she is unsure how to prepare for leadership responsibilities. What are some actions that Meredith could take?

FOR MORE INFORMATION

1. The United Way Board Development Guide explores options for possible board models in more detail and provides a Models Comparison Chart Matrix.

   www.boarddevelopment.org/importance.cfm

2. Imagine Canada has compiled extensive resources on issues related to governance in nonprofit organizations. The resources are useful in understanding the possible duties and responsibilities and preparing information for board members. They are also useful for early childhood educators who are considering positions on boards of nonprofit organizations.

   www.nonprofitscan.ca/page.asp?boards_governance

3. The *Thomson Nelson ECE Resource Centre* is intended to enhance the teaching and learning experience for both instructors and students. The website provides extensive and helpful resources in many different criteria related to early childhood education.

   www.ece.nelson.com

OPERATIONS

CHAPTER OUTLINE

Downtown Squire Early Childhood Centre

Downtown Squire Early Childhood Centre is in a beautiful renovated space licensed for 78 children from 12 months to 10 years. It is open 12 months a year, five days a week, from 8 A.M. to 6 P.M. The centre is organized into four groups—a group of 12 infants/toddlers (aged 12 months to two and a half years), a group of 16 preschool children (two-and-a-half- and three-year-olds), a group of 20 kindergarten children (four- and five-year-olds), and a group of 30 school-age children (aged six to ten years).

Some of the children aged 12 months to six years attend part-time, and some attend full-time. Flexible arrangements are made to suit families whenever possible, although children do attend on a regular basis (a minimum of three half days per week). In total, the centre is licensed for 78 children and over 100 are currently enrolled. The waiting list is long—more than 100 children.

The indoor play space and the outdoor playgrounds of the centre make use of natural light and materials. There are separate playgrounds for the toddlers and three-to-five-year-olds; each one has a garden that the children tend. All the climbing equipment is made of wood. Thanks to a number of large covered areas, the children are able to be outside on rainy days and there is protection from winter's icy blast.

Each of the four groups of children has four types of space: a main play area; a gross motor area; a room for small groups to have some time together away from the larger group; and a resource room where the special-needs resource staff works daily with small groups of three or four children who are in need of additional support.

Chapter Objectives

This chapter will:

1. Discuss how regulatory requirements, program policies, and procedural guidelines can work together to ensure the smooth operation of early childhood programs.
2. Outline the components of a healthy and safe environment for young children and families.
3. Consider the design of the physical environment.
4. Discuss a family-centred approach.
5. Describe effective record-keeping and information systems.

OPERATIONAL FRAMEWORK

Early childhood programs are social institutions that must meet a variety of general and program-specific legal requirements. Early childhood programs have individual histories, strengths, challenges, and opportunities. Programs may be set up for infants, toddlers, preschoolers, and/or school-age children. Parent or other caregiver participation may be encouraged or required. Activities may take place in the child's home, in a caregiver's home, or in centre. Programs may be located in urban, suburban, or rural communities. They may be in church basements, school classrooms, office towers, or in their own buildings. Early childhood programs need policies and procedures that are based on their individual philosophies, goals, choices, and priorities that also meet legal requirements.

The following discussion considers legal requirements, insurance, and program policies and procedures for early childhood programs. The rest of the chapter considers specific program policy areas—health, safety, and nutrition; physical environment; a family-centred approach; diversity, equity, and inclusion; and record-keeping. Much of the focus of this chapter is on full-day child care centres and part-day nursery schools/preschools, as they have defined space requirements and other health and safety measures contained in regulations.

Legal Requirements

Early childhood programs that are incorporated as commercial or not-for-profit must adhere to financial record-keeping, labour standards, and incorporation requirements.

Understanding how legislation affects early childhood programs helps to meet legal requirements and avoid legal problems. Early childhood programs must comply with two types of regulatory requirements:

- Provincial/territorial legislation that is specific to the operation of regulated child care centres, family child care, public health programs, child and family services, or kindergarten programs.
- Provincial/territorial regulations related to employment standards and human rights requirements.
- Local zoning, public health, and fire department regulations.

The following sections summarize legislative requirements relevant to specific early childhood programs.

Regulated Child Care Programs

All nonprofit licensed child care programs must operate in ways that comply with federal, provincial, and local regulations. Legal requirements impose common features on all child care centres. Other legal requirements dictate financial record-keeping practices, labour standards, and incorporation.

A licence to operate a child care program is obtained from the provincial or territorial government. Such a licence is required for all child care and education programs for more than a designated number of children under 10 or 12 years of age who are not siblings. Exceptions include public schools, separate schools, private schools, recreation programs run by the municipality, and children's mental health centres. Table 5.1 summarizes program licensing by province or territory.

Provincial/territorial licensing requirements include requirements for program content, physical premises, equipment and furnishings, playground, staff, health, nutrition, funding, and record-keeping. Specific requirements will be outlined later in this chapter. Almost all jurisdictions require some of the staff in centre-based programs to have some training in early childhood education. However, Canadian requirements for early childhood education training are considered to be minimal (OECD, 2004).

■ Table 5.1

Provincial/Territorial Child Care Programs

Province or Territory	Child Programs That Are Regulated	Child Care Programs That Are Not Regulated
Newfoundland and Labrador	Day care centres, school-age child care centres, family child care agencies, individually licensed family child care homes	Family child care (four children; three if all are under 24 months, including caregiver's children under seven years); nursery school programs for up to six children, who participate in a program for no more than nine hours per week
Prince Edward Island	Early childhood centres, school-age child care centres, family day care homes, occasional centres	Family child care (five preschool children if not more than two are younger than age two, three if all are under 24 months, six in mixed-age group up to ten years with no more than two younger than two years—figures include caregiver's preschool children); on-reserve Headstart
Nova Scotia	Child care centres, child development centres, family day homes	Family child care (six children of mixed age groups including caregiver's own preschool children; eight if all children including caregiver's own are school age); on-reserve child care
New Brunswick	Day care centres, school-age child care centres, community day care homes	Family child care (five children mixed ages from birth to age 12, four children if all are two to five years, eight children if all are school age, no more than two infants allowed and numbers include caregiver's own children under 12) Note: On-reserve child care centres and nursery schools are approved/licensed upon request
Quebec	Centre de la petite enfance (CPE), which delivers centre-based and family child care for children up to age five; garderie (for-profit day care centre); milieu scolaire (school-age child care), on-reserve child care	Family child care not affiliated with a CPE (six children or fewer including caregiver's own); jardins d'enfants (nursery school); haltes-garderies (stop-over centres)
Ontario	Day nurseries (child care centres, nursery schools, before- and after-school programs), private home day care agencies (family child care)	Family child care (up to five children not including caregiver's own children), other types of informal care (e.g., nannies), family resource centres
Manitoba	Day care centres, nursery schools, school-age child care centres, family day homes, group family day care homes, occasional day care centres	Private home day care (four children, no more than two under two years old, including caregiver's own children under 12 years); First Nations programs on-reserve
Saskatchewan	Day care centres, school-age child care centres, family child care	Family child care (up to eight children including the caregiver's children under 13 years); nursery school programs for no more than nine hours per week
Alberta	Day care centres, nursery schools, approved family day homes, licensed drop-in centres	Private babysitting (six children, with three under the age of two, including caregiver's own children under 12 years) Note: On-reserve child care approved at request of band (approval indicates that the centre complies with provincial licensing requirements)
British Columbia	Group child care centres, preschools, out-of-school care, family child care, emergency care, child-minding, ski hill or resort care, on-reserve child care	Family child care (two children, not including caregiver's own)

■ Table 5.1

Provincial/Territorial Child Care Programs *(continued)*

Province or Territory	Child Programs That Are Regulated	Child Care Programs That Are Not Regulated
Nunavut	Day care centres, nursery schools, after-school care, family day homes	Family child care (four children, including caregiver's own under 12 years)
Northwest Territories	Day care centres, nursery schools, after-school care, family day homes	Family child care (four children, including caregiver's own under 12 years)
Yukon Territory	Child care centres, school-age child care, family day homes	Family child care (three children, excluding caregiver's own children under six years); preschools

Sources: Beach et al., 2004; Friendly & Beach, 2005; McCain et al., 2007.

Application for a licence to operate a child care centre is made to the provincial/territorial department or ministry responsible for regulated child care programs. A representative from the department inspects child care programs for initial licensing and renewals, and provides guidance for new centres and those already in operation, including guidance on incorporation.

Each child care centre that meets provincial requirements is issued a regular licence valid for a designated period of time, usually one year. (In Quebec, licences are renewed every three years, and monitoring visits are generally more frequent.) If the centre does not meet the requirements, the government may issue a time-limited provisional licence that indicates the requirements not being met and the improvements necessary within the specified time frame.

In not-for-profit organizations, the board of directors should receive a full report from the program director or supervisor concerning all visits and conversations with the government staff.

Kindergarten Programs

Kindergarten is typically delivered within the public education system (except for Prince Edward Island) for five-year-old children and sometimes four-year-olds as well. In Prince Edward Island, kindergarten is offered

Most regulated child care programs in Canada are required to include qualified early childhood educators as staff members.

From the Past

CANADA'S FIRST CHILD CARE LEGISLATION

In 1946, Ontario became to the first province to specify standards that had to be met in order to receive provincial funding. During World War II, the federal government introduced emergency legislation, the *Dominion-Provincial War-Time Agreement,* to establish day nurseries for children of working women, with provisions for federal/provincial cost-sharing. Both Ontario and Quebec entered into agreements and established preschool and school-age programs (Schulz, 1978). The Institute for Child Studies provided a model of operation for the day nursery programs and directed a shortened training program for staff (Raymond, 1991; Wright, 2000).

The history of the *Day Nurseries Act* (DNA) dates back to 1946. Significant revisions were made in 1978 and 1983 to include the licensing of private home day care and improve staffing and ratio standards. In 1998 the legislation was amended to include authority for the newly formed Consolidated Municipal Service Managers (CMSMs) to administer and manage the regulated child care system and funding for other prescribed services (including special needs resources, family resource programs, and social assistance subsidies through Ontario Works).

The general orientation of the DNA and its regulation retains the original 1946 perspective. The operational standards primarily relate to daily care routines and protect children's health and safety. The funding standards promote parents' attachment to the paid labour force as the primary purpose for licensed child care.

by regulated child care programs. Provincial/territorial education legislation stipulates regulations for public education. Regulations in all jurisdictions stipulate degree qualification requirements for all teachers, including kindergarten teachers. Class size and age of eligibility are also included in the legislation. Except in New Brunswick, kindergarten is not compulsory, but over 95 percent of all five-year-olds in Canada do attend. The federal government is responsible for on-reserve kindergarten programs in First Nations communities.

Family Support Programs

Family support programs are typically community-based organizations offering parent/caregiver education and/or adult–child activities to families with young children and caregivers. Federal, provincial/territorial, and local governments (municipal, school, and public health authorities) may be involved in the funding, planning, delivery, and oversight of family support programs. Ontario Early Years Centres have operational guidelines from the Ministry of Children and Youth Services, Strong Start Centres in

British Columbia are supported by guidelines from the Ministry of Education, and Alberta's Ministry of Children's Services has guidelines for Parent Link Centres.

Insurance

In choosing insurance policies for the program, consider every aspect of the premises and the program's operation. This includes excursions off the premises, volunteers, transporting children back and forth to schools, physical property indoors and outdoors, signed contracts, and activities of the board of directors. Each program must make sure all aspects of the program and the people involved in it are taken into account when insurance is obtained.

The board of directors of a nonprofit organization should be aware of the insurance arrangements. Policies are usually renewed on an annual basis, at which time the board of directors should review the program's coverage and decide whether additional coverage is necessary.

The purpose of liability insurance for early childhood programs is to protect children and staff's interests if there is an injury. Provincial/territorial child care legislation states that all licensed programs must have insurance that includes general liability coverage, personal injury coverage, and motor vehicle coverage. Other early childhood programs that receive public funding are likely to be required to have similar types of coverage.

Board of directors' insurance, which provides protection for board members, is discussed in Chapter 4. It does not protect members who knowingly make poor decisions. Board liability insurance does protect members who are well intentioned and make decisions in a responsible manner that create problems.

Property insurance covers the loss of a building and its contents through theft, fire, and other disasters. If the building is leased or rented from a church, school board, or community centre, ensure that the landlord insures the property against damages to the building and its permanent equipment and fixtures. The program should insure whatever contents belong to it. In order to make sure there is adequate insurance coverage, list the contents and the estimated value of each item, and update this inventory annually.

Program Policies and Procedures

Policies and procedures for early childhood programs must take into account that each program is unique and that all programs are subject to some form of government regulations. A policy is a general rule that covers a specific issue or situation. A procedure refers to the specific steps needed to ensure that the general rule is followed. A policy is a rule that states what to do and the procedures describe how to do it.

HEALTH, SAFETY, AND NUTRITION

Health, safety, and nutrition policies and procedures protect children and adults from harm and promote their well-being in early childhood settings. Effective health, safety, and nutrition practices are central to the quality of early childhood programs. Many health and safety policies are determined by requirements of provincial and territorial child care legislation and local municipal regulations.

From the Past

EARLY ROLE OF PUBLIC HEALTH IN EARLY CHILDHOOD PROGRAMS

In the 1900s public health outreach programs played a role in helping to support mothers and their infants and young children. Immigration, urbanization, and industrialization brought larger numbers of people together and increased the risk of infectious disease and mortality that did not respect the boundaries of income or social class. Diseases that thrived in crowded, dirty living conditions could not be contained, and their transmission to upper-middle class environments was inevitable. Therefore, prevention of diseases attracted attention and interest from all socioeconomic groups.

Research evidence identified health prevention measures that could greatly reduce the spread of infectious disease and reduce mortality, particularly among infants and children (Sutherland, 1976). Canadian historian Neil Sutherland identifies three events in 1882 that shaped the direction of public health: "Louis Pasteur proved the effectiveness of immunization for anthrax in sheep, Robert Koch discovered the tuberculosis germ, and Ontario established a board of health" (1976, p. 40). The establishment of public health boards in other provinces followed. The emerging public health movement in Canada built upon the achievements of nineteenth-century improvements in sanitation and on the dramatic bacteriological discoveries of the 1880s and 1890s. Public health initiatives brought prenatal and well-baby clinics, milk depots, and home visiting to communities throughout Ontario (Arnup, 1994; Sutherland, 1976). These measures reduced infant deaths and improved maternal health (Sutherland, 1976).

The public health nurse's responsibilities for well-baby clinics and home visits encompassed a parent education role. In many instances, they became a friendly adviser who was able to suggest changes in caregiving practices and promote healthy habits (Sutherland, 1976). The approach to parent education was often patronizing and didactic (Kyle & Kellerman, 1998) but was typically directed at all families with young children, not just those living in poverty, consistent with the notion that everyone was vulnerable and it was in everybody's best interest to avoid or prevent disease.

By 1914 the public health nurse's role in the schools was becoming central in school health programs (Sutherland, 1976). In addition to preventative health (such as routine inspections, maintenance of medical records, and teaching healthy habits including nose-blowing and tooth-brushing drills), school nurses often led health clubs after school, such as the Little Nurses League in Winnipeg and the Little Mothers in Vancouver, Regina, Victoria, and Stratford (Sutherland, 1976). Such clubs provided after-school activities for school-aged children while promoting health.

Health, safety, and nutrition policies and practices in early childhood programs are shaped by current evidence from pediatrics, child welfare, public health, and nutrition. Regular attention to bulletins from municipal public health departments and child welfare organizations, and monitoring of information from organizations such as the Canadian Institute of Child Health and the Canadian Pediatric Association can help.

Health, safety, and nutrition practices are basic to childrearing. Many of the difficulties that arise between staff and parents in early childhood settings are related to differences in approaches to childrearing and related differences in what are considered to be appropriate health, safety, and nutrition practices. Preferred childrearing practices are grounded in parents' personal and cultural values. A balance needs to be maintained to ensure that requirements are met, children are protected, and parents' wishes are respected.

Injuries are the number one cause of death and disability for children and youth in Canada. Research shows that the vast majority of what people usually consider to be accidents are really predictable and preventable events. Safe Kids Canada (www.sickkids.ca/safekidscanada/default.asp) promotes effective strategies to prevent unintentional injuries.

Risk Management

A written **risk management plan** may prevent disasters from occurring and prepares for emergencies that do happen (Clark, 2002). It develops a set of procedures to respond to or recover from a crisis when it does occur, limiting the impact on people and property. Being prepared by having a risk management plan is about understanding the risks, trying to alleviate the risks, and getting ready for a possible crisis.

An early childhood program's risk management plan begins with planning to assess the possible impact of a variety of possibilities. It should include clear procedures to follow in the event of an emergency such as a severe storm, fire, power outage, intruder, or illness, and it should have guidelines to reduce the risk of child abuse or neglect incidents or allegations.

PHYSICAL ENVIRONMENT

The physical layout and design of most early childhood programs reflect the notion that children are not adults. Spaces are set up for smaller people who are continually meeting new challenges in their growing independence but who still require physical security and safety. The space defines areas for quiet and active play, individuals and groups, storage, eating and sleeping, and indoor and outdoor activity.

Design

Provincial/territorial child care regulations include indoor and outdoor physical environment requirements, including:

- minimum space requirements per child;
- designated space for washing, eating, napping, resting, storage, food preparation, isolation of sick children, staff room, and office area;

Innovations

QUALITY BY DESIGN

PHYSICAL ENVIRONMENT

The program setting that includes:
- Sufficient well-designed indoor and outdoor space
- First-rate equipment and program resources
- Amenities such as staff room, outside play space, kitchen, windows for natural light
- Connections to the surrounding community

Elements of ELCC environments such as amount of space, access to the outdoors, arrangement of rooms, availability of a variety of materials, air quality, equipment, and lighting play a role not only in safety and health but in children's well-being, happiness and creativity, their learning to live in and with the natural environment, and their cognitive and social development. In addition, elements of the physical environment such as how easy or difficult it is to carry out a program in, whether there are physical amenities that support staff—a staff room and adequate program resources—and whether the nature of the facility conveys that early childhood education is a respected, valued career have an impact on the morale of the people working in the program and, thus, on the quality of the program. In addition—as some commentators have pointed out—as children are the least powerful stakeholders, it is important to find ways to involve them in considering ELCC's physical environments.

Supporting good physical environments means not only high standards or regulations regarding, for example, the number and placement of toilets, windows, exit doors, kitchen and food preparation requirements, placement of sinks for hand washing, and height of fencing, although these are clearly important and cannot be overlooked. In addition to these basic health and safety considerations, today there is considerable interest in and knowledge concerning design and architecture of children's environments with emphasis on creativity, physical activity, social and cognitive development, aesthetic considerations, and how the physical environment can support rather than hinder implementation of excellent early childhood programs and ensure their visibility as a valued community institution.

Source: Reprinted with Permission from Childcare Resource and Referral Unit.

- premises that are approved by municipal, fire, health, and zoning departments; and
- requirements for outdoor play space.

The required amount of space in child care legislation is a minimum and does not usually provide for an adequate amount of space needed for quality programs.

The design and setup of the physical environment is central to the quality of early childhood programs.

In the process of selecting a site or a building, consider the overall amount of space required by provincial or territorial regulations as well as other requirements such as parking, staff and parent meeting areas, and storage. Local government or building design guidelines or requirements may also be a consideration. Local zoning bylaws, building codes, allowed occupancy, and vehicular access will also need to be taken into consideration.

Outdoor Space

If possible, the outdoor space should be connected to the indoor space, with direct access to the children's indoor space, so children can have freedom to move between their indoor and outdoor space at will. Covered areas provide a transition from indoor to outdoor areas and shade and protection in inclement weather. There should be various textures, heights, and activity areas.

The majority of design time and renovation cost of early childhood programs is usually allocated to the indoor space, and the outdoor play space is designed after the interior space. All provinces and territories require that children have access to an outdoor playground, but it many cases it does not have to be immediately adjacent to the indoor space.

In some playgrounds a manufactured piece of climbing equipment is ordered from a catalogue and that is the base around which the playground is developed. Fortunately, there is a growing body of knowledge about the importance of the outdoor environment and an understanding that children need natural environments with numerous possibilities.

The outdoor space is central to quality early childhood environments.

In many Canadian early childhood programs, children spend very little time outdoors—if the weather is inclement, they may not go out at all throughout the day. Some lessons can be learned from the outdoor activities in some other northern countries, where sometimes young children spend the whole day outside in all kinds of weather, gaining an appreciation for their climate and the activities it affords (OECD, 2006).

In July 2003, the Canadian Standards Association (CSA) published the third edition of its guide to playground standards, *Children's Playspaces and Equipment* (see www.csa.ca/news/releases/Default.asp?articleID=7894&language=english). The standard serves as a guide to the proper design and maintenance of public playspaces and equipment for children aged 18 months to 12 years.

The standard applies to new playspace equipment, as well as additions to and replacement parts for existing playspaces and equipment. It is not retroactive. Compliance is voluntary unless mandated in government legislation or enforced by local authorities. For example, Ontario's child care legislation regulations require licensed child care programs to adhere to the CSA playground standards.

Routine Maintenance

Routine maintenance of the physical space includes contracts for cleaning services; maintenance of the furnace, cooling system, and playground equipment; and fire extinguishers and an emergency fire alarm system. A system of routine maintenance includes records of sanitation procedures that are posted daily, and signed records of daily safety checks.

Innovations

VANCOUVER DESIGN REQUIREMENTS

The City of Vancouver child care design guidelines (see http://199.175.219.1/commsvcs/socialplanning/initiatives/childcare/) stipulate that there should be a total of 85 square metres of outdoor space for a group of 12 infants; 170 square metres for a group of 12 toddlers; and 350 square metres for a group of 25 three- to five-year-olds.

Children need to be active, to be challenged, and to be free to run, to jump, to climb, and to ride tricycles. They also need spaces in which to be creative and reflective, to explore their natural environment, to learn about science and nature, and not be confined by equipment with predetermined use.

FAMILY-CENTRED APPROACH

An early childhood program exists to meet the needs of young children *and* their families. Planning a program that promotes children's well-being and development and supports the primary role of parents/guardians involves attention to the needs of both. Partnerships with families are encouraged through policies and procedures that promote increased communication between program staff and families.

Everybody agrees that it's a good thing, but what is exactly meant by **"family involvement"**? Is it communicating regularly, and sharing information and ideas between staff and family members? Is it attending parent education sessions to discuss strategies for effective child guidance? Is it participating directly in the program? Is it taking part in decision making by being a member of the board of directors or parents' advisory committee? These are very different kinds of activities, yet all can be considered "family involvement." All of these activities support families' capacity to participate in, and enhance, their children's early learning and development.

The focus on parents as caregivers, learners, and teachers is prevalent in the rhetoric about early child development but is often absent in actual practice (UNESCO, 1998). The actual practice often involves "telling parents what to do" rather than providing opportunities to become engaged in their children's early development. Parents' active engagement in early learning and development is associated with better developmental outcomes and academic achievements. Parents' direct participation in early childhood programs can increase their engagement and amplify opportunities for early learning in the home environment.

Early childhood programs can provide a platform to increase parents' literacy. Early childhood education programs provide an entry point to engage parents in literacy programs and engage them directly in their children's early learning. Such programs are most effective when they are based on principles of adult education.

Daily informal conversations between early childhood educators and parents provide a key opportunity to exchange information about a child's early development and learning.

Effective early childhood programs engage parents' participation and transfer strategies that support early learning to home environments. Program strategies that have an explicit role for parents are implemented. When parents participate, there is an increase in literacy rates among disadvantaged children whose parents are not literate. However, it may be difficult to engage parents who themselves are illiterate.

Family support programs have developed a set of principles for working with families that can be applied in any early childhood setting. They provide a foundation for early childhood educators who want to actively engage parents' participation in their child's early learning and development.

Communication

Parents and other family members benefit from information about early childhood programs. This may include a written program statement and program policies. Communication with parents on an ongoing basis can include daily conversations, telephone calls, scheduled meetings, newsletters, bulletin board notices, and developmental profile reports.

Parents/guardians and other family members need regular, ongoing communication with the staff members who are with their children for many hours each day. They also need information about how the centre is run, what decisions are made, and how they can influence decisions.

Basic information sharing can be achieved through:

- regular daily conversations and charts;
- parent bulletin boards;

- newsletters;
- family handbooks;
- parent–staff interviews and meetings;
- orientation meetings; and
- family events such as pot-luck suppers, film nights, performances, and other social events.

Most programs use several strategies to communicate with parents/guardians in a way that responds to their particular needs. For example, in a rural or suburban setting where families often travel long distances, evening meetings may not be realistic, but Friday family suppers are a welcome opportunity for parents to chat with each other and with staff members.

Enrollment and Registration

Many early childhood programs, such as regulated child care programs, require that children be accepted into a program based on space availability. A program's admission policies reflect the purpose of the program and set priorities to fulfill that purpose. If the purpose of the program is to provide work-related child care for a consortium of employers, the admissions policies will give priority to children in these families. In other settings, a first-come-first-served policy will best reflect the program's purpose.

Admission policies guide procedures for:

- recruiting children;
- maintaining a waiting list;
- accepting children; and
- registering children at the centre.

Family Handbook

The purpose of a family handbook is to introduce the program to new families and to provide an up-to-date reference for all families whose children are enrolled in the program. It should be offered to families at the orientation meeting. Features of the handbook are outlined below.

Content Information about the children's program, the protection and program policies, and procedures that affect parents and the organization's operation is usually included. If there are specific services in a community that are related or connected to an early childhood and family program, include an overview of what is available.

The program statement (which is discussed later in this chapter) provides a complete summary of program policies and procedures. Several items from the current board of directors' handbook can be copied into the family handbook. This is one way of making sure that the board's policies and decisions are reflected in the information that parents receive.

Most families do not know a lot about how programs work and who is running them. Some parents think that because a centre is located in a school building, the local district school board is running the program and staff are employed by the school board. Other parents may be eligible for a fee subsidy or the Child Care Tax Deduction but not know anything about it. A section of the family handbook can cover the basics of different types of early childhood programs in that community.

Format Information must be easy to find. Most people will not sit down and read the handbook from beginning to end, but will refer to it as questions and concerns arise. Here are some suggestions:

- Arrange information in logical order.
- Divide different topics into sections, chapters, or units.
- Organize the material with clarity in mind. Use consistent headings, subheadings, boxes, lines, and other graphics to help create divisions. White space (where there is no text or graphics) helps to focus attention on the written text.

Style A conversational tone is user-friendly, while a formal style can alienate the reader. As the handbook is a publication of the program, it should reflect the program's philosophy and goals. At the same time, the writing should not interfere with the communication of information.

Daily Schedule

When children attend early childhood programs without accompanying family or caregivers, staff can provide a verbal report or written note that shares the child's day-to-day experiences inside and outside of his or her home environment. Daily opportunities to exchange information and conversation between parents/guardians and staff are powerful vehicles for communication. Drop-off and pick-up times are hectic times for staff members and parents, who are often rushing to work or home duties. However, schedules, space, and activities can be organized to maximize these opportunities. Much can be communicated if staff members can be available for a few moments of conversation with specific information about the child's day and accomplishments. A quick comment about a child's newly acquired abilities in following the narrative in a storybook offers families useful information and guidance that can expand learning opportunities at home.

Orientation

A specific process to introduce and familiarize new children and their families can ensure all families are welcomed. Orientation is a critical step in the development of an important relationship with parents who are new to a program. In the majority of full-time child care programs, the board of directors establishes the enrollment and program policies while senior staff put the appropriate procedures in place. The program director or a designated early childhood educator is then responsible for discussing these policies and expectations with families who are enrolling their children in the program.

A comprehensive family handbook and family-centre contract outlining the obligations of parents and the program are important documents. Board and staff should be familiar with the information included in these documents. The information should be revised as needed to ensure accuracy. Also, both documents should be reviewed annually to make sure any changes are noted.

From the Past

DAILY ROUTINES IN CANADIAN NURSERY SCHOOLS, 1935

ROUTINE EQUIPMENT

The ideal cloakroom equipment is an individual locker for each child, equipped with hooks, and a shelf along the top for hats and other accessories. The locker should be open and adapted to the child's height. It is particularly important that the child have his own section. This not only helps him by making his procedure quite definite, but also reduces general confusion and helps to keep the clothing of individual children separated. (The latter is a real problem in a nursery school, and all school clothing should, of course, be marked.) An apron for play and bedroom slippers for the indoor period may be kept in the lockers, where the child can get them. The procedure is facilitated by means of a separate cupboard in which each child has a compartment to hold the extra set of clothing he needs.

PROCEDURE

The objective for the child in the cloakroom routine is to learn to dress and undress efficiently and within a reasonable length of time. The degree of conformity expected is a cooperative attitude toward learning and participation in the procedure according to ability. Ideally, this routine should be taken slowly, the children entering from the preceding activity in groups of two or three. They very quickly learn to proceed directly to their lockers and to begin to dress or undress, doing this alone or with assistance, according to their ability. The adult can help the children most easily and unobtrusively if seated on a low chair by the locker.

It is difficult in the nursery school to adapt the dressing routine to the child's capacity. Even a four-year-old child should not be expected to manage all his fastenings, especially those of his winter gear, and a two-year-old should be expected to do little more than get out and put away his clothes. Dressing, from the child's point of view, is a long and intricate process, and occurring, as it does, twice in the nursery school day, the learning should be taken gradually if it is not to become an unpleasant and tedious episode for both adult and child. If the child acquires a negative attitude toward dressing through repeated failure and boredom, learning will be retarded and behavior difficulties may arise. When the two-year-old enters the school he is usually utterly oblivious to and uninterested in the whole affair, and furthermore has not the physical ability necessary for dressing himself. Instruction in the skill itself at this stage may do more harm than good to the child, and the adult expends much energy, which would not be necessary if she waited until the child showed spontaneous effort. The first step, then, is to keep the child's attention on the job in hand, by preventing distraction and play, and by directing him in doing the simplest parts

(continued)

of the routine. Though doing practically nothing, if kept busy he will feel that he has accomplished a great deal. By this method an interest in the proceedings is stimulated and an attitude of personal responsibility is developed. The adult's attitude should always be that of assisting the child, although she may actually be doing everything for him. Once a real interest and desire to try and dress himself appear, together with the necessary physical ability, then teaching how to dress will be easy and profitable. Patience is the main requisite during this period of interested effort, but the adult must be alert to the capacity and staying power of each child, and ready with assurance, suggestions, and timely but unobtrusive assistance. Within the next year the process should become fairly efficient and sufficiently automatic so that the child can dress although his mind is on other matters. It is important that the period of interest should be capitalized, and efficiency well on its way by five years of age. With the growth of the child's other interests, and a consequent increase in opportunity for achievement, the dressing process loses its initial attraction for the child. Thus, if this period of genuine interest is not utilized and learning is postponed until the child is over four years of age, teaching him becomes an increasingly difficult task. His lack of skill combined with his divided interest results in dawdling and playing, and the shifting of the responsibility to the adult. Trying to teach a five-year-old child to dress, when he has not been given sufficient previous training, would be comparable to asking the child to tidy his room while a circus is passing on the street. In brief, pre-school development in the dressing procedure may be divided roughly into three main periods. In the first period the child is uninterested and lacking in ability and the adult's role is that of stimulating an interest and developing a sense of responsibility in regard to dressing, while doing the greater part of the dressing herself. The second period appears with the development of an interest in the proceedings and a growing skill in manipulating clothing. For the adult this period is one of instruction and assistance. In the third period the child loses his interest but, if he has been properly instructed, he has become sufficiently proficient to handle the situation with comparative ease. The adult's role is reduced to directing proceedings and maintaining order.

Source: Blatz et al., 1935 p. 56–58.

Program Statement

Early childhood programs should have a program statement that is reviewed with families. This statement should outline the program's policies and procedures, including the following information:

- Program goals that have been developed from the program's philosophy (discussed further in Chapter 8).
- Breakdown of how the children and staff groups are organized.

- Daily schedules and routines describing both basic care and developmental or enrichment activities.
- Organization of the physical environment.
- Description of the program plans for each group of children and for children within the group.
- Communication approaches used by staff to guide behaviour and promote learning.
- Health policies that promote the children's well-being and are consistent with licensing requirements.
- Nutrition policies that guide menu planning and meet individual needs and requests.
- Procedures for fire drills and emergency evacuations.
- Steps taken if child maltreatment is suspected.
- Procedures for admission to the centre, including registration and orientation.
- Attendance policies, including holidays, fee payment, and withdrawal notice.

The program statement should reflect the purpose, philosophy, and goals of the centre and should be consistent with all legal requirements, including the provincial child care legislation. Each organization will have its own unique circumstances to reflect in a program statement. Board members should be familiar with this statement to ensure it is an accurate reflection of established policies. Management is responsible for developing program policies but all staff members can help to articulate the related procedures and put them into practice.

The program statement helps parents understand how the program really works and if it is appropriate for their family. It outlines the program's activities and the expectations of families who choose to use the services.

The content of the program statement should be included in the family handbook.

The contract is an agreement between two parties (family, usually represented by the child's parents and the program) that outlines clear guidelines for each party's responsibilities and obligations. The agreement should clarify expectations and set up a framework to resolve issues that may arise.

Mutual respect between parents and early childhood educators benefit young children.

It can also protect the financial interests of the organization. If the parents/guardians of the children enrolled in the program become members of the organization, the membership agreement should be included in the contract.

The agreement should explain:

- family responsibilities;
- the program's responsibilities to the child and parent/legal guardian;
- payment and notice of withdrawal; and
- the program's health, safety, and nutrition policies

A family-centre contract should be introduced and explained to new families at the orientation meeting. Both parties can then sign two copies, one for the child's file and one for the family.

Childrearing Practices

Care routines are a crucial part of life in an early childhood program. Eating, sleeping, and toileting routines should follow the centre's protection policies and procedures. The care routines must also be responsive to individual children's needs and family wishes, and reflect the family's and community's cultural childrearing practices.

Early childhood and family programs can provide opportunities and information to parents/guardians that will develop knowledge about early childhood and parenting skills.

Participation

Parents/guardians and other family members may work directly with staff in the program. In cooperative nursery schools and some cooperative child care centres, regular parent participants make up part of the required staff complement. In other instances, regular parent participation increases the overall resources available and enhances the ability of the program to meet the individual needs of children. For example, a regular parent participant might read stories to children from 4:30 to 5:30 P.M., thus offering a welcome new source of stimulation and comfort to children at the end of the day while freeing up staff attention for conversations with other parents as they arrive to pick up their children. The benefits from such arrangements are two-fold: participants provide additional resources to the program and participants learn more about their children and the program activities.

Policies and procedures describe the roles and responsibilities of participating parents. Here are some ideas to consider:

- Identify the time commitment needed from each family and set consistent guidelines for families with more than one child in the program.
- Consider alternatives to direct program participation, including preparation of play materials, administrative tasks, and shopping.
- Consider financial consequences of participation, missed participation, and alternatives to participation.
- Develop mechanisms for missed participation times.
- Communicate roles, responsibilities, and tasks.
- Recognize variations in parents' experiences and skills.

Innovations

COMFORT, PLAY & TEACH: A POSITIVE APPROACH TO PARENTING™

Comfort, Play & Teach translates recent science and best practices into a simple and practical approach to parenting. It is based on activities that parents and caregivers share with their child every day.

Handouts for parents and caregivers can be adapted to meet individual program needs.

Comfort, Play & Teach is a parenting approach developed and supported by Invest in Kids (see www.investinkids.ca). Invest in Kids is a national, charitable organization that supports the healthy social, emotional, and intellectual development of children from birth to age five by strengthening the parenting knowledge, skills, and confidence of all those who work with and live with Canada's youngest children.

Invest in Kids translates the science of parenting and child development into engaging, easy-to-understand, relevant resources for parents and professionals.

- Consider staff skills and available resources.
- Communicate program activities, daily schedule, and child guidance expectations.

Early childhood programs must allow parents/guardians to visit their children at any time, regardless of whether the visit is scheduled. If family visits are encouraged throughout the day, children become accustomed to these comings and goings. A few minutes at lunch, in the playground, or at group time provide another opportunity for families to participate in their child's daily life and ongoing early learning and development.

If parents and other family members are welcome in a program, their needs need to be met. For instance, consider having an adult-sized chair or sofa in the children's play area; there should be a place for adults to hang their coats and leave their bags.

Decision Making

Parent/guardian involvement in the decision-making process ranges from opportunities to advise or make recommendations to a board of directors to situations where parents/guardians have the majority vote on the board. Parent involvement in decision making can only work if parents know *how* to take part in the process.

Possibilities for input into decision making include:

- suggestion boxes;
- parent questionnaires;
- program evaluation feedback; and
- participation on board of directors or advisory group.

EVERYONE BELONGS

Planning for early childhood programs in Canada needs to take into consideration the range and forms of difference each child and family brings to the early learning setting, including appearance, age, culture, ethnicity, race, language, gender, sexual orientation, religion, family environment, and developmental abilities. Additionally, there is particular consideration for the unique characteristics of specific groups, such as the Francophone, Aboriginal, rural and remote, and different ethno-cultural communities.

The overall implementation of an early childhood program should be respectful of the unique perspectives of communities. Programs can conduct a needs assessment to identify the early care and education needs of immigrant families in their communities, and the gaps in service provision and participation (Matthews & Ewen, 2006). Many children live in mixed-status families, so the information collected should include migration history and details about extended family networks (Ali et al., 2003; Bernhard et al., 2006a; Orellana et al., 2001; Yau, 1995; Young, 2002). This information can be used to improve access to services. Achieving meaningful participation will require additional training for early childhood educators to implement teaching strategies for second language acquisition and more skills and knowledge to work with children from linguistically and culturally diverse families (Chumak-Horbatsch, 2004; Pacini-Ketchabaw, 2001).

Early childhood programs can provide ongoing support to sustain diversity, equity, and inclusion. Specific supports include (Bernhard et al., 2006b):

- additional staff beyond ratio as needed to support inclusion;
- technical support and special consultancy;
- special equipment and materials; and
- interpreters to ensure effective communication with parents.

Young children with different abilities, challenges, resources, and cultural backgrounds and their families come together in early childhood settings. They bring unique life experiences and orientations. They and their families benefit most when they are fully included and when they feel that they belong. Children grow up with a strong sense of self in environments that promote attitudes, beliefs, and values of equity and democracy and support their full participation (Bennett, 2004). To include everyone, early childhood settings must encourage healthy dialogue about the principles and shared beliefs that relate to inclusion, diversity, and equity. They must recognize every child as a citizen with equal rights and unique views about how to participate in the world. To turn belief statements and principles into practice at the community level requires an infrastructure that actively promotes engagement of all children and their families (see Bernhard et al., 2006b).

Early childhood settings can be proactive in identifying strategies that will respect families' diverse linguistic, cultural, ethnic, and religious backgrounds and value this diversity as an asset that enriches the environment for everyone. It is important to consider the following:

- Effective strategies begin by identifying the early learning and child care needs of families in their communities, and taking this information into account when planning the curriculum and pedagogy of the program (Ali, 2005; Bernhard, 2003). Because many children live in newcomer, immigrant, and refugee families, information that is collected should include migration history.

- Meaningful participation for all requires strategies for second language acquisition (Chumak-Horbatsch, 2004; Tabors & Snow, 2001). Children who are learning English or French as an additional language benefit when their first language is valued. It is a challenge to know what children are capable of learning when early childhood practitioners and children and their families do not share the same language. In order to be able to determine a child's capacity to learn, the child needs adequate opportunities to learn in a language that she or he can understand. Interpreters can increase the level of effective communication with parents.

- Preconceived notions about children's ethno-cultural backgrounds, gender, abilities, or socioeconomic circumstances create barriers that reduce engagement and equitable outcomes (Bernhard et al., 2004). Addressing prejudices increases the involvement of all children. Early childhood practitioners can take actions to avoid prejudice and to counteract bias when it occurs in early childhood settings.

- Early childhood settings in Francophone communities can contribute to the protection, enhancement, and transmission of the French language and culture. Aboriginal early childhood settings require programming that values Aboriginal languages and culture and is generated from the community rather than imposed on the community (see Ball, 2005).

- Rural and remote communities require flexible early childhood settings that can adapt to the challenges of geographic distances and isolation (Gott & Wilson, 2004).

- Early childhood settings can organize programming to use the diversity of the participants as an asset that enriches the environment for everyone.

RECORD-KEEPING

Each program must keep official written legal, financial, program, and personnel records. Records are also kept on each child enrolled in the program and each staff member employed by the program.

Records must be organized so information can be easily retrieved; storage procedures are established to ensure security and confidentiality. Board members and designated staff members should be familiar with the record-keeping system so that they can access necessary information and documents in the event of an emergency in the supervisor's or director's absence.

There are many different systems for information organization—alphabetical, subject, numerical, and colour-coding are all viable options.

The following records should be kept:

- *Legal records.* Current legal records should be readily available and on the premises. Copies can be made to include in a handbook for the board of directors. Past legal records should be stored for as long as the organization is in existence.

- *Financial records.* The books of account and financial statements must be stored for six years.
- *Children's records.* Individual child records should include developmental records; letters from medical practitioners, child welfare agencies, or the courts; legal documentation of custody arrangements; and forms that indicate parental/guardian permission for participation in research studies, field trips, photographs, or videos.
- The information in children's files is confidential. Each program should develop policies that outline who has access to the information, what information is collected, and how the information is stored. Programs are required to share information related to the child's identity, family physician, health insurance, history of communicable diseases, and immunization record with the medical officer or designate.
- Parents should have access to all information. Written parent consent is needed before information can be released to a third party, unless it is demanded by court order or by an official for a child welfare agency.
- Children's records must be kept for at least two years after the child has been withdrawn from the centre.
- *Program records.* All program records must be kept for two years. Children's records must be kept for two years after the child withdraws from the program.
- *Personnel records.* Employers are usually required to keep complete individual employee records for two years after employment is ended. Records of employee names, addresses, date of commencement and termination of employment, wages for each pay period, and vacation pay must be kept for five years after employment is ended.

Keep official documents and other records on the premises. The records must be organized, usually in a filing system, and located in a cabinet that can be locked.

EARLY CHILDHOOD EDUCATORS AND OPERATIONS

When the physical environment is well taken care of, records are in order, policies are in place to protect children and promote their well-being, and families are welcomed into the centre's community, then the program is well managed. Regulatory requirements, program policies, and procedural guidelines are the foundation, but it is the early childhood educators who must take an active role in making sure day-to-day operations are smooth.

Making sure that the paperwork is complete, the physical environment is organized and well maintained, and families are engaged is part of the scope of responsibilities for every ECE. Finding opportunities to participate in managing the operations of early childhood programs expands the knowledge and skill level and enhances future career opportunities. Consider the following:

- Discuss how regulatory requirement, program policies, and procedural guidelines can work together to ensure smooth operation of early childhood programs.

- Outline the components of a healthy and safe environment for young children and their families.
- Consider the design of the physical environment.
- Discuss a family-centred approach.
- Describe effective record-keeping and information systems.

KEY TERMS

family involvement   risk management plan

REFLECTION QUESTIONS

1. How does the organization of the physical space support the daily program and children's activities?
2. Consider strategies to support a family that is new to Canada and does not speak English to help them participate in an early childhood program.
3. Sasha is two years old. Her mother, Michelle, does not want Sasha to play in the sand because she will get dirty. How might you respond?

FOR MORE INFORMATION

1. Examples of outdoor play environments for children can be found at the *Places for Play* exhibition by Playlink and the Free Play Network in Britain.

   www.freeplaynetwork.org.uk/playlink/exhibition/index.html

   The section "woe and possibility" shows poor as well as creative playground possibilities.
2. The *Government of Ontario* has design guidelines for the development of child care facilities.

   www.children.gov.on.ca/NR/CS/Publications/PlanningAndDesign_en.doc

3. The *Thomson Nelson ECE Resource Centre* is intended to enhance the teaching and learning experience for both instructors and students. The website provides extensive and helpful resources in many different criteria related to early childhood education.

   www.ece.nelson.com

HUMAN RESOURCES

Downtown Squire Early Childhood Centre

Sabiha's day begins at 8:30 A.M. in the toddler program at Downtown Squire Early Childhood Centre and she is soon joined by a couple of older children who want to "help with the babies." Staff members find many ways for children and staff to visit different groups, and to spend time together in the playground.

"The focus of my work is on both children and families, and the needs vary considerably," says Sabiha. Some families need the additional services of community organizations; many families are not aware of the availability of fee subsidy. We are well connected with agencies in the community in an effort to make sure the extra support needs of families of children with disabilities are met.

"Keeping the operation running smoothly means making sure that the physical environment is as good as it can possibly be, thus freeing up staff for more interaction with children and families," she says. "Policies that work are a foundation that allows us all to do more of what we like to do best—play with the children and engage parents in the wonder of early development."

Sabiha is an early childhood educator who graduated from a community college with an ECE diploma six years ago. She was employed in another centre immediately following graduation, but after a few months she started to look around for another position. Sabiha was dissatisfied by the quality of care in her first centre, and was discouraged at the lack of opportunity she had to focus on interacting with children and plan activities and the environment based on their development. Sabiha accepted an offer at Downtown Squire Early Childhood Centre because of the opportunity to practise quality early childhood education.

Chapter Objectives

This chapter will:

1. Outline staff roles and responsibilities.
2. Review compensation policies and procedures.
3. Discuss working conditions.
4. Explore support, guidance, and supervision practices.
5. Review employment practices.
6. Consider how human resource issues impact the work environments of early childhood educators.

ROLES AND RESPONSIBILITIES

The quality of working life in early childhood programs influences the quality of programs that children and families receive. Clear staff roles and responsibilities and reasonable levels of compensation certainly contribute to a positive work life and high quality of care. The governance structure defines the "employer" for all staff members who are working in an early childhood program. The first step in establishing positive employer–employee relationships is to develop consistent, fair personnel policies that put the program's purpose, philosophy, and goals into practice. Clear, consistent personnel policies contribute to a shared understanding of staff responsibilities. Written personnel policies outline responsibilities and expectations of the staff. The lack of clearly defined roles is a common source of conflict in early childhood programs, as well as many other workplaces.

The current societal circumstances, scientific findings, and government requirements described in Section 1 expand expectations for the role of early childhood work educators:

- Families using early childhood programs are under stress as a result of factors such as trying to balance work and family responsibilities, poverty, trying to adjust to a new culture, being a lone parent, and the increased incidence of stressed families.
- There are increasing numbers of vulnerable children from all socioeconomic backgrounds who have emotional, social, linguistic, and cognitive difficulties and need additional supports.
- Families and professionals have expanded expectations for the provision of appropriate education and care for children with special needs and for children from diverse cultural backgrounds.
- The early childhood work force is expected to have knowledge of pedagogy (the development and implementation of purposeful activities designed to support and enhance children's learning), as well as skills in translating knowledge obtained through observing a child into activities that build upon the child's current

Early childhood educators usually work together in teams to plan and carry out the daily program.

developmental level and interests and enhance the child's holistic development, including basic literacy and numeracy skills.

- There is increasing demand for accountability to a number of different sources, such as child welfare, public health, and children's services.

Human resource management policies and practices are part of an administrative infrastructure that can support early childhood educators in meeting increased demands. The director or supervisor and early childhood educators have specific roles and responsibilities in early childhood programs. The expectations are shaped by the program's purpose, philosophy, and goals, and by regulatory requirements. Job descriptions and behaviour guidance policies help to define and understand early childhood educator roles and responsibilities.

The following sections in this chapter focus on human resource policies and practices for early childhood educators employed in child care programs. However, as is indicated throughout the chapter, much of the content will be relevant in other early childhood settings.

Child Care

Early childhood educators are central to staffing of child care settings. The roles and responsibilities of early childhood educators and other staff are outlined in a set of **occupational standards.** While intended for practitioners working in child care settings, many of the standards are applicable to early childhood educators working in other types of early childhood programs.

In 2003, the Canadian Child Care Federation (CCCF) published occupational standards for a person who is responsible for a group of children in an early childhood setting (Doherty, 2003). This document was developed under the guidance of a steering committee and subjected to review and amendment through extensive Canada-wide consultation with all parts of the early childhood sector. In addition to incorporating the CCCF's *Code of Ethics,* the document articulates the following roles and responsibilities:

- Protect and promote the psychological and physical safety, health, and well-being of each child.
- Develop and maintain a warm, caring, and responsive relationship with each child and with the group of children.
- Plan and provide daily experiences that support and promote each child's physical, emotional, social, communication, cognitive, ethical, and creative development.
- Use observations to assess children's skills, abilities, interests, and needs.
- Recognize signs and symptoms of emotional or developmental delays or challenges, and take appropriate action.
- Establish and maintain an open, cooperative relationship with each child's family.
- Establish and maintain supportive, collaborative relationships with others working in the child care setting.
- Establish and maintain collaborative relationships with other community service providers working with the child.
- Reflect on one's own knowledge, attitudes, and skills and take appropriate action as indicated.

A list of the specific responsibilities and the required knowledge, skills, and abilities is provided for each standard. The standards incorporate the responsibilities resulting from the expanded expectations on early childhood educators in that they:

- Include the establishment of a warm, supportive relationship with each family and through the *Code of Ethics* provide guidance regarding the ethical limits associated with addressing parents' social, family, or personal problems.
- Refer to the provision of appropriate environments and experiences for *all* children, and in their articulation of the required knowledge, skills, and abilities, make explicit reference to respecting and responding sensitively and appropriately to diversity. They also incorporate responsibilities such as making environmental and program accommodations for children with special needs.
- Identify the responsibility to support and promote each child's development in all areas, including offering "experiences that set the stage for literacy and number skills and developmentally appropriate experiences related to reading, science, mathematics and social studies" (Doherty, 2003 p. 16).
- Discuss responsibilities associated with observing children and interpreting observations.
- Discuss reporting responsibilities related to infectious diseases and possible neglect or abuse.

The role of the person responsible for a group of children has become increasingly more complex. It requires "an ability to make critical judgments about practice, to communicate and network with children, parents, colleagues in other children's services and the wider community, to work with the complexity and diversity of group settings and of children and employing a holistic approach" (Cameron, 2004, p. 3).

Family Child Care Providers

Family child care combines the roles and responsibilities of managing a small business with caring for children and communicating with parents (Cox, 2005). The family child care provider makes an emotional commitment and the role requires constant attention to the children in care. Regulated family child care providers must equip and maintain their residences in compliance with child care, health, and safety regulations.

Job Descriptions

Job descriptions for those working in early childhood settings have two purposes:

- To satisfy the requirements of the program for quality of performance and reliability.
- To satisfy the needs of early childhood educators and other staff members for challenge, security, and accomplishment.

Job descriptions usually include:

- position title;
- qualifications;
- responsibilities; and
- salary (optional; this may be included in the employment contract).

Innovations

OCCUPATIONAL STANDARDS FOR CHILD CARE PRACTITIONERS

The Canadian Child Care Federation's *Occupational Standards for Child Care Practitioners* (see www.cccf-fcsge.ca/subsites/training/pdf/occupational-final-e.pdf) presents nine standards that outline the skills, abilities, and core knowledge required for competent practice.

The occupational standards are intended to be applicable to all settings providing care and education to children and for children of all ages. Read the standards and then think about:

1. Are these basic standards realistic for an ECE responsible for a group of children in a centre-based setting? If not, why not?
2. Are these basic standards realistic expectations for family child care providers? If not, which standards are unrealistic?
3. Are these basic standards applicable for all age groups? If not, why not?
4. Is any standard crucial for competent practice missing? If so, what?
5. Is any standard unnecessary? If so, which?
6. Do you have any concerns about the standards in general or about an individual standard? If so, please describe your concern.
7. Can you identify specific situations or positions in which additional skills and/or knowledge are necessary?

Job descriptions are not static but evolve over time as the priorities of the program change and as legislation and general practices in the field change. Job descriptions can include goal and objective statements that describe the centre's expectations of staff members *and* are consistent with the organization's overall philosophy and purpose. See the Appendix for an example of a job description.

Job Title

Role titles are confusing in early childhood settings. Manager, coordinator, director, supervisor, and administrator are all terms that may be used for the person "in charge" who is primarily responsible for carrying out the centre's policies. Early childhood teacher, program staff, and early childhood educator are terms used to describe the people who directly plan and carry out children's daily care and activities. Parenting workers or family support staff are terms that may be used to describe staff who work with parents or parents and children in family support programs. Other categories may include assistants to the supervisor or assistant to program staff.

Different titles may indicate different types of responsibilities, but there is no consistent use within the field of particular titles that have corresponding roles and responsibilities. Early childhood programs can select the titles that are most acceptable

Beyond Our Borders

INTERNATIONAL QUALIFICATIONS COMPARISON

FINLAND

Staff in day care centres are required to have at least a secondary-level (equivalent to high school) degree in the field of social welfare and health care. One in three of the staff must have a post-secondary level degree (bachelor of education, master of education, or bachelor of social sciences). Preschool teachers are required to have either a bachelor or master's degree in education, or a bachelor degree in social sciences with an additional pedagogical course.

Family child-minders are required to have training (the amount varies) and are recommended to have the new vocation training for family child-minders. The adult-to-child ratio in family day care is one to four, including the child-minder's own under–school-age children (in addition, a child-minder can provide part-time care for one preschool or school-age child).

NEW ZEALAND

All New Zealand's early childhood teachers must complete three-year post-secondary training programs, and most of them are in faculties of education that also prepare elementary and secondary teachers. Under the country's ten-year strategic plan, there is a move toward requiring 100 percent of regulated staff to be registered teachers (by the year 2012). Funding is provided to centres to enable teacher release time to assist provisionally registered teachers to become fully registered. (These requirements do not apply to home-based care, play centres, and licence-exempt services. Kindergartens have required registered teachers in every classroom since 1989.)

SWEDEN

Preschool teachers complete a three-year free university training program. Child-minders, family day care providers, and leisure-time "pedagogues" receive their training in secondary school, supplemented by a wealth of in-service opportunities.

Sources: OECD, 2006; Dickinson, 2005; Oberhuemer, 2005.

and use them consistently. Job titles should reflect the organizational structure and hierarchy.

Qualifications

Early childhood programs should have written statements of qualifications for each position in the program. The minimum *required* qualifications can include education/training and work experience. Also, it is possible to include additional qualifications that would be beneficial to the position but not required. For instance, the ability to communicate in a language other than English may be a bonus skill in an early childhood program if families are unable to communicate in English.

Research on quality early childhood programs have found that senior staff in quality programs are more likely to have:

- a university degree;
- a strong background in child development and/or early childhood pedagogy;
- several years of experience working in early childhood and family settings; and
- training in administration.

Responsibilities

The job responsibilities can begin with a summary that states the purpose of the job within the program and identification of the supervision that is given and received. Next, the description of responsibilities can identify what is expected in order to achieve the purpose, philosophy, and goals of the program. For example, the program director will provide the board with support to make informed decisions. Such statements are really performance goals. Next, the description can explain how the performance goals can be carried out by outlining specific tasks and responsibilities. For example, provide a supervisor's report at each board meeting and at the annual general meeting.

These statements are performance standards or objectives that describe how to carry out each goal. In establishing job responsibilities, it is a good idea to consider how the work can be set up to promote staff satisfaction and motivation. If possible, organize work so that each staff member has some measure of autonomy and decision making with the operation of the program.

BEHAVIOUR GUIDANCE

Each early childhood program needs policies and procedures that describe acceptable and prohibited behaviour guidance practices for the staff, volunteers, caregivers, parents, and other family members who may be interacting with young children in the program. Guidelines include:

- Discipline should be appropriate for the age and developmental level of the child, related to the problem at hand, and carried out as soon as possible.
- Behaviour guidance practices should be developed to promote cooperation, support autonomy, and set limits.
- Behaviour guidance problems and discipline issues should be discussed with parents.
- Corporal punishment, including hitting, spanking, pushing, shaking, pinching, biting, grabbing, and slapping, is prohibited at all times.
- Humiliation of children—physically and verbally—is prohibited.
- Food, drink, shelter, clothing, or bedding cannot be withheld from the children as a threat or punishment.

- Children cannot be confined or locked in any room or left alone.
- If parents or other caregivers are present with the child, expectations for their role in behaviour guidance should be clear and explicit.

The behaviour guidance policy also needs to outline disciplinary actions that will be taken if a staff member contravenes the stated procedures. Serious violations may be reported to local child welfare authorities as suspected child abuse. In child care programs early childhood educators and other staff members must read and sign the behaviour guidance policy when first employed in the program. Volunteers, participating parents, and students must also read and sign the policy before interacting with the children. The policy must be reviewed annually with staff, volunteers, and students.

In nonprofit programs, the board of directors is responsible for reviewing the behaviour guidance policies and procedures at least once a year. A written record of each review and the changes made should be signed by an officer or staff member who has knowledge of the review, and can be kept on file.

Regulated child care programs need to have a written procedure for monitoring the behaviour guidance practices of staff, volunteers, and students. It is also a good practice to carry out in other early childhood programs. A written record of the monitoring that is done must be kept on file. For example, the supervisor might observe each staff member's behaviour guidance practices on a quarterly basis. A written record of the quarterly observations would then be kept on file.

Reporting Child Maltreatment

Early childhood educators have the same obligation as any member of the public to report a suspicion that a child is in need of protection. In fact, child protection legislation recognizes that professionals who work closely with children (including anyone who is employed in a regulated child care setting) have a special awareness of the signs of child abuse and neglect. Therefore, they have a particular responsibility to report their suspicions, and provincial requirements make it an offence to fail to report.

Early childhood educators are not experts on child abuse and neglect and do not investigate or judge situations. This is the responsibility of child welfare or protection agencies. Child care staff members, however, are legally responsible for noting any possible signs and symptoms that might be related to child abuse, neglect, or risk of harm, and for reporting these suspicions accordingly. Individual child care staff must make the report directly to the local child protection authorities rather than rely on anyone else (including the supervisor or director of the child care program) to report on his or her behalf.

The duty to report is an ongoing obligation. If a child care staff member has made a report about a child, and has additional suspicions that the child is or may be in need of protection, that staff member must make a further report to the local authorities.

Provincial/territorial child protection legislation does protect early childhood educators and other staff who make a report of a suspicion of a child in need of protection. If a civil action is brought against an early childhood educator, the system provides protection from liability unless the staff member acted maliciously or without reasonable grounds for his or her suspicion.

COMPENSATION

The capacity of individual early childhood programs to compensate staff is set within the broader context of public policies and funding. The challenges of early childhood policies identified in Chapter 2 impede the ability of many programs to improve the work environment, particularly wages and benefits. Human resource management in early childhood programs must address limited resources for adequate compensation. Recruitment and retention of qualified staff in early childhood programs is often difficult.

Compensation for employees includes salaries and benefits. Employees working in early childhood programs are covered under provincial and territorial employment standards legislation. Employers are obliged to meet minimum requirements for staff remuneration and benefits. Minimum wages are established in each jurisdiction. The maximum number of hours per day and per week varies, but eight hours a day and 40 hours a week is the most common. Statutory holidays (New Year's Day, Good Friday, Victoria Day, Canada Day, Labour Day, Thanksgiving Day, Christmas Day, and Boxing Day) with pay are recognized across Canada. Employment standards call for a minimum of two weeks' paid holidays annually, and some jurisdictions call for increased holidays after five years' employment.

Employment Legislation

Provincial and territorial ministries and departments administer and enforce several pieces of legislation that set down basic rules for employment practices in workplaces, including early childhood programs. Federal laws include income tax reporting and deduction requirements, employment insurance contributions, record of employment, and Canada Pension Plan.

Provincial/Territorial Legislation

The provincial/territorial employment legislation includes basic rules about employing people. It stipulates minimum employment conditions including minimum wages, maximum hours of work, required vacation pay, statutory holidays, and pregnancy and parental leave. Employment standards also set out the employer's responsibilities for employment termination, layoff notice, and pay administration.

Labour legislation regulates the collective bargaining process, including:

- definition and formation of a trade union;
- certification of a union;
- negotiation towards a contract or collective agreement between management and staff;
- strikes; and
- unfair labour practices.

In Ontario and Quebec, pay equity legislation requires that job comparisons be made between female-dominated and male-dominated job classes. Work performed by women that is comparable to work performed by men in the same establishment should receive the same pay. Proxy pay equity allows child care staff in community-based, nonprofit centres to compare their jobs to comparators in child care centres directly operated by municipalities.

Employee health and safety legislation protects workers against health and safety hazards on the job. It sets out the rules for employees and employers to work together to ensure a healthy and safe workplace environment, identifies the rights of workers and responsibilities of employers, and stipulates mechanisms for enforcement.

Workers' compensation legislation provides for compensation for employee injuries received while working. Early childhood programs typically are not required to participate in plans (unless they are part of larger multi-service organizations), but it is strongly recommended. Workers' compensation provides financial protection for employees, including wage compensation, payment of medical expenses, and rehabilitation costs. Under the program, the employer receives protection against legal action by employees who are injured at work or are affected by work-related diseases. If the employer is covered under the plan, employees have the right to compensation and do not have the right to sue.

Human rights legislation protects against discrimination based on handicaps, age, marital status, family status, sex, sexual orientation, record of offences, or citizenship unless there is reasonable or genuine disqualification based on the nature of the job. The legislation also prohibits sexual harassment.

Federal Legislation

The *Employment Insurance Act* provides for reduced income while someone is not employed after a period of employment. All employers and employees are required to pay into this fund through mandatory payroll deductions. Parental leave benefits for new parents are offered through Employment Insurance.

The federal *Income Tax Act* specifies employers' responsibilities to remit income tax deductions, Employment Insurance, and Canada Pension Plan deductions and employers' contributions to the Canada Revenue Agency each month.

Salaries

Salaries usually account for 85 percent of the expenses in most early childhood program budgets, so this is a critical item in financial calculations. Salaries in most of the early childhood sector seem to be chronically low—so low that staff members are really subsidizing programs by working for substantially less money than they could earn in similar jobs in other fields. Employers have a tough time raising salaries to a reasonable level and still keeping the program financially viable.

Remuneration levels and benefits do vary by program and jurisdiction. Overall, caregivers in regulated family child care earn less than staff working in centre-based programs. Remuneration levels are usually decided by boards of directors or owners of individual centres or family child care agencies or through negotiation between individual parents and caregivers who are not affiliated with an agency. Salary levels may or may not vary with education and experience. Government policies related to grants have an impact on compensation levels, but overall (outside of Quebec), remuneration and benefit levels are usually determined by the fees that parents pay and/or government parent fee subsidy levels.

In comparison, kindergarten teachers receive salaries and benefits that are established between provincial/territorial teachers' associations and provincial/territorial governments in ten jurisdictions and the local school authority in Ontario, Manitoba, and Alberta (Canadian Teachers Federation, n.d.). Salary levels increase with additional education and experience.

Salary and benefits in early childhood programs, apart from regulated child care and kindergarten, are usually established by the programs' funding guidelines. Most are funded programs that are accessed by parents for no cost or minimum fees. The funding usually includes a dedicated amount for salaries and benefits.

Family child caregivers who are individually licensed are self-employed. However, the employment status of those who are affiliated with a family child care agency is less clear and has been debated in the courts on several occasions. At this time, caregivers affiliated with an agency are treated as if they were self-employed for purposes of administration of federal and provincial/territorial employment and income tax legislation. Therefore, they are not eligible for maternity and parental leave benefits, Employment Insurance, and protection under labour legislation (such as paid vacation days).

The work the family child care provider does is at the core of several problems associated with the failure to recognize the value of women's work. The lack of recognition of the value of caregivers' work is particularly acute in early childhood care (Beach et al., 1998, p. 8). Within the child care sector, work done by caregivers in the home, and often concurrently with unpaid work (such as taking care of their own children), is also undervalued.

Salary Scales

In spite of the serious problem of limited financial resources, early childhood programs usually have some options when setting up a salary scale: Will all staff members earn the same salary, or will there be a salary grid based on education and/or experience? This decision is usually based on the organizational structure for staff in the program. If some staff members supervise others, it is logical that they will receive additional pay. If the staff works together as a collective, equally sharing all responsibilities, it makes sense to equalize salaries. Possible options include:

- annual salary increases based on a COLA (cost of living allowance) percentage;
- additional increments for each year a staff member has worked at a particular centre; and
- salary increments related to performance.

Whatever the format chosen for the salary scale, it should be consistent and fair. Salary scales should be based on the staff positions, not on the particular people in the positions.

Decisions about salary increases are made by boards of directors, usually based on recommendations from both the personnel and finance committees, in consultation with staff members.

Pay Equity

Pay equity is a process designed to ensure that equal monetary compensation is given for work that is of equal value, and is often an issue in female-dominated jobs. The fair value of work is assessed by comparing pay for predominately female jobs with that of pay for predominately male jobs.

Pay equity programs aim to identify and correct wage gaps that are due to systemic discrimination against women. Generally, the traditional work of women has been undervalued and underpaid. As reported by Ruth Rose and Elizabeth Ouellet: "The problem of low wages is common to all workers who perform, in the labour market, a type of replacement of housewives' unpaid work" (2000, p. 13).

Public sector employers have the legal obligation to pursue a pay equity program in only seven provinces (British Columbia, Prince Edward Island, Manitoba, New Brunswick, Nova Scotia, Ontario, Quebec) (Bakan & Kobayashi, 2000). Further, pay equity legislation applies to private sector (including not-for-profit) employers only in Ontario, Quebec, and fields under federal jurisdiction.

In Ontario, the *Pay Equity Act* requires employers in the public sector to file pay equity plans in the workplace, effective January 1, 1990, and to make the necessary pay equity adjustments. Pay equity is a process designed to ensure that equal monetary compensation is given for work that is of equal value. Proxy pay equity allows child care staff in community-based not-for-profit programs to use municipal child care programs as comparators.

The *Pay Equity Act* requires programs to make annual payroll adjustments at a rate of 1 percent of the previous year's total payroll until the rates of pay established by the pay equity process are reached. Adjustments up to 1998 were funded by the provincial government. Since 1998, funding has been the responsibility of the boards of directors of not-for-profit child care programs. Pay equity adjustments are a legal requirement, but boards of directors and child care programs were typically unable to pay without pay equity grants.

In 2001, four child care staff and five unions launched a court challenge of the Ontario government's decision to stop pay equity funding in mostly female public sector workplaces, including child care centres. In 2003, the challenge was successful, resulting in $414 million in proxy pay equity payments for public sector employees (Ontario Coalition for Better Child Care, 2003). The settlement applies to Ontario non-profit community-based programs that receive public funding through fee subsidies and/or wage grants. The pay equity settlement will translate into monies available to child care centres to meet pay equity obligations.

Benefits

Benefits are items provided by employers for the benefit of employees apart from salary compensation. Some benefits are mandatory; that is, employers are required by law to provide them.

Early childhood programs must provide employees with:

- Canada Pension Plan;
- employment insurance;

- vacation pay; and
- pregnancy and parental leave.

A good benefit package is an effective way to attract and retain staff. A package might include some of the following features:

- A percentage amount (10–15 percent) of the total annual payroll is set aside for benefits.
- Employer's share of mandatory benefits is deducted.
- The remaining budget allocation is used to purchase a combination of benefits that suits the needs of staff members. Possibilities include extended medical care, dental care, life insurance, pension plans, child care, and long-term disability.

It's a good idea to investigate opportunities to join other group plans offered by umbrella organizations, and to compare packages from a number of insurance companies.

Leaves of Absence

Paid leaves of absence cover sick leave, holidays, and sometimes other days. Unpaid leaves of absence are usually granted when a staff member wishes to take an extended period of time off or paid leave has already been used. Provincial/territorial employment legislation stipulates bare minimum provisions, but many employers in not-for-profit organizations try to provide much more.

Policies concerning staff absences should be consistent for all staff. They should also be:

- established by board members, owners, or managers in consultation with staff;
- consistent with the legal requirements of the *Employment Standards Act;*
- responsive to a working environment that often is physically and emotionally demanding; and
- adequate to compensate staff who are in frequent contact with infections.

A generous sick leave policy—such as 1.5 days per month for staff members, which begins as soon as employment commences—takes into account the nature of the working conditions. Staff members are often in direct contact with children who are infectious with any number of illnesses, and their jobs are physically demanding. Programs may also choose to include provision for staff members to take paid leave to be with their own sick children or other family members.

WORKING CONDITIONS

The working conditions are shaped by the policies and procedures that structure schedules and routines in the workplace. When working conditions meet the needs of early childhood educators, their involvement with young children and family tends to be more responsive and supportive and program quality is higher (Doherty, 2000). Reasonable work schedules, paid preparation and meeting time, and reasonable staff-to-child ratios increase staff satisfaction and program quality and reduce staff turnover. The working environment (the nature of the interactions among people) contributes to the overall conditions of work.

Hours of Work

The structure of the program determines the hours of work for staff members. A half-day program operating four or five mornings a week is likely to employ staff on a part-time basis. Hours of work for kindergarten teachers follow the school day and are usually set in union collective agreements. In full-day, full-year child care programs, hours of operation are typically more than ten hours per day. Staff members are generally assigned seven- or eight-hour shifts, which may be permanent or may rotate on a regular basis.

The environment and working conditions of regulated family child care providers are defined both by the framework of child care policy and the legal framework that governs employment and self-employment or independent contracting (Cox, 2005). Working conditions in family child care typically include long hours without contact with other adults, the absence of breaks, and a lack of outside support (Beach et al., 1998; Beach et al., 2004). Regulated family child care providers work a 56-hour week, of which 47 hours are dedicated to the care of children, and nine hours to preparation of children's activities and meals. They care for an average of 5.4 children and 80 percent work all year (Beach et al., 1998).

Meetings

Many early childhood programs operate between nine and eleven hours each day, particularly if they are offering full-day, full-year options that meet the needs of working parents. Program staff, who work together with a group of children, have early and late shifts and different lunch and break times. Effective staff teams must have opportunities to meet when they do not have responsibility for children. This may require hiring casual staff to supervise children during the day or holding meetings outside of the program's hours of operation.

Staff members should receive financial compensation or time off when they attend meetings outside of regular work hours.

Preparation Time

High-quality early childhood education programs require staff preparation time, just as teachers in grade school, high school, college, and university. Time for planning and preparation may be built into the weekly staff schedule, or staff may receive overtime pay for planning and preparation outside of the regular work week.

Paid preparation time is generally available for kindergarten teachers working in the school system and for staff in early intervention programs. It is less common in family support programs or child care settings.

Work Environments

Each program has the opportunity to maximize the potential of early childhood educators in spite of inherent limitations to wages and benefits. The human resource management of individual programs can make a big difference to the work environment and to the motivation of early childhood educators.

A number of interrelated elements make up the work environment of an early childhood program. The style of administration and supervision, organizational

Early childhood educators respect children's documentation by carefully displaying drawings and paintings.

climate, compensation, and working conditions influence staff and caregivers' interactions with young children and their ability to organize the physical environment and learning experiences. Early childhood administrators play a pivotal role in creating work environments that promote high performance and personal fulfillment.

Organizational Climate

The organizational climate is the collective perception of staff about the work environment. It is based on their collective perceptions of the culture, atmosphere, and conditions in their workplace. Organizational climate exerts a powerful influence on motivation and behaviour in all workplaces. In early childhood programs, organizational climate affects the well-being of staff and influences their performance, program quality, and recruitment and retention. The role of the director or supervisor in setting the organizational climate is discussed further in Chapter 8.

Workplace Safety and Health

Healthy and safe conditions for staff members are important elements to consider. Policies and procedures to protect the children's health and safety may help, but there are additional conditions to consider. There are significant issues related to child care staff health and safety in their work environments, notably, infectious diseases, musculoskeletal disorders, and stress.

Health and safety challenges are reduced by good working conditions that minimize the risks. When illness or injury happens, sick leave and extended health-care benefits can make a big difference.

Physical Conditions

Working with young children is physically demanding. Babies and children are often carried and lifted, and furnishings and equipment get moved throughout the day's activities. Thus, backs, knees, and joints can suffer.

The organization physical environment can reduce musculoskeletal disorders. Here are some suggestions:

- Provide adult-sized furniture in the children's activity areas.
- Ensure staff have assistance before moving or lifting equipment.
- Offer information about correct bending and lifting from the knees to avoid back injury.

Infectious Disease

Getting sick is an occupational hazard in early childhood settings. Young children get colds, with runny noses and crusty eyes. They get gastrointestinal viruses and may vomit or have diarrhea. Chicken pox is a common childhood disease. Staff who are exposed to these germs through constant physical contact with children do risk becoming sick. Personal health-care and preventative measures, as well as excellent hygiene practices, in child care settings do help to reduce the likelihood of illness. But, compared to most work environments, there is increased exposure to infectious diseases in work with young children.

Provincial child care regulations require program staff to have a health examination and current immunization as recommended by the local medical officer of health. Immunization requirements usually cover rubella, measles, tetanus, diphtheria, and poliomyelitis.

SUPPORT, GUIDANCE, AND SUPERVISION

Early childhood educators are more likely to value their work and strive to improve their practice when their efforts are recognized and encouraged. Reasonable compensation, appropriate personnel policies, and positive working environments contribute to good practices. Employers can also ensure that there are specific policies and procedures in place that promote good practice. Consistent practices to support, guide, and supervise staff can enhance staff performance.

Staff Meetings

Communication between staff members is necessary to build a strong team and plan the children's program, review their progress, and discuss parental requests. Many issues concern all staff members and thus require time for group discussion and information-sharing.

Regular staff meetings can be structured to maximize the opportunity to meet together as a group. The agenda is an important tool. The supervisor or director needs an opportunity to bring forward information from the board of directors, the community, the municipality, or the province/territory that should be shared with all staff members. Program staff members should have the opportunity to bring forward items for the agenda. Agendas become a more useful tool when they are developed in advance of the meeting. This can be accomplished with a sign-up sheet for topics for discussion that program staff members identify and an advance listing of the supervisor's announcements and discussion items. The agenda can also identify actions from the previous staff meeting. The meeting's agenda should be known to all participants and the meeting's time can be allocated accordingly.

Staff Performance Review

Staff performance review is a process that should be established as a regular annual or semi-annual event. This type of evaluation can be used to:

- ensure program and staff performance goals and objectives are being carried out;
- identify areas of strength and interest, and areas where additional effort is required;
- recommend that staff be moved to permanent status from probation, fired, reassigned, or promoted;
- determine merit increases;
- meet requirements of funding agencies;
- lay the foundation for staff development and training plans;
- motivate staff; and
- identify resources and support needed by staff.

Managers should determine the purpose of the evaluation before deciding who the participants shall be and how the process will unfold. If merit increases and staff promotions are tied to the outcome of the performance review, staff members are likely to be more reluctant to identify performance problems as part of the permanent record.

If the results of the performance review process are not used in making decisions related to probation, promotion, reassignment, and termination, some other form of evaluation will be necessary to make these decisions.

Possible participants include the manager (supervisor/director), staff members who are being evaluated, peers, members from the board of directors, and parents. When all participants have a role in performance evaluation, it can be time-consuming and may not be completed. Sometimes called "360 degree performance review" (considered from all perspectives), this is usually too cumbersome a process for early childhood settings.

The manager usually evaluates the performance of all staff members as part of her or his staff supervision responsibilities. The manager who is doing performance reviews should be familiar with each staff member's performance over a period of time and bring a broad information base to the evaluation process. Also, the manager has an overview of the program's operation and is familiar with the human and physical environment.

Effective staff performance reviews are not something that is done to the staff. Staff members can be active participants in the process. Self-evaluation is an opportunity to consider one's own performance and reflect on changes that have occurred.

In some settings, staff members who are peers participate in each other's performance reviews. Because staff members who work together in a group program for young children become quite familiar with each other's practices, this can be another valuable source of information. However, this is not appropriate if the performance review is used to make hiring, firing, or promotion decisions.

In not-for-profit centres, the board members represent the centre and are the employer. Board members may have some involvement in performance reviews. The supervisor/director usually reports directly to the board of directors in early childhood programs and it is the board's responsibility to review the supervisor's/director's performance. Usually, board members are not directly involved in the evaluation of other staff but monitor performance reviews and can use the information in making staffing decisions.

Parents have another perspective to offer in reviewing staff performance. Typically, they do not see staff in action throughout the entire day, but they do observe staff members' communication skills and their own child's responses during arrival and departure times.

Here are some staff performance review guidelines:

- Evaluation of staff performance is a disruptive policy if it is only applied when there are perceived problems with one staff member's performance. To be fair and effective, a consistent process must be developed for performance review.
- This process must consider the purposes of the performance review and the participants who will be involved.
- The process should include plans for staff development opportunities.
- Performance review is a time to look back and consider what has happened and to look ahead to what should happen.
- Staff should have a clear idea of the criteria or performance standards that will be used for the performance review.

The joint performance review meeting and summary report identify specific training needs for each staff member and establish a time frame and needed resources. This becomes an individual professional development plan. Further discussion on program-wide professional development is found in Chapter 9.

The program review may identify training needs for a group of staff members. The recommendations and program review summary report outline specific plans for staff training such as workshops, journals and books for a staff library, and centre-wide staff development days.

Professional development plans can be presented to the board of directors or personnel committee that can monitor their implementation. If financial resources are needed, this information is integrated into the budget process.

A performance review process that is directly connected to the job description and involves both the staff member and the supervisor in reviewing performance can be used to create professional development plans for further growth. The personnel committee monitors the performance reviews and uses the information in making staffing decisions. Self-evaluations are *not* a required part of the documentation that is placed in staff members' files, and the information is not used to determine salary increases.

Input in Decision Making

Staff and programs benefit when staff members have avenues into the decision-making process of the early childhood programs. Staff that are invested in providing a quality program for young children and their families have much to offer to the decision-making process. The staff perspective should be sought out and respected by the supervisor, other management, and the board of directors.

In unionized settings, program staff have established structures and requirements for staff participation in the operation of the centre. In non-unionized settings, the board of directors can seek out staff input through ex-officio membership, participation on committees, and by attending staff meetings to discuss specific issues.

EMPLOYMENT PRACTICES

Employment practices include procedures for the recruitment of staff and the termination of employment. In not-for-profit settings, board members have a legal obligation to ensure equitable employment practices that meet employers' legal obligations. In a unionized setting, employment procedures are negotiated and recorded in the collective agreement.

RECRUITMENT

Attracting and hiring qualified staff to work in early childhood programs is a key management concern. Finding the right applicants and then making the right selection choices challenge most managers.

Recruiting a Diverse Work Force

Diversity refers to diversity of gender and diversity of culture, race, and language. As indicated in Chapter 1, Canada's population includes a wide variety of cultural backgrounds. Early childhood programs that aim to be sensitive to the varied backgrounds of the children and families being served want to reflect that diversity in their early childhood staff team. Furthermore, male and female models benefit young children.

Cultural and Linguistic Diversity

Recruiting employees to match the diversity of the children being served in early childhood programs has become a priority. However, "countries face the challenge that as the requirements for formal education increase, the diversity of backgrounds of staff decreases" (OECD, 2001, p. 106). Newcomers to Canada may not meet the entry requirements for post-secondary programs or be hesitant to apply because of limited skills in written English or French. One possible solution is to hire untrained people from the immigrant community served by the ECE program to work as assistants and then seek out opportunities to access further professional education. Newcomer applicants may have out-of-country qualifications that could be eligible for Prior Learning Assessment and Recognition (PLAR) at local colleges. Managers can encourage applicants to access PLAR and provide assistance in completing the process.

Beyond Our Borders

MEN IN CHILD CARE

In England and Scotland, targeted marketing to men includes television, newspaper and poster campaigns featuring male workers, handing out brochures (including one with the provocative title "Are You Man Enough for Childcare?") at venues where men are likely to be found, and providing men-only orientation sessions at secondary schools and career fairs. Several Nordic countries also use targeted marketing. But targeted marketing is not sufficient to attract men. Barriers such as low remuneration and poor career mobility must be addressed—to attract qualified men and women. Based on the premise that being part of a small minority could be off-putting for potential male workers, male support networks and mentoring for male students and for men already working in child care have been developed by Men in Childcare Scotland (see www.meninchildcare.com/).

Gender

In all countries, early childhood work is dominated by women. In 2001, women comprised over 96 percent of the early childhood work force in Canada (Beach et al., 2004). The Equal Opportunities Commission of the European Union (Rolfe, 2005) identified key barriers to recruiting men into services for young children:

- low wages and poor benefits in ECE services;
- the perception of child care as "women's work," simply an extension of mothering;
- the low status associated with working with children under age six; and
- insufficient information for boys in secondary school about early childhood education as a career.

Hiring Policies

Hiring policies can make it clear who has the responsibility for hiring individual staff. In not-for-profit programs, the board is usually responsible for hiring the supervisor/director. The supervisor/director is responsible for recruiting and hiring all other program staffs. A member of the personnel committee may participate in the process. In some centres, hiring committees are formed with board members and/or parents in addition to the supervisor and perhaps other staff.

Hiring Process

Before recruiting job applicants, decide what is wanted. Starting with the job description's list of responsibilities for a particular position, determine what the basic requirements are. Then think about the present staff team and add in other criteria.

The program director and a parent representative are interviewing early childhood educators.

Recruit applicants through advertisements in newspapers and notices to other child care centres, community centres, and early childhood organizations. Be specific—if the position requires an ECE diploma, say so. It helps to screen out applicants who do not meet the basic requirements.

Review the applicants, keeping the basic requirements and other identified criteria in mind. The appearance and presentation of the applicant's résumé is important. It is difficult to imagine how a supervisor would represent the centre if unable to prepare a concise résumé and covering letter.

Criminal Reference Check

Provincial/territorial regulations require that employers obtain a criminal reference check on all successful applicants for employment (and anyone over the age of 12) who will be working with young children. The purpose of the criminal record check is to protect children from persons whose criminal record indicates they present a risk to children.

Criminal reference checks are intended to screen out individuals who are not suited to work with children and to protect children from the risk of abuse or neglect. Used alone, criminal reference checks are limited in their effectiveness. They should be used in combination with other aspects of hiring, such as checking references and conducting interviews with applicants.

Programs need to establish criteria for which criminal convictions can be overlooked and which establish clear grounds for not pursing a job offer. A minor civil disobedience incident involving a noisy street party five years ago or a conviction resulting from unpaid parking violations does not present the same security issues as convictions related to theft or assault.

Probation

A **probation period** is a clearly defined trial period for new employees. In early childhood programs, a probation period serves the interests of both the program and the staff member. During the probation period, the supervisor or designate should meet regularly with the new staff member to provide feedback and guidance on job performance. The probation period should conclude with a formal performance review and either a permanent appointment, an extended probationary period, or dismissal. If the program is unionized, the collective agreement will include rules governing the probationary period.

Orientation

Early childhood educators should expect an orientation session at the beginning of employment in an early childhood program. An effective orientation is a positive beginning to employment. The session typically presents the program's philosophy, program goals and objectives, as well as an overview of policies and procedures.

Performance Issues

Personnel policies and procedures, along with regular staff performance reviews, staff development opportunities, and constructive discussion, help to avoid frequent performance problems. Straightforward job descriptions and rules make clear what performance standards are expected of staff. All staff have a responsibility to be aware of what is expected of them and what actions are not acceptable. They should also be aware of possible consequences of actions that are contrary to the child care program's policies. Managers have a responsibility to address specific problems. If sloppy practice is ignored, it is actually promoted because the message to staff is that it is okay. There is a clear obligation to discuss specific issues with staff members as they arise.

If problems do arise, job descriptions and other policies and procedures help ensure equity and justice in dealing with the situation. Early childhood organizations need to have a process to address the performance problems when staff members violate the centre's policies or are not carrying out their responsibilities. If the program tolerates unacceptable performance, the problem may get worse and become more difficult to solve. Staff performance problems are more likely to be dealt with in a consistent manner if there is a process in place.

The supervisor or director is usually responsible for addressing performance problems with other staff members. The board is responsible for addressing problems concerning the supervisor's performance if they arise. Disciplinary actions usually include verbal and written warnings that indicate the problems and the necessary performance changes. Staff should also be informed of what further consequences may be involved if the performance problem persists. Serious staff misconduct, such as negligence or harsh and unacceptable communications with children or families, must be addressed immediately.

Grievance Process

Each staff member has the right to know how to deal with concerns about performance and have a process to appeal any actions taken. A grievance policy provides checks and balances to the power of the supervisor. The staff can ask that the supervisor's actions be reviewed by the board of directors or an appropriate committee of the board.

Termination of Employment

Provincial/territorial employment legislation stipulates minimum notice requirements for individual termination of employees. Typically, after one year of employment, employees who are terminated receive one to two weeks' compensation for each year of employment. The notice provisions do not apply where a staff member has been dismissed for misconduct, poor work, or willful neglect.

Staff may be terminated:

- *Without notice* for just cause, which includes criminal acts, child abuse, or property destruction.
- *With notice* for incompetence or failure to meet stated job responsibilities *if* the proper steps outlined in the disciplinary procedures have been taken to inform the staff member, verbally and in writing, of problems during the probation period.
- *With notice* if enrollment is low and staff members are no longer needed.

Sometimes called de-hiring, altering terms of employment, or realignment of human resources, firing is unwanted and unpleasant for both the one who does the firing and the one who gets fired. Effective personnel policies and a good organizational structure can reduce the frequency considerably. But when hiring mistakes have occurred or performance has changed, and written and verbal notification is not effective, the board of directors and/or supervisor must take charge and do it, for the good of the centre. Here are some guidelines:

- Notice of termination should be delivered by the supervisor or board member in a face-to-face meeting and in writing. Review the content in advance with a lawyer.
- Try to hold the termination meeting at the end of the day.
- Keep it short and simple. Outline the problems and steps taken. Be clear about notice of termination, pay benefits, and references to future employers.
- This is a management decision and should not be discussed with other staff members ahead of time.

Employer–Employee Relationship

The employer–employee relationship is a legal contractual relationship. In a not-for-profit program, the employer is the board of directors.

Contract of Employment

A contract of employment outlines the terms or "rules" of the employment arrangement. Such a contract is a binding agreement between the employer (the early childhood program) and the employees (program staff and support staff). In a unionized setting, it is called a collective agreement and is negotiated by a process of collective bargaining.

Personnel policies may be included in the contract or letter of employment; together, the personnel policies may constitute the contract of employment. The contract of employment should include the job title, employment status, salary, benefits, working conditions, and employment procedures (e.g., hiring, firing, and grievance procedures).

Unionization

Staff in many early childhood programs have chosen to join or form a recognized trade union. About 35 000 members of the regulated child care work force belong to unions (Beach et al., 2004). Almost all unionized child care staff in Canada are centre-based. Kindergarten teachers in the public education system also belong to unions. Staff in community family support programs are generally not unionized. Staff working in home visiting or other types of family support services that are operated by local health departments or municipalities are usually unionized.

In unionized settings, personnel policies are negotiated between the employer and the employees through a process called collective bargaining. Provincial or territorial legislation regulates collective bargaining for employees, employers, and trade unions. The legislation defines a number of legal rights for employees, employers, and trade unions. For example, all employees have the right to form a union without interference in any way from the employer and they have the right to participate in a legal strike in support of a trade union. Employers and employees have the right to demand both parties and the trade union honour the terms of the collective agreement. A trade union that holds the bargaining rights for employees has the right to require the employer to bargain in good faith to make a collective agreement.

Personnel Handbook

Personnel handbooks or manuals orient new staff members and provide a reference document. Personnel handbooks can include information about the program including organizational information, program policies, and procedures. Most importantly, personnel handbooks include the personnel policies that should ensure fair and consistent working conditions for all staff. They outline responsibilities of all employees, including managers and other staff members.

The personnel policies create a framework for dealing with personnel issues. They are rules that are in place and can guide actions when there are problems. Typically, each individual policy has procedures, which are specific actions for implementing the policies.

Personnel handbooks need to be kept up-to-date. Changes in internal or external policies can be distributed immediately either as replacement pages or addenda. The entire handbook can be reviewed each year.

EARLY CHILDHOOD EDUCATORS AND HUMAN RESOURCE POLICIES

Programs that employ early childhood educators and other staff must comply with federal and provincial/territorial requirements related to employer obligations.

Human resource policies and procedures structure the work environment. Early childhood educators should expect to work in environments that can articulate clear expectations of what is expected and how the work is valued and rewarded. Financial compensation is certainly one important aspect of the work environment but it is not the only one. If the infrastructure for human resource management is poorly structured—or nonexistent—it will be difficult to maintain enthusiasm and commitment to the daily work. Provisions for preparation time and professional development contribute to a positive work environment.

KEY TERMS

compensation
occupational standards

pay equity
probation period

REFLECTION QUESTIONS

1. What do you want to know about the work environment in an early childhood program before accepting an offer of employment? What are the elements of a work environment in an early childhood setting that are most attractive to you? Why?
2. What are the benefits and challenges of unionization for the early childhood work force?
3. Describe differences in the roles and responsibilities of an early childhood educator employed in a child care program and in a family resource program.

FOR MORE INFORMATION

1. The *Child Care Human Resources Sector Council* (CCHRSC) is a Canada-wide, non-profit organization that addresses pressing human resources issues in the child care sector. Its projects develop research, strategies, and tools to meet the needs of the child care work force and achieve related goals.

   www.ccsc-cssge.ca/english/aboutus/

2. The *Thomson Nelson ECE Resource Centre* is intended to enhance the teaching and learning experience for both instructors and students. The website provides extensive and helpful resources in many different criteria related to early childhood education.

   www.ece.nelson.com

FINANCIAL MANAGEMENT

CHAPTER OUTLINE

Downtown Squire Early Childhood Centre

Downtown Squire Early Childhood Centre has an annual budget of almost $1 million. About 85 percent of the budget is spent on salaries and benefits, and the rest is allocated to the cost of the space, program supplies, and equipment.

Parent fees account for about 75 percent of its revenue. Half of the parents pay a full fee and half receive a partial or full fee subsidy. The centre also receives $200 000 in government operating grants.

Each year, fund-raising events raise almost $10 000 that is used for special events and program equipment. This supplements what can be allocated for the program from the operating revenue. The staff decides how best to allocate the fund-raising revenue to meet their program objectives.

Downtown Squire Early Learning Centre has a financial management system. The board of directors is responsible for seeing that the finances are well managed. Its director and part-time bookkeeper help the board carry out its responsibilities by summarizing the daily financial activities and communicating this information on a regular basis. The centre's annual budget is a financial plan that reflects the goals and objectives of the organization. This year, the annual program review identified professional development related to oral language development as a priority. The budget set aside $10 000 for professional development in this area.

The centre's financial records, or books, track the details of financial activity (revenues and expenses) as they occur. Monthly and annual financial reports summarize the record of daily transactions into a report for the board that can be compared to the budget or financial plan. The board is responsible for ensuring that adequate financial resources are available. This includes monitoring government resources, determining fee levels and payment policies, and seeking out other revenue sources if necessary (e.g., fund-raising).

Chapter Objectives

This chapter will:

1. Outline the components financial planning, including the annual budget.
2. Describe financial record-keeping appropriate for early child development programs.
3. Discuss different types of financial reporting.
4. Review sources of financial support for early child development programs.

Early childhood organizations, like all organizations, need strong, effective financial management systems. There are four elements to an effective financial management system: financial planning, financial record-keeping, financial reporting, and financial resources.

FINANCIAL PLANNING

Budgets are financial plans. There are four main types of budgets:

- operating budgets;
- capital budgets;
- start-up budgets; and
- long-range financial plans.

Annual Operating Budget

The operating budget is the most commonly used budget. The annual operating budget projects the expenses and income for a one-year period.

The annual operating budget of an early child development program is an important policy tool that shapes the operation of the program. In not-for-profit programs, the budgeting process helps the board of directors decide what can be achieved during the year. Items in the budget should reflect the organization's priorities and long-term goals in financial terms. Once a budget is in place, the supervisor/director and board can use it to monitor the program's financial performance by comparing actual results against the budget each month and understanding the reasons for differences.

Early childhood educators are reviewing program objectives and identifying priorities as part of the annual budget process.

An annual budget states what it will cost for an organization to achieve a realistic set of objectives within a year. It also describes where the money will come from to pay for the program's expenses. The annual budget usually tries to balance income and expenses over the one-year term.

The budget is usually drafted by the director/supervisor and reviewed by the finance committee, and it must be approved by the board of directors. The process is best begun about three months before the end of the current year. The budget process can be part of annual planning that considers the priorities for the upcoming year. Annual budgets are the backbone of management in most programs. The basic approach is simple and can be understood by staff members. It is an estimate of money coming in and how it will be spent.

Program Objectives

The program objectives for the upcoming year reflect an organization's long-term goals, feedback, and recommendations from recent program reviews, input from parents and program staff, and any changes planned for the program.

The first step is to identify the steps needed to accomplish identified objectives. For instance, if increased opportunities to support positive parenting are an objective, the operating budget might need to accommodate:

- parenting workshops for staff members;
- purchase of resources for parents;
- parenting specialist to participate in the program alongside staff on a regular basis;
- substitute staff to enable additional planning time for program staff; or
- costs of evening sessions with parents.

Current Financial Situation

To prepare the budget for the next year, it helps to have up-to-date financial reports. Budget preparation takes the financial health of an organization into account. Note fluctuations in income and consider whether these patterns will continue, or if they were related to one-time-only circumstances.

Project the revenues and expenditures to the end of the year, based on an understanding of the current financial situation.

Estimate Costs

Prepare an estimate of projected costs for the upcoming year. Identify expense categories that are consistent with actual cost areas, and with reporting requirements for external parties (including governments and funders). These same categories need to be reflected in the financial records.

The largest expense in early child development program operating budgets is staff salaries. The total staffing costs include salaries and benefits, and need to consider potential compensation increases. Sometimes additional staff costs are associated with meeting identified program objectives for the upcoming year. Staff costs are usually about 65 to 90 percent of the expense budget.

Costs from the current year can be used as a base, and then anticipated increases to staff compensation costs and to the cost of equipment, supplies, food, and so forth, can be added on to that base. Early child development program budgets should be realistic and include a margin for unforeseen expenses or unexpected drops in revenue.

Estimate Revenue

Consider all sources of revenue—fees, operating grants, and donations—to estimate the program's revenue.

Fees are the largest source of income for child care programs. Fee payments come directly from families or from governments on behalf of families who are receiving fee subsidy assistance. When estimating income from fees, base figures on enrollment estimates, not the total licensed program capacity. Consider the previous year's enrollment and enrollment at other child care programs in the area to get a sense of what enrollment trends are occurring. If you enroll children in different age groups at different fees, estimate the number of children that will be enrolled in each different category.

Family support programs usually receive a grant, or small grants from several sources. Most do not have user fees and those that do only raise a small proportion of revenue this way. Often programs are able to acquire a one-time grant for special programming or projects. The annual budget needs to consider whether or not grant revenue is recurring.

Kindergarten programs are operated as part of the publicly funded school system. Their budgets may be centralized at the local school board or provincial/territorial department level. Parents do not pay fees for basic kindergarten programs.

A word about fund-raising—some groups include fund-raising (bake sales, bingo, bazaars, and carwashes) as part of their operating income. Others carry out fund-raising events but do not count on the money as part of their operating income. Still other organizations consider fund-raising frustrating and refuse to do it. Organizations should decide their own policy, but be cautious about counting on the income from fund-raising events for necessary operational costs. It often is not as successful as groups anticipate. It is prudent to budget and record fund-raising revenue and expenses separately. Fund-raising is a valuable strategy to increase revenues for specific projects or one-time expenditures if the expectations are realistic and the goal is clearly articulated in advance.

Compare Income Estimate with Costs

Once the costs and income are estimated, compare them to whether the revenues will cover the expenses. The goal of the annual budgeting process is to construct a balanced budget: the income equals the expenses. Most programs try to budget so that the revenue slightly exceeds the expenses and there is a small surplus. However, if the previous year's balance is a deficit, the goal will be to have a larger surplus. On the other hand, if the previous year's balance is a large surplus, the goal will likely be to operate with a deficit in order to end the current year with a small surplus.

If costs exceed revenue, the bottom line is a deficit. Consider ways to increase revenues, what activities will have to be scaled back, or where costs can be cut. Adjust the budget. As changes are made, remember the program objectives. Try to make changes that make it possible to achieve as many objectives and priorities as possible.

In nonprofit programs, the treasurer and the finance committee may decide to present a number of options to the board of directors, including further fee increases, reduction of expenses, elimination of program areas, or a combination of measures. Staff input into the impact of various options is a useful source of information.

The board should make decisions based on what is viable and what is consistent with the recommended program objectives.

Approve the Budget

In nonprofit programs, the final budget is presented to the board of directors for approval, thus completing the annual planning cycle. The approved final budget usually sets the parameter for staff compensation and determines fee increases for the upcoming fiscal year.

Monitor the Budget

A final budget is not written in stone. It is a working document that projects an estimate of expenses and revenue. If estimated costs or income sources change significantly over the year, the budget can be amended. Changes to the final budget require the board's approval.

Capital and Start-up Budgets

Capital budgets are projected plans of expenses for large pieces of equipment and furnishings, land costs, building costs, and renovations. These are usually one-time expenses that are sometimes covered by one-time fund-raising campaigns, grants, and/or donations.

A **start-up budget** outlines the income and expenses for the initiation of a new program or program component. It may include some capital expenses, salary costs to develop the program, and operating expenses for the first three to six months of operation. Income may include start-up grants, donations, and parent fees.

Long-Range Financial Planning

Longer-term (beyond one year) financial planning is useful in projecting the financial impact of new program components, applying for a bank loan, or preparing a proposal for a grant from a government or a foundation.

A long-range financial plan for a grant or a loan application usually includes the following elements:

- *Title page*. Include the program name and the names, titles, and telephone numbers of contact individuals.
- *Purpose*. State reasons for financial assistance.
- *Program*. Describe the operation, including who uses (or will use) the program, the geographical area served, composition of the board of directors, program goals, unique program services, and how this financial loan or grant will be used and/or repaid.
- *Financial information*. Supply the current annual budget, annual audited statement, income and expense projections for the next three years, cash-flow projections for the next year, and a break-even analysis.
- *Corporate and legal documents*. Include a copy of letters patent, annual incorporation updates, copies of leases, purchase of service agreements, and collective agreement if the centre is a unionized setting.

Talk to the prospective funder to find out what he or she needs and expects.

Recording Financial Transactions

Bookkeeping (sometimes called **accounting**) is financial record-keeping that tracks all financial transactions—income and expenses, or money earned and spent. Not-for-profit organizations must set up bookkeeping systems that help to manage finances and meet professional standards. A good bookkeeping system records all financial transactions, leaving clear footprints that are easy to trace back. There are internal checks to make sure that the whole system is accurate.

There are many benefits in maintaining good accounting records:

- providing accurate information about the organization's financial position;
- helping to prepare necessary financial reports;
- helping to measure actual financial performance against the financial plan or budget;
- improving ability to obtain credit;
- meeting government requirements; and
- taking less time to maintain books of record.

There is no one correct method of bookkeeping, but not-for-profit programs must follow accepted accounting practices. Today, financial record-keeping is usually

Finding a skilled bookkeeper to keep the financial records benefits many early childhood programs.

computerized in a customized spreadsheet program or in a software program that is designed specifically for early childhood (particularly child care) programs. The best option for most programs is to find a competent accountant or bookkeeper who can tailor a set of financial reports and do the bookkeeping.

The general method outlined here is based on an approach that provides a record of actual cash transactions and a record of revenue (accounts receivable) and expenses (accounts payable) that are recorded when they are earned or due, not just when cash is actually received or paid. The recording of actual cash transactions is known as **cash accounting,** and the recording of revenue and expenses is known as accrual accounting. This method is incorporated into computerized programs.

Cash accounting is only concerned with reporting when cash comes in or goes out of the bank balance. It does not record what an organization owes, or what it is owed. Under cash accounting, there is no account of either creditors or debtors. Money received is recorded as receipts. Money spent is recorded as payments.

Cash accounting takes no account of the future. If a bill is received in June that must be paid in July, cash accounting will record the payment of the bill in July when the cheque is sent.

In order to maintain a complete set of financial records, it is necessary to record some transactions every day (or every week or each month) and others on a recurring, but less frequent, basis.

Cash Receipts and Cash Payments

It is advisable to keep up-to-date records of the money that comes in and the money that is paid out. By maintaining these records daily or weekly (depending on the size of the program), it is possible to know the cash position of the organization at all times.

The board of directors, owner, or government department is responsible for ensuring that financial resources are used appropriately. A bookkeeping system that requires regular documentation of how money is received and spent is key to ensuring that the treasurer and board of directors are able to monitor the program's use of financial resources.

The payments that are taken in are called the **cash receipts** and the funds paid out are the cash payments or **cash disbursements.** Cash receipts and cash payments are recorded in two separate books called journals.

Cash receipts are cheques, cash, or credit card invoices, usually for fees or grants. Child care subsidy payments, wage subsidy payments, and operating grants are also cash receipts. Most fee payments (from parents/guardians or government child care subsidy payments) are paid by cheque.

It is important to know who has and who has not paid fees, so cash receipts are recorded in the cash receipts journal at the end of each day. Each cash receipt should also be reported separately in the bank deposit book and then deposited in the bank. Bank deposits should be made at least once a week.

Payment by cheque is preferable to receiving cash payments. It is more difficult to monitor that all cash received is deposited and can be traced back to the source. However, sometimes parents/guardians will make child care fee payments in cash or there will be cash received from fund-raising events. In order to control cash payments:

- Ask parents/guardians to make cash payments directly to the supervisor.
- Immediately provide the parent/guardian with a receipt for the cash payment (with a copy retained in the centre's receipt book). The parent/guardian can initial the receipt when it is issued. This can help to prevent misunderstandings as to the actual amounts paid and accepted.
- Deposit all cash received into the bank account with the weekly deposit. A photocopy of the parent/guardian receipts can be attached to the duplicate deposit book sheet.
- Cash from fund-raising events (e.g., bake sales, flea markets) can be deposited into the bank account as soon as possible—especially if it is a large amount of money. Details of the event and the money raised should be recorded in the deposit book and initialled by at least one other staff or board member.
- *Never* put cash received directly in the petty cash box.

It is important that purchases are approved and that the amounts paid are reasonable. Purchases are usually made by cheque, with petty cash, or by credit card. All non-routine expenditures in excess of a set amount (e.g., $1000) should be authorized by the board of directors. The board can give the supervisor permission to authorize purchases less than the set amount, provided that the purchases are within the program's budget.

Cash payments are recorded in the cash disbursements journal. Paying by cheque or regular automated payment arrangements makes it easy to keep track of payments. Each payment is recorded separately.

All cheques should be signed by at least two signing officers and one of the signatories should be a board member. The person preparing the cheques (i.e., the bookkeeper) should include an invoice approved for payment by the supervisor. The invoice should note the cheque number, the word "paid," and the date on the invoice. Registered charities must have two signatures on each cheque.

Cheques should not be pre-signed. If there are three individuals authorized, necessary payments are less likely to be delayed if one person is not available. Both signatories should review the supporting documentation before signing the cheque for payment. In situations where the amount to be paid will not be known until it is actually time to pay (e.g., when paying for a food purchase by cheque):

- the cheque should be made out to a specified payee before it is pre-signed;
- the inscription "not to exceed [specified dollar amount]" should be written below the space for the amount of the payment; and
- the cheque to be pre-signed should be accompanied by documentation from the supervisor indicating exactly what the cheque is for and why it must be pre-signed.

A petty cash fund allows for the use of cash for small purchases. For most not-for-profit organizations, the monthly total of petty cash does not exceed $300. A petty cash float should be for a preset amount (e.g., $300). The total of the cash on hand and the receipts for purchases should always equal the preset amount. The petty cash float should only be replenished by cheque on submission of an itemized expense report with receipts attached. The treasurer should review the petty cash box once or twice a year to ensure that the sum of invoices and the cash on hand equal the preset amount. The petty cash float should be kept in a locked box that is kept out of open view (e.g., a drawer or file cabinet). If receipts are lost or not obtained for a purchase, a note should be submitted indicating the circumstances and signed by the person seeking reimbursement.

The use of credit cards for purchases can be a convenient way to make payments. It is important to establish procedures for authorization of credit card purchases. Identify what can be purchased with a credit card and require credit card purchases to be pre-authorized by a board member. It is advisable to have low credit limits (e.g., $1000) to avoid problems if the card is lost or misused. The monthly credit card statement should be accompanied by a copy of every credit card receipt, the actual invoice, and a note authorizing the credit card purchase when the monthly payment is prepared.

Payroll is the cash payments for salaries paid to staff members. It is recorded in the cash payment (or cash disbursements) journal each payday. Payroll records note payroll deductions from each staff payment. Employee withholdings should be sent to Canada Revenue Agency on a timely basis, as required by law. There are substantial penalties for not remitting or remitting late. A Record of Employment form must be filled out promptly for any employee who leaves his or her job. T4 forms must be prepared annually for all employees. Employer contributions to Employment Insurance, Canada Pension Plan, and health tax are recorded as cash payments when they are remitted to the government.

The cash receipts and cash payments or dispersals are individual transactions. An overall review of receipts and payments for the month is important to help identify problems or irregularities. Bank reconciliation and a report of the cash balance with a statement of cash receipts and payments are two monthly review procedures that help to make sure cash transactions are appropriate.

Bank reconciliation is carried out each month to make sure that the bank statement is in agreement with the operation's bookkeeping records. Once a nonprofit program has completed the incorporation process and is applying for a licence, a chequing account should be opened at a local bank. At the end of each month, the bank prepares a monthly bank statement showing all deposits made and cheques issued during the month. The bank will return cheques that have been issued by the organization.

Revenue and Expense Records

Accrual accounting records income and expenditures against the period they are for, not just when cash changes hands. Therefore, revenue and expenses are also recorded when they are earned and due, not just when cash is received or paid. Two journals are kept for this purpose—an accounts receivable journal and an accounts payable journal. The general ledger is a book of final entry for financial transactions once they are complete.

Accounts receivable are amounts of money owed to the organization, usually by parents or by the government. Accounts payable are the amounts that the centre owes to suppliers, landlords, and other creditors.

Monitoring Financial Record-Keeping

The board of directors, owners, or government (depending on the auspice of the program) is responsible to ensure there are approved policies and procedures in place that describe how financial record-keeping will be performed. The actual record-keeping system should be reviewed periodically (often by the treasurer) to see that actual practice is consistent with these approved policies and procedures.

Every early childhood program is unique and should establish financial record-keeping procedures that meet its needs for financial monitoring (internal and external) and reporting. A competent bookkeeper can set up the program's financial record-keeping so that it meets both internal and external requirements, both in tracking and summarizing financial details. If the program is small and does not have the financial resources to pay for a bookkeeper, it is possible to seek professional financial advice on the adequacy of its accounting system.

FINANCIAL REPORTS

A well-maintained bookkeeping system allows organizations to routinely produce financial reports that paint an accurate picture of the health of the organization.

Access to accurate financial information helps the board make better financial decisions. Financial reports also provide documentation to funders. Financial statements must be accurate, timely, and readable.

Monthly and annual financial statements should include information about all money received and dispersed, assets and liabilities, and any other financial transactions that affect the organization's financial position. Financial statements can be used to measure the organization's success at meeting its budget objectives. The most common financial statements for a not-for-profit organization are:

- the statement of operations (sometimes known as an income statement);
- the statement of financial position (sometimes known as a balance sheet);
- the statement of changes in net assets (often combined with the statement of operations); and
- the statement of cash flow.

Related information that cannot be translated into dollar terms is usually added as "notes to the financial statements."

Monthly Financial Statements

Effective bookkeeping systems enable program managers to produce financial statements of operation each month. Organizations can use this information to monitor the financial health of the organization and to make good financial decisions.

A financial statement of operations report helps to make financial information (monthly, quarterly, bi-annual, or annual) more accessible to board members in not-for-profit programs and can be shared with staff members to build a better understanding of the financial situation, particularly in smaller organizations. Financial statements compare the actual spending and earnings to the projected amounts in the budget.

There are a number of useful questions to ask about financial statements of operations or other forms of financial statements:

- What are the differences between projected and actual amounts?
- Do plans need to be changed?
- What else is happening that will affect this?
- Do the explanations make sense?

Cash Flow Statements

An analysis of cash flow tracks the cash coming into the centre and the cash going out to determine how much cash the centre has at a given point in time.

Annual Balance Sheet

The balance sheet or statement of financial position shows the net worth of an organization. It is usually prepared at the end of a financial year. Figure 7.1 explains how to understand an annual financial sheet.

Annual Auditor's Report

The purpose of the annual audit is to lend credibility to financial reports. The auditor, who is a chartered accountant, is appointed by the membership at the annual general meeting in a nonprofit organization.

■ Figure 7.1

Annual Balance Sheet

Assets: Value of the Organization's Resources		**Liabilities:** Value of the Organization's Debts		**Net Worth:** Actual Financial Value of the Operation

 Minus   Equals

- Either cash or something that can be converted to cash
- Current assets include money owed to the centre (such as outstanding fees), cash on hand, and petty cash float.
- Fixed assets include equipment, inventory, and property.

- Current liabilities include unpaid bills, goods or services received but not yet paid for, bank overdrafts, and payroll deductions due.
- Fixed liabilities include long-term bank loans.

- What is left after subtracting liabilities from assets

A year-end statement of money in and money out is called a comparative statement of operations. Instead of comparing the actual results to the budget figures, this type of statement compares them to prior year's actual results.

The annual audited report includes:

- a balance sheet;
- an audited statement of income and expenses; and
- auditor's notes.

The auditor's notes can include recommendations for changes in financial record-keeping, clarification of accounting principles used, any weaknesses found in the accounting system, and the corporate status of the organization.

The auditor makes certain that the financial statements have been prepared in accordance with generally accepted accounting principles.

FINANCIAL RESOURCES

The management of early childhood programs has a responsibility to ensure that adequate financial resources are available to meet the income targets identified in the annual budget.

Parent Fees

Child care programs rely on receiving a fee for each space in the program. Either the parent/guardian pays for the child care services or the municipality/district social service administration board pays on behalf of the family if there is an approved subsidy.

Provincial/territorial governments set the eligibility criteria and amounts of child care fee subsidies. Other than in Ontario, child care fee subsidies are managed and administered by the provincial/territorial governments. Variation in the organization of child care fee subsidies is discussed in Chapter 2.

In Ontario child care fee subsidies are managed and administered by municipalities or district social service administration boards. The provincial government is responsible for 80 percent of the costs and the local government picks up the other 20 percent. The province places a maximum limit on the total subsidy budget for each municipality or district social service administration board. Families who are eligible for fee subsidies may enroll their child in a child care program that has a purchase of agreement with the municipality or district social service administration board.

Eligibility requirements for child care fee subsidies are established by the province through the *Day Nurseries Act*. Applicants must complete an income assessment that considers assets, income, and expenses. Fees are calculated taking into account family income and family size.

In many jurisdictions there is a waiting list for child care fee subsidies, so parents/guardians should be advised to apply well in advance.

Setting and Collecting Fees

Child care fees are determined as part of the operating budget process. If a child care program has a purchase of service agreement for subsidized spaces, the municipality/district social service administration board will request an operating budget that meets its guidelines, and usually establishes ceilings for budget items.

Fee collection policies must be clear, consistent, and firm. Here are some guidelines:

- Establish a reasonable due date each month. Some programs collect fees weekly but this is time consuming and inconvenient for everyone. Most programs collect fees at the beginning of each month.
- Prepare invoices for each parent outlining the amount owed one week in advance of the due date.
- Encourage parents to pay by cheque rather than with cash.
- Issue receipts for fee payments.
- Determine a late payment fine for fees outstanding after the due date.
- Establish a process for families who wish to negotiate a payment extension, clearly stating who has the authority to make the arrangement.

Operating Grants

Operating grants for early childhood programs vary among programs and vary across provincial/territorial jurisdictions. Most family support programs are funded through operating grants. In Quebec, the provincial government provides operating grants to Centres des Petits Enfants based on specific costs. Child care programs in other provinces rely more on child care fees.

The Ontario government introduced wage subsidy grants to child care staff in the late 1980s. The wage subsidy is a direct provincial grant to child care agencies to allow them to raise staff salaries without raising parent fees. In 1994, wage subsidies were capped, meaning that only existing positions within child care programs are still eligible for funding. The result is that there are no wage subsidy grants for new not-for-profit child care centres. If an existing program expands and hires new staff, the wage subsidy grant must be divided among more people.

Since 1999, municipalities in Ontario have had the responsibility for allocating wage subsidy grants and can reallocate the wage subsidy grants. The wage subsidy is intended to improve salary and benefit levels of permanent full- or part-time employees working in a child care program. Early childhood organizations that receive wage subsidy grants are expected to distribute the wage subsidy to each employee in a manner that is consistent with achievement of the organization's pay equity plan.

Child care organizations may use a portion of the wage subsidy to cover mandatory employer contributions that result from increased salary and benefit costs related to implementing the wage subsidy. If a child care program has downsized, reducing the numbers of children enrolled and the numbers of employees, the amount of the wage subsidy will be reduced accordingly.

Fund-Raising

Fund-raising can supplement special programs or one-time capital costs for a new piece of equipment or furnishings. Events can be an opportunity for families to work together in a social context and participate in the life of the early childhood program.

A careful record of fund-raising income along with related expenses gives a clear idea of how profitable the fund-raising activity actually was. For instance if it takes $5 of ingredients and two hours' time to bake two dozen cookies and they sell for 25 cents each, what is the "profit"?

Successful fund-raising is based on the idea that a contribution is a satisfying mutual exchange that takes place between the donor and the organization. From buying cookies at a bake sale to making a major financial contribution to a new building, donors want to give money to an organization that provides a program or service they support.

Charitable nonprofit early childhood organizations may have annual campaigns or ongoing drives to raise funds. Programs that are part of larger, multi-service programs may be supported by local United Way grants and take part in annual fund-raising.

Regular fund-raising for special projects or a proportion of operational expenses is usually tied to strategic planning and communication planning.

In larger fund-raising drives, board members, senior staff, advisors, and special friends of the organization are bridges to donors. Their efforts are supported by clear, logical material that describes the needs of the organization, how it supports early child development, what the costs are, and what results it is hoping to achieve. When the exchange happens, the organization receives the funds, and the donor receives the satisfaction of knowing that he or she has helped to provide early child development programming for young children and their families.

Fund-raising—whether selling raffle tickets or chocolate bars or holding bake sales or craft fairs—can be very time consuming and, as noted earlier, is not an effective way to acquire regular operating funds, such as salaries, rents, or day-to-day materials.

Fund-raising events that involve the program's families and community have benefits beyond the dollars raised.

A Business Plan

A business plan is a recognized management tool used by operating and prospective businesses of all sizes to document business objectives and to propose how these objectives will be attained within a specific period of time. It is a written document that describes the organization, what the organization is trying to achieve, where the business or project will be located, the expected timeframe, and how risks will be overcome and returns on investment met. A business plan provides information on proposed ventures to lenders, investors, funders, and suppliers to demonstrate how their money will be used and to establish a basis for the credibility of a project or business.

Even though most business plans are written for profit-making enterprises, the objectives are equally applicable to nonprofit organizations. They are a useful organizing tool for public, commercial, or not-for-profit early childhood programs that are starting up or expanding their services.

EARLY CHILDHOOD EDUCATORS AND FINANCIAL MANAGEMENT

Most early childhood educators do not enter the sector with a solid understanding of financial management. But many will find it necessary to manage money while working directly with young children and families. Collecting fees or raising funds for new playground equipment are common. Those who work in family child care will need to maintain financial records of a small business. Staff members who are seeking higher wages and benefits are more likely to be successful if they can present proposals within the actual financial context in which the program operates.

In larger organizations, following how resources are allocated helps child care staff to understand the impact of board and management decisions. Staff input on strategic directions and operational management is always more informed if staff members have an understanding of how money comes in and how it is spent.

Understanding budgets and financial statements does not mean actual financial record-keeping or accounting. Basic understanding of financial statements provides an overview of how organizations work and a perspective that is essential in learning to manage program goals.

KEY TERMS

accounting

capital budgets

cash accounting

cash disbursements

cash receipts

start-up budget

REFLECTION QUESTIONS

1. If you were employed in a program that has identified professional development about emergent curriculum as a priority goal for the upcoming year, what would you expect to see in the annual budget?

2. Why are early childhood educators' salaries so low in child care programs?
3. What is the difference between income that is based on an operating grant per child and income that comes from parent fees?

FOR MORE INFORMATION

1. For a fuller discussion of budgeting, see *Cowperthwaite Mehta Chartered Accountants.*

   www.187gerrard.com/financial/budgeting.htm

2. *Imagine Canada* (formerly the Canadian Centre for Philanthropy) is a great resource for nonprofit organizations. This site provides a list of core resources held by Imagine Canada's Nonprofit Library Commons.

   www.nonprofitscan.ca/page.asp?core_resources

3. The *Thomson Nelson ECE Resource Centre* is intended to enhance the teaching and learning experience for both instructors and students. The website provides extensive and helpful resources in many different criteria related to early childhood education.

   www.ece.nelson.com

Leading Early Childhood Programs

Leadership is taking a broad view to help an organization confirm clear values, set goals, articulate a vision, and chart a course of action to achieve that vision (Talan & Bloom, 2004). Leadership skills include the ability to guide, direct, or influence people, particularly to confront challenges, changes, and problems that need to be solved. Leadership in early child development programs begins with a vision of what the best possible early environments could be for young children. The next step is to guide the vision into daily activities, environments, practices, and policies that shape early childhood programs and make those environments a reality.

Continuous learning is the foundation of leadership. Early childhood educators who seek out opportunities for learning through continuing education and professional development are becoming leaders. Learning organizations value new ideas, learn from existing practices, and encourage the exchange of new information. The concept of a learning organization can be applied in early childhood programs. Clear goals, the active participation of all in achieving them, continuous improvement based on reliable feedback, and effective communication and collaboration are the key features that can create early childhood learning organizations. Early childhood educators, who bring a depth of knowledge about early child development and parenting, and the programs that can support both, are ready to be active participants in early childhood learning organizations.

Early childhood programs are entrenched in the Canadian landscape. They exist alongside schools, small shops, and community centres, from Iqaluit in the north, to Victoria in the west, and St. John's in the east, and all points in between. They are part of the daily world that young children and their families live in. Early childhood educators are finding that their role extends beyond the boundaries of individual programs and out into the local community. Who else is there and what are they doing?

Early childhood educators can advocate for early childhood programs in a local community or develop system-wide policies that merge the patchwork into a more coherent system. Early childhood educators have the depth of knowledge about early child development to bridge across the existing patchwork and pull the pieces together. These leaders can generate sound policies and practices in the field, and they can advocate for changes that will benefit Canada's children, families, and communities.

VISION AND ACTION

CHAPTER OUTLINE

Patricia Chorney-Rubin

A quality early childhood program needs a leader with a clear vision of what the program is trying to accomplish and the ability to drive the vision into action. Much of the ability has to do with communicating a compelling vision to others—to early childhood educators and to families.

There is clear value in having a curriculum approach and direction in early childhood programs that prepares children for success in their school years. But what is the right approach and direction?

Currently in the United States, a holistic, developmental approach, skilled early childhood practitioners, clear and specific programs, and early learning standards are prevalent.

In Canada we are less convinced about the value of designated early learning standards for young children. Instead we tend to view children as independent agents who can have an active role in shaping their learning environments. The focus is on enriching and extending learning opportunities that emerge, based on the early childhood educator's knowledge of child development, observation and documentation of the child's activities, and the child's family and community context. Children's acquisition of early literacy and other pre-academic skills are really the byproducts of an excellent, purposeful play program that is guided by what we call emergent curriculum.

The critical element that runs across all discussions of effective early childhood programs is a skilled early childhood work force. Early childhood educators who are reflective and responsive practitioners are essential in establishing preschool programs as early learning environments.

Source: Interview with Patricia Chorney-Rubin, Chair, Centre for Early Child Development, George Brown College.

Chapter Objectives

This chapter will:

1. Explain components of vision, including purpose, philosophy, and values.
2. Describe how program coherence puts vision into action.
3. Define the leadership roles and responsibilities of early child development program directors and supervisors.
4. Outline preparation for early child development program leadership.

VISION TO REALITY

Vision begins with an understanding of the purpose of early childhood programs. From there, the philosophy of a centre or an early childhood educator emerges. The **philosophy** of early child development considers what children learn, how they learn, and what is important for them to learn. Each early childhood educator is guided by a personal philosophy of education that is brought into programs, which also have a philosophy. Program coherence emerges at the intersection of personal and program philosophies.

Purpose

What is the primary purpose or intention of early childhood programs? Early learning? Parenting capacity? Community social capital? Support to parental labour force participation? School readiness? Family support? The discussion about the purpose of early childhood programs began in Chapter 1 and is reintroduced here because it is closely tied to the vision and the implementation of that vision.

Chapter 1 presented human capital and children's rights as arguments for early child development programs. Therefore the broad purpose of early childhood development programs is to do the right thing for children now and for their and society's future.

Having a clear purpose in an early child development program is an essential first step of leadership. It sets the direction of people and their actions. Purpose is a shared platform for team efforts.

A moral purpose is the intention of making a positive difference in the lives of children, families, communities, and society as a whole (Fullan, 2001). A "make a difference" purpose tends to inspire greater collaboration than a purpose that is solely about remuneration, keeping people employed, or financial profit. It is about both means (how things can be accomplished) and ends (the long-term vision of what is to be accomplished).

Think about why individuals choose to become early childhood educators. For some, it is an occupation that earns a living, perhaps until something better comes along. But for most, there is a strong desire to make a difference in the lives of young children.

What's in a Name?

Debates about the purpose and names of early child development programs are often linked together.

One such debate took place in Ottawa on November 7, 2003, at the national symposium titled Training for the Delivery of Quality Early Childhood Development and Care Services in Canada. The symposium, part of a two-year study by the same name, was sponsored by the Canadian Child Care Federation (CCCF) and the Association for Canadian Community Colleges. The 61 participants included representatives of federal and provincial/territorial child care organizations, the Child Care Human Resources Sector Council (CCHRSC), centre-based programs, family child care programs, community college ECE programs, organized labour, and federal and provincial governments. The debate focused on what is the appropriate name for people working directly with young children in a variety of child care settings—candidate names included *early childhood educator, child care educator, child care worker,* and *child care and development specialist.* The group did not reach consensus, but the debate engaged participants and there was agreement that a common name (representing a common identity and purpose) was a difficult, but necessary step in finding common ground in gaining greater recognition for the occupation.

The debate about a name for the sector and for the occupation and the related structural issues is not a new debate. It does reflect an underlying tension—is the purpose of child care *primarily* to support children's early development and learning or is it to support labour market participation? Are early childhood educators part of a "caring" occupation or part of an "early educator" occupation that is aligned to the larger teaching profession?

Early child development is a sector that straddles early learning and early care. The regulated child care sector is part of early child development. Indeed, many consider regulated child care the core program for early child development.

Defining care work is difficult. Its borders are neither clear nor settled and many occupations include elements of care. An occupation can be described in one country or discipline as "care work" and as part of early education or early pedagogy in another country or context (Moss & Cameron, 2002).

Quality early education is not possible without caring, and quality caring is not possible without early education. But there is a disjoint between how governments view and fund child care and how it is perceived by many in the work force, particularly those with ECE qualifications.

Most early childhood educators want to work in an environment that allows them to practise their profession.

Post-secondary ECE programs' *primary* intention is to prepare individuals to support the optimal growth and development of all children, regardless of setting. Responsiveness to children and understanding of developmental trajectories is central. Child care centres are central as sites to apply the principles of early childhood education. Graduates enter the work force with the *primary* intent of practising early childhood education (and earning a living).

But regulated child care is primarily viewed by provincial and territorial governments as a service that supports labour force attachment. Government policies and regulations continue to tie the provision of child care fee subsidies and operating grants to parental labour force participation. Outside of Quebec, the primary role of regulated child care from the provincial/territorial government's perspective is to care for children while parents are working. Other types of early child development programs and services are supported by governments because they promote optimal development and early learning.

Common Purpose

Why do early childhood educators stay working in early childhood programs? For the most part, it is not about the money (this is not a sector for those who want to become wealthy). It may be because it is employment and other options are limited. But for the most part, it is likely because they find their working environment purposeful. Early childhood educators are similar to others in the work force. An American survey found that three out of four employees cited "personal satisfaction for doing a good job" three times as often as "getting ahead" or "making a good living" (Galinsky et al., 1993). In two recent studies of Canada's child care work force, early childhood educators across the country cited the satisfaction of supporting children's early development and learning and of supporting their families as the primary reason that they stayed working in the sector (Beach et al., 2004; Beach & Flanagon-Rochon, 2007).

Early childhood program leaders can forge a common purpose that converges with the reasons that early childhood educators come into the field in the first place. The purpose can be used to bring early childhood educators and families together as part of a shared collective effort.

The purpose must also be specific enough to define the program's parameters and provide direction to the program's activities. Early child development programs are typically legal entities. The type of legal status of the program has an impact on its purpose. Not-for-profit organizations exist to operate a public service for a particular group of people. Publicly operated organizations, such as school boards or public health agencies, have a stated or implied mandate of equity (i.e., a mandate to serve everyone who is eligible). Commercial organizations are geared to earn a profit for the owners.

In addition to stating the primary intention of the program, the purpose should state whom the program is for and where it will be located. For example:

Purpose:

ABC Centre offers an early learning and care program for children aged one to six years that nurtures children's optimal development, enables parents to work or study, and supports parents in their parenting role.

ABC Centre is located at 461 Blackwell Ave, Blackley, Ontario.

Children may be enrolled in the program part-time or full-time, Monday to Friday, between 7:30 A.M. and 6:00 P.M. Parents and other caregivers are welcome to attend with their children anytime.

Philosophy

A philosophy is a statement of the values and beliefs that underlie the purpose. It defines how the purpose will be put into action. The purpose and philosophy are the program's vision and become the public statements that are often the families' and communities' first introduction to the program.

Philosophy:

ABC Centre believes that

CHILDREN are entitled to opportunities that support their social-emotional, cognitive, and physical growth and development in an environment that fosters active learning, autonomy, respect for diversity, and a sense of responsibility.

PARENTS have the primary responsibility for the care and education of their children. They also have the right to pursue financial security, further education, and/or personal fulfillment. The centre will support parents' participation in their children's early learning and development and their participation in other pursuits.

STAFF members have chosen their work because of a belief in the importance of the task and suitability of their skills and education as well as a strong commitment to the development of children. Staff are entitled to open communication, job descriptions, performance reviews, financial recognition of the value of their work, opportunities for professional development, and direct input into making decisions.

ABC Centre believes that an optimum early child care and education centre must support positive relations between children, parents, and staff. Such programs supplement and complement parental care in a nurturing, learning environment that promotes nonsexist, anti-racist values.

ABC Centres believes that all young children and their families should have access to early child development programs.

Beliefs

What early childhood educators believe about how children learn and develop and their views of childhood affect the programs they develop (Astington & Pelletier, 1996). Much of this is based on their understanding of childhood, as discussed in Chapter 1.

Broadly speaking, early childhood educators' beliefs fall into one of three orientations: maturationist (nativist), behaviourist (empiricist), or constructivist (Piagetian or Vygotskian).

- Maturationists, or nativists, believe that abilities unfold with development. They wait until the child is ready. The early childhood educator is viewed as a nurturer and sometimes a parent figure. Maturationists emphasize social-emotional development and promote affective programs that satisfy emotional needs.

- Behaviourists, or empiricists, believe that children acquire skills and knowledge through instruction. The early childhood educator is viewed as a teacher who instructs the child. Behaviourists believe that effective programs are structured to instruct children and set up processes for feedback.
- Cognitive constructivists believe that children develop through cognitive disequilibrium and problem solving. The environment sets challenges, and the early childhood educator is a facilitator. Programs typically emphasize cognitive development and set up opportunities for discovery through which the child builds his or her understanding of how the world works.
- Social constructivists hold beliefs similar to those of cognitive constructivists, but they believe that children develop in a social context and the social environment is central to building knowledge. The early childhood educator is viewed as a collaborator, and programs provide opportunities for shared learning of cultural expectations.

The beliefs of early childhood educators affect the way they work with young children. Pelletier (2002) has found that children's understanding of kindergarten is related to teachers' practices—or the way they work with children. Pelletier points out that teachers' beliefs affect the transition of children from early childhood settings such as preschool or child care to kindergarten. In fact, many children must make the transition from one set of beliefs to another.

Personal Philosophy

A personal philosophy of early childhood education is a set of beliefs and values about how young children learn and develop. It also lays out personal goals. It is based on a general philosophy of life. Knowing what research says about early development and what others believe is important and helpful in developing a personal philosophy. But each early childhood educator must decide on what his or her own personal philosophy is.

A personal philosophy is based on core values and beliefs. Core values of life relate to beliefs about the purpose of life, individual responsibilities, and relationships to others. Core values and beliefs about early childhood education include beliefs about the nature of children, the purpose of early child development programs, the way people learn, the role of early childhood educators, and what is worth knowing.

A personal philosophy of education will guide and direct daily work with young children and their families. It clarifies intentions and is a guide that helps determine actions. For example, beliefs about how children learn determine whether to instruct children or facilitate their activity in a planned environment.

The process of preparing a personal philosophy helps clarify your ideas and refine your thoughts about working with young children and their families. A personal philosophy should be understandable to others—although they do not have to agree with it.

Program Philosophy

The philosophy considers the purpose of the centre and the children, parents, and staff who will be part of the life of the centre. Children often live in early childhood settings for many hours each day. Early childhood educators also live there and are part of the environment that evolves. Parents rely on programs to support them in carrying out childrearing responsibilities. *How* the centre operates must depend on *what* is important to children, parents, and staff.

The philosophy of an early childhood program is based on:

- assumptions about how children develop and learn;
- what's worth knowing; and
- the underlying values of parents and staff.

Theories about early human development influence assumptions about how children develop. These theories range from those that see development as a result of the environment to those that view development as a result of maturation. Related teaching strategies range from adult-directed instruction to child-initiated activity.

Decisions about what's worth knowing depend on what kind of knowledge is thought to be important. Some people believe that specific pieces of information and particular skills are the most important things to know. This perspective is often called a content approach. Others think that it is more important to know *how* to learn—problem-solve, explore, compare. This perspective is known as a process approach.

The underlying values of parents and staff are tied to culture, ethnicity, religion, language, and experience. These values influence childrearing and education approaches. Values determine what priorities parents and staff set for children, and influence views on children's development and learning and on deciding what's worth knowing.

Which philosophical approach is the best? Well, it all depends on what you want. Research to date suggests that having a direction is more important than which direction is taken.

The philosophy of an early childhood program serves as a starting point to:

- build board and staff commitment;
- determine goals and objectives that guide the board of directors and senior staff in managing and administering the centre's operation; and
- make decisions in setting and implementing policy and procedures.

The philosophy is developed to fit a program's purpose and reflect the needs of children, staff, and parents.

Program Coherence

Program coherence or **implementation integrity** is the extent to which the early childhood program is focused on a clear vision and developmental goals, and is able to implement those goals (Newmann et al., 2000).

Early childhood programs are made up of separate parts and people. Fitting them together to form a harmonious whole is complex and often messy. Complexity often generates stress and confusion. Fragmentation is one way that early childhood programs may attempt to handle complexity. People try to master the situation by working on their own and only concentrating on their piece of the overall program. For example, an early childhood educator who is working with preschool children may prepare activities without taking into account what others are doing. Her morning group time is separate from the other morning activities, and she does not pick up on earlier interest in the front-end loader just outside the playground that has galvanized children's attention for the past week. When she is finished, she carefully puts away her picture book, *The Hungry Caterpillar,* and bright felt figures she used to illustrate the story. They are not made available to other early childhood educators or to the children. Next the children head to lunch where another early childhood educator (who has just arrived to begin her shift) asks everyone to join her in singing "I'm So Hungry" while waiting for lunch to arrive from the kitchen. She then reads a story until lunch arrives. The story is not finished, but the book goes away before we know if Benjamin finds his favourite blanket or not. No reference is made to the earlier group time or to any other experiences the children have shared that morning. Each staff member is prepared to engage in activities, carry out daily routines, and bring resources to the program. But they are working alone, isolated from each other.

Another response to complexity is control, but complexity doesn't let itself be so easily controlled. Top-down program plans may be posted on the walls but remain quite distant from children's actual activities. Structured parent education classes may present information and offer handouts but have little impact on what parents do with their children. Home visiting checklists may be completed but have little impact on the conversation that takes place during the visit. What's more, it is likely that top-down control will hamper the emergence of experiences that are more meaningful to young children and their families. The teachable moments that appear when a child's interest is captured by a bug, or puddle, or new friend, can be lost. A parent's openness to learning more about his or her child's immediate language development may shut down when the topic is about bedtime routines. An early childhood educator who makes a great find for the dramatic play area at a garage sale may not bother picking it up and bringing it to the centre. There is a plan in place and following the plan becomes more important than making connections or extending spontaneous experiences.

In approaching complexity in organizations, Fullan (2001) draws a parallel between living organisms and human organizations. Complex living systems are known to "self-organize." New forms and new ways of working emerge spontaneously from the complexity of the system. Living systems cannot be constrained to follow linear paths. They may appear to do so in the short term, but not over time. Unforeseen and unintended consequences are inevitable.

Program coherence begins with a commitment to the vision (the purpose and philosophy) and goals that can be sustained over time. It is reinforced by supports and pressures that keep the balance between chaos and order. It is supported by organizational capacity that provides a stable infrastructure for exploration and experimentation.

Setting Goals

Goals are planning tools that define what results are wanted based on the centre's purpose and philosophy. Goals remain constant over a period of time but must be revisited when the purpose and philosophy shift or change to meet new circumstances and expectations. The purpose and philosophy set the stage for action. Goals release the energy to take action with a common purpose. Goals are standards that outline what is expected. Goals remind us what is important and where to focus our attention when

Beyond Our Borders

CURRICULUM APPROACHES

ITALY

The Reggio Emilia approach from northern Italy is a continuous process in which children raise questions and construct theories and meaning in an interplay with the surrounding world. Reciprocity of interaction, relations and communications, and concepts such as subjectivity and inter-subjectivity are at the core of Reggio Emilia pedagogy. Children enrich their conceptual maps if they have the opportunity to make these shifts in a group context, and if they both listen and are listened to, express their differences, and are receptive to the differences of others. The result is knowledge that is bountiful and enriched by the contributions of many.

SWEDEN

In Sweden, the child's learning is grounded in play and meaning making. Knowledge is not to be found in the child or in the world (including adults) but in the relationship between them. Consequently, the child's search for knowledge should be developed through play, social interaction, exploration, and creativity, as well as through observations, discussion, and reflection. Language, learning, and identity are closely entwined; meaning is created in children's communication and play.

NEW ZEALAND

The New Zealand curriculum known as Te Whariki (meaning "the woven mat") emphasizes the critical role of socially and culturally mediated learning and of reciprocal and responsive relationships for children with people, places, and things.

The level of specificity about the adult's role in relationship to infants, toddlers, and young children is very clear, thus providing direction to all adults working with these three age groups and a clear focus for program evaluation. Te Whariki is written for *all* adults who interact with these children in whatever setting, and it encompasses bi-cultural values. The empowerment of the child is an overriding principle, as is continuity with the school curriculum.

JAPAN

The environment should be created with the intention of ensuring voluntary activities among children, based on an understanding and anticipation of the individual actions of each child. Teachers should create a physical and psychological environment in view of the importance of the relationship between a child and other people and things. Teachers should also play various roles in response to the situations of individual children's activities and should strive for making activities more enriching.

The curriculum is conceptualized through health, human relationships, environment, language, and expression. There is a strong focus on social-emotional development and the development of positive social interactions.

TASMANIA, AUSTRALIA

Beliefs and values underpinning the early years curriculum include partnerships, learning, educating, and diversity. Partnerships refer primarily to building strong relationships with families as well as related professionals. Learning implies that young children are actively involved in making meaning of experience and are in control of their own learning, which should be rewarding, enjoyable, and based on play and exploration. The educative role of adults is realized through providing a stimulating environment, positive interactions with children, and the fostering of productive interactions between children. All children and families deserve equal respect, and the diverse needs of all children should be met. The curriculum framework includes creating personal and world futures (essential learnings), learning markers (benchmarks), and learning stories (evidence).

FINLAND

The principal target of Finnish early childhood programs is to promote the child's overall well-being so as to ensure the best possible conditions for growth, learning, and development. The child is able to enjoy the company of other children and educators, experiencing joy and freedom of action in an unhurried, safe atmosphere. Children are interested in their environment, and can direct their energy to play, learning, and everyday activities with an appropriate level of challenge.

This vision is encouraged in an environment that honours children's individual needs, personality, and family culture in a fair and equitable environment. Relationships with parents, educators, and other children are fostered so that they have a feeling of belonging within a peer group.

The Finnish early childhood curriculum framework is organized into three major sections—overarching categories, the child's way of acting, and content orientations.

Source: Dickinson, 2005; OECD, 2006; Valimaki & Lindberg, 2004.

day-to-day details bombard us with demands and distractions. Experience in businesses, schools, social services, governments, sports teams, and just about anywhere else where people are working together, finds that program goals or standards are best set by the team rather than externally imposed by regulations or leaders.

All programs in early childhood education are not equally effective in promoting the learning and development of young children or supporting parents. The overall effectiveness of an early childhood program is dependent upon several factors: quality staff, suitable environment, appropriate grouping practices, consistent schedules, and parent involvement. Decisions about these factors often are made early in the planning and organizing process for an early childhood program. These decisions have important ramifications because they affect the child, the family, and the community.

Goals can guide the kinds of decisions that are made in setting up an early child development program. They provide a framework for how space and time will be organized and how people will work together. If the purpose and philosophy are clear and focused, program goals can be established by the initial team that comes together to set up the program. If the vision changes, it is time to review the goals to guide specific program changes.

Possible Program Goals

Some possible program goals include the following:

- To support emotional development by encouraging caring and responsive relationships, providing opportunities for independence and autonomy, and attention to individual needs.
- To ensure support for social development by encouraging ongoing verbal communication, promoting opportunities for sharing and cooperating, guiding children's behaviour through example and positive redirection, and promoting self-regulation skills.
- To support physical development by encouraging large and fine motor play, a balance between active and quiet activities, and sensory exploration and discrimination; by providing nutritious meals and snacks; and by ensuring safe and hygienic practices.
- To create an inclusive setting by promoting an appreciation of each child's own culture and the culture of others, accommodating developmental diversity, and by demonstrating the same expectations for boys and girls.
- To support each child's creative development by providing opportunities for creative self-expression and exploration.
- To ensure support for cognitive development by stimulating language skills and promoting conceptual and problem-solving abilities.

Think about how these program goals might influence decisions about how the daily routines are organized, how children are grouped together, or how space is shared among different age groups. Think about how these program goals can support program coherence.

Finding the Balance

In the story of Goldilocks and the Three Bears, Goldilocks is looking for balance: "Not too big and not too small; not too hot and not too cold; not too hard and not too soft." Program coherence finds a balance between fragmentation (everyone doing their own thing) and linear, top-down planning (superficially in place but largely ignored in day-to-day activities). Complex organizations (such as early child development programs) thrive when there is enough structure to point in the right direction but enough flexibility to let patterns emerge rather than following someone else's plan. Program coherence is connecting the elements (people, space, materials, and time) and building on moment-to-moment experiences.

Think about a parent who is excited about how fast her two-year-old is using new vocabulary. That parent is probably very interested in what books to read, different ways to read books, and how books build language and later literacy abilities. It could be an opportunity to talk about how the program uses books, the value of repeating the same books over and over again, what books are popular among the children right now, what specific books her child is enjoying, and to make suggestions about books to take home. The mother may respond with anecdotes from home and offer to share the child's favourite bedtime stories with the whole group of children. What happens is that the parent's capacity to be involved in the child's early learning and development is enhanced and the program's resources are increased.

But the message needs to be consistent and reinforced by a shared commitment and understanding about child development and the kinds of experiences that benefit that development. If the program is able to connect its philosophy to daily practice and, at the same time, allow the daily practice to be shaped by the contributions of children, families, and staff, emerging patterns will reinforce the overall purpose and goals of the program and excite its participants.

Coherence building does not mean everyone must follow a preset plan. Rather, coherence building can guide people through their differences and enable those differences to surface. Creative ideas and novel solutions are often generated when the status quo is disrupted. The parent who asks "why" may open up a new way of thinking about a simple routine or activity.

Organizational Capacity

Organizational capacity is the ability to organize human, technical, and social resources in an effective collective enterprise. In early child development programs, the collective enterprise can be defined as a quality program that will benefit young children and their families.

People are the key factor in quality early child development experiences for children. Quality programs allow early childhood educators to build the kinds of experiences and relationships associated with positive early child development. Skilled and educated individual staff members are less likely to be able to apply their knowledge and abilities and behave in a sensitive and responsive manner in a poor-quality program.

In the recent studies of Canada's child care work force (Beach et al., 2004; Beach & Flanagon-Rochon, 2007), focus group surveys of early childhood education students close to graduation revealed that the quality of a program can be a determining factor in deciding where to work, particularly if compensation levels are similar. Several focus group discussions with early childhood educators pointed to poor-quality programs that provided little opportunity for reflective practice and application of early childhood pedagogy as a strong disincentive in attracting the skilled staff necessary for a quality program.

Quality begets quality. Early childhood programs are faced with the reality that quality is dependent on people and people are attracted by the quality of the program. As the organizational capacity increases, a program is better positioned to attract more skilled early childhood educators who have the knowledge and ability to ensure higher-quality programming.

The organizational capacity of an early childhood program includes practices, policies, and procedures. Some are critical to achieving the best possible environments for children and families and ensuring quality programs. Others may be in place because of tradition or "that's the way we've always done things," and nobody has given much thought of late as to how they are contributing towards the goals and vision of the program.

Organizational Challenges Common in Early Child Development Programs

Structural realities present tough challenges to the organizational capacity of most early child development programs:

- *In full-day child care centres, the hours of work are long and child care work is physically and emotionally demanding.* Child care staff in such programs typically work a 40- to 45-hour week. Outside of lunch and breaks (often only an hour daily), child care staff are working directly with children, responsible for their physical safety and well-being. Child care programs operate full days, often in excess of ten hours per day, and ECEs are sometimes required to work split shifts to accommodate the length of the day. Centres are open every working day of the year and are busiest during school holidays when school-age children attend full days. Ratios are 1:10 for preschool groups and 1:15 for school-age children. In addition to planning and preparing the program and environment, ECEs are also required to assist with meal preparations, lay out cots for naptime, sweep and mop floors, and clean toilets. During naptime—the only downtime in the day—some staff take lunch breaks while those left supervising napping children are expected to do double duty, using the time for program planning and administrative tasks. Staff meetings, professional development activities, and required courses such as first aid and CPR are usually scheduled in the evenings or on weekends, requiring ECEs to have additional time away from their own families and personal lives.
- Family child care providers, who generally work alone for up to ten hours a day, have no breaks or time away from the children during the day. Scheduling appointments for themselves or their own children, attending parent–teacher meetings at school, attending child care–related meetings, or participating in training during the day all prove very difficult. Some individually licensed caregivers hire substitutes so that they can be away from their program during the day, but paying substitutes reduces the caregivers' income and makes it costly for them to be away for any reason.
- *Custodial care often overtakes early learning and child development focus.* Child care staff and caregivers in regulated family child care have chosen to work with young children. ECE college programs prepare them to take a developmental perspective and actively encourage children's emerging abilities. But they often find themselves in work environments that do not permit them to pursue developmentally appropriate educational plans or activities. Instead, they must focus on supervising groups of children to ensure their safety and taking care of immediate needs for food, toileting, and sleep. The notion of embedding the curriculum into routines is lost in the need to ensure diapers are changed before a lunch break, or crowd control ensures no one is hurt at the end of the day, with only the late shift

staff and a large group of children. Child care staff sometimes report that a significant proportion of their day is spent on maintenance or cleaning tasks, compared to the amount of time they are able to spend with children, apart from leading them through daily care routines. The problem seems to be compounded in some jurisdictions by the requirements that are intended to ensure minimum standards.

- A Canadian study of the child care work force reported that one-quarter of centre-based child care staff reported that the nature of the work (e.g., cleaning and maintenance, lack of adult contact, insufficient planning time, and collection of parent fees) was a negative aspect of their job (Doherty et al., 2000). The same message was repeated in front-line staff focus groups across Canada (Beach et al., 2004).
- *Early childhood programs often face instability*. Child care centres and regulated family child care frequently offer unstable work environments. Low enrollments (which can be related to several possible factors, including changes in parents' employment, changes in child care fee subsidy eligibility criteria, or even a change in a commuter train schedule) can result in layoffs in child care centres or termination of contracts in family child care settings.
- Many early child development programs are located in schools or other community spaces, and few have lease agreements that protect the centre from eviction if the school or community group requires the space for other purposes.
- Stand-alone small child care centres typically exist with thin margins and have little credit at the bank. Payroll is dependent on payments from individual parents and government.
- *Families require flexibility*. There is a higher demand for part-time care and more flexible enrollment in full-time programs. Staff must work with a greater number of families and children due to children "sharing" spaces, and increased difficulties in providing quality care when there is not a consistent group of children attending on a daily basis.

Planning for Early Childhood Programs

A strategic plan is a leadership tool that sets the future direction for the entire organization. It spells out the organization's mission, vision, primary goals, and strategies. From time to time, early child development organizations are faced with significant changes in their mandates. The annual review of goals and objectives will not be adequate for planning new directions. Strategic planning considers different options based on the organizations' strengths, weaknesses, opportunities, and threats.

A business plan is a management tool that sets short-term objectives and defines the steps necessary to achieve them.

Operational Review

From time to time, complex problems may emerge in the operation of an early child program that are not easy to solve. New external demands, combined with limited resources, or sudden changes in staff or board members, may trigger issues that cannot be resolved within the regular planning and management framework.

An operational review is an opportunity to take an orderly look at how the organization is working—what could be done better and how. It tries to determine "what is" versus "what could be." An operational review should set the stage for positive change.

An operational review is an analysis and assessment of how efficiently and effectively an organization uses its human, physical, and financial resources to provide programs for young children and their parents that meet the centre's stated purpose, philosophy, goals, and objectives. It helps to identify specific steps to better achieve the goals and objectives.

Early childhood programs face increasing demands and expectations. Early childhood educators indicate greater pressure on them to address broader family and social issues that they were not equipped to deal with—issues such as family violence, concerns related to family poverty, child welfare concerns, and family counselling. Many programs have made efforts to offer a more inclusive environment for children with special needs, but additional funding to provide the necessary supports is often dependent on an identified diagnosis. Many of the children requiring additional supports have behavioural problems—often associated with attention-deficit disorder (ADD) or attention-deficit/hyperactivity disorder (ADHD), for which funding is often not available. There is increased emphasis on "school readiness," which is often interpreted as ensuring that children have formal numeracy and literacy skills before they enter kindergarten. Parents may arrive at summer preschool programs, family resource programs, and child care centres armed with information packages from their local schools, containing lists of skills that their children are expected to master before entering kindergarten.

Michael Fullan (2002) warns schools to be careful about taking on too many strategies for improvement. If can be ineffective and frustrating. The same holds true for early child development programs that are anxious to respond to increased demands and expectations. Piling on staff in-service workshops and multiple program review plans can serve to distract staff from the core purpose, philosophy, and goals of the program. The program director or supervisor is the early child development program leader who is instrumental in incorporating plans for improvement that increase program coherence.

THE ROLE OF THE EARLY CHILDHOOD PROGRAM LEADER

Early childhood programs benefit from skilled management and leadership. International and Canadian research findings point to the child care centre manager, supervisor, or director as the gatekeeper of quality (Goelman et al., 2000; Mill et al., 2002; National Research Council, 2001). A positive organizational climate, which includes opportunities for caregivers to be involved in decision making, creates a coherent administrative framework to support caregivers in centres. In family child care, support and contact with other caregivers is part of a positive organizational climate.

The education and training of centre managers influences centre quality. Managers who have higher educational levels seem to be better able to provide curriculum and

A knowledgeable and engaged program director encourages early childhood educators to excel.

pedagogical leadership to front-line staff. Overall, there seems to be a gap in the abilities of centre managers to implement good human resource practices that can help to retain staff. One U.S. study of the director's administrative style in 400 child care centres found that a director's involvement in both curriculum planning and in the professional community of early childhood education was associated with higher levels of overall quality (Helburn et al., 1995).

When a capable leader or manager in a child care centre demonstrates and encourages practices that support the interpersonal and structural elements of quality, the likelihood is increased that child care staff who are working directly with the children will do likewise.

The Program Director

The early childhood program director/supervisor is the keystone to carrying the program's vision (purpose and philosophy) forward. He or she can bring clarity or confusion, calm or chaos, stability or fragility to the daily lives of children, their families, and the staff team. The director's responsibilities are varied and he or she must hold multiple roles. The program director is responsible for the day-to-day and long-term operation of an early childhood education setting or the management tasks necessary to carry out the organizational purpose. The program director is also the leader who guides the organization's vision and goals and then leads the way in achieving that vision.

Chapter 8 Vision and Action

Innovations

SUPERVISOR, ADMINISTRATOR AND MANAGEMENT OCCUPATIONAL STANDARDS

The Child Care Human Resources Sector Council developed occupational standards for this position. Its standards identify the following broad leadership and management responsibilities:

- Development of the children's program, including the development of curricula, and the monitoring and evaluation of the overall program.
- Creation of a child-centred environment, including the development of a culture that respects children's needs and a child-friendly learning environment.
- Recruitment, hiring, and orientation of new staff.
- Staff management, including motivating, supervising, evaluating, and taking appropriate action when there are concerns about a staff member's behaviour, and maintaining staff records.
- Staff development, including determining and prioritizing staff training needs.
- Labour relations, including developing and implementing processes for the identification and delivery of wages and benefits and the communication and implementation of labour codes.
- Management of external human resources such as volunteers, ECE students, other professionals, and support services.
- Budget management, including the projection and prioritization of expenses and the determination of probable revenue, preparation of yearly operating and capital budgets, monitoring of revenue and expenditures and taking of appropriate action as indicated, implementation of procedures to maintain accountability to funders and reporting to the program owner or board of directors and relevant government authorities.
- Facility management, including the development and maintenance of a safe, secure, and healthy physical environment, development of emergency procedures, and identification and provision of necessary maintenance, repair, and replacement.
- Creation of a family-friendly environment, including the provision of information and referral to families and the promotion of parental involvement in the program.
- Relating to and communicating positively and effectively with a broad range of stakeholders including other community services, collaborating with other services, informing the public about early childhood education, and advocating on behalf of early childhood education.

- Participating with the owner, parent body, or other body responsible for governance in program policy development. Developing, monitoring, and evaluating policies and procedures.
- Planning for the centre, including gathering relevant data required for planning, developing plans, implementing communication plans, and marketing the program's services.
- Working collaboratively and effectively with the centre owner or governing body (i.e., board of directors, municipality, or sponsor such as a multi-service organization), including providing advice and support, preparing reports, and following the directions of the owner or governing body.

Source: Child Care Human Resource Sector Council, 2006.

In summary, the role of the program director includes a wide and complex array of responsibilities, including:

- developing and maintaining a positive environment and program for children;
- supporting families;
- developing and maintaining a positive workplace for staff;
- ensuring the financial viability of the centre;
- hiring, managing, and developing staff;
- developing and maintaining positive relationships with the community, the centre owner or governing body, and the provincial government; and
- engaging in strategic planning for the centre.

In some programs, some of the tasks associated with the above responsibilities are delegated to other staff members. Nevertheless, the director or supervisor in an early child development program remains ultimately responsible to the owner or governing body and the provincial government for how the tasks are performed.

Leadership Style

Daniel Goleman (2000) defined six different leadership styles:

1. *Coercive: "Do what I say" (demands compliance).* Coercive leadership is a commanding leadership style that works well in any emergencies. But most day-to-day situations are not emergencies. Leaders who rely only on this style also tend to take an assumption that the emergency is so important that it doesn't matter how individuals feel. They tend to ignore the emotional reality and they have no empathy. They typically bark orders.
2. *Authoritative: "Come with me" (mobilizes towards a vision).* A visionary leader articulates a shared vision and gives clear direction to motivate people toward a shared hope or dream. This model of leadership can have a positive impact on the team's

emotional climate. For example, a visionary leader clearly articulates where the team is going but not how it will get there. People are free to innovate, experiment, and take calculated risks. To be effective using this style, a leader needs a well-developed sense of empathy. He or she must be able to read people in order to sense what they are feeling and if they resonate with the broad vision. Leaders can't inspire people without understanding their perspectives.

3. *Affiliative: "People come first" (creates harmony and builds emotional bonds).* The affiliative style creates harmony in the group by getting people to connect with each other. Affiliative leaders create settings in which people can spend time together, get to know each other, and then bond together. They focus on people and their feelings more than on tasks and goals, and use praise lavishly. The affiliative style builds emotional capital among the team, so that the group can work together more harmoniously, even under pressure, and team members are also more likely to be there for the leader when needed. The downside to this style is that its focus on praise and making people feel good can allow conflicts to be ignored and poor performance to be tolerated.

4. *Democratic: "What do you think?" (consensus through participation).* The democratic leader is a consensus builder who really listens to other people, who takes their opinions into account in making a decision. This style is not appropriate for a crisis situation, or when expert knowledge is required. The ability to listen gets people engaged and makes them feel that they matter. Its downside can be endless team meetings, discussions that go on and on, and never reaching any conclusion—except, perhaps, to hold another team meeting.

5. *Pacesetting: "Do as I do, now" (high standards for performance).* A pacesetter shows up most often in technical fields. The pacesetter is typically someone who, as an individual contributor, was outstanding, which led to the promotion to team leader. Pacesetters lead by example and become impatient when people cannot meet that standard, which is very high because pacesetters are very good. They don't give positive feedback, only negative feedback. This leadership style may work well in leading a highly motivated, highly competent team, such as a team of research scientists, but most teams are not like that. People have a range of talents and a spectrum of abilities in each of those talents, and this reality is difficult for pacesetter leaders to recognize.

6. *Coaching: "Try this" (develops people for the future).* The coaching style is the least-used leadership style. It doesn't look like leadership. The coaching style involves talking to someone off-line, outside the team setting. It is often based on one-on-one conversation, not about shared tasks or the job at hand, but about the person. The conversation opens up an ongoing dialogue that lets the leader articulate the task in ways that make sense to the team member, in terms of where to go, or to find a challenge to lead that person in the direction where he or she wants to be moving anyway. Coaching can create intense loyalty and commitment to the leader and the team. Sometimes leaders may think they are coaching when they are actually micromanaging.

In most work settings, people can become overwhelmed or burned out when leaders demand compliance and have very high performance standards. Each of the styles impacts the emotions of the people who work with that leader and shapes the organizational climate. Think about how the six different leadership styles work in early child development settings.

Leadership can be, and probably should be, dispersed across the team. In early child development programs, staff teams can work together and take on leadership for different aspects of the program.

Pedagogical Leadership

Directors define pedagogy in early child development programs. Pedagogy in early childhood settings is the deliberate cultivation of early learning and development (National Research Council, 2001). It includes:

- curriculum or content of programs, including the content that is intentionally designed to promote learning processes, skills, and specific information;
- methodology or the strategies used to implement the curriculum, including the planned interactions of people, use of physical space and materials; and
- techniques for socializing children in the cognitive, social, and emotional skills necessary to get along with others.

Pedagogical leadership refers to the establishment and reinforcement of a climate and culture that expects staff members to provide an environment that deliberately supports the learning of young children. It implies the ongoing supervision of a process of planning, implementing, and reviewing what children do and how they are doing.

Pedagogical leadership skills and the ability to support and nurture recent ECE graduates who are entering the sector are important. But a recent survey of directors in child care centres reported that only 2 percent of their time was spent in activity planning and preparation, compared to 3 percent doing maintenance tasks (Doherty et al., 2000). About 10 percent of their time was spent on staff supervision (presumably some of which is spent on pedagogical issues), while 18 percent is spent on administrative tasks. It seems that the increased demands on child care directors and supervisors for record-keeping and documentation related to safety, health requirements, and financial accountability may be limiting their ability to provide pedagogical leadership.

Preparing for Early Childhood Program Leadership

"Leadership is everyone's business" (Kouzes & Posner, 2002, p. 383).

Effective program leadership is widely accepted as necessary to successful organizational development in early child development (Beach et al., 2004; Bloom, 1997, 2000; Doherty et al., 2000; Kagan, 2005; Rodd, 1998). Leaders' experience and education have been related to the quality of child care centre programs in a number of studies (Bloom, 1992; Goelman et al., 2000; Kontos & Fiene, 1987; Beach et al., 2004). An American study of Head Start programs reported that competent and stable leadership had a significant influence on how well the program was implemented (Ramey et al., 2000).

Preparing for leadership responsibilities in early childhood programs begins when aspiring early childhood educators start their first part-time job or begin their first field placement in an ECE training program. Direct work with young children and their families is the foundation of developing the skills of a program leader. Further academic training, networks and relationships, learning from other fields, and acquiring specific leadership skills and knowledge help too.

There is limited research on the nature of specific early childhood program leadership that is effective (Mujis et al., 2004), and much of what is available is anecdotal. In contrast, research findings confirm the contribution of leadership to improving school performance and raising academic achievement (Fullan, 2001).

The research that does exist is consistent with the findings in school-based programs. The characteristics associated with successful early child development program leaders are similar to the kinds of characteristics that are associated with successful principals in primary schools (Bloom, 2000; Rodd, 1996). These include:

- knowledge about child development and teaching strategies;
- a clear vision that includes moral purpose, philosophy, and goals;
- the ability to establish good working relationships;
- responsiveness to parents' needs and the ability to communicate with them; and
- the necessary administrative skills to keep the program's infrastructure (financial, legal, and record-keeping matters) operating.

Early childhood educators who are entering the work force may want to start thinking about how best to prepare for a future program leadership role. First-hand experience working directly with young children and families is a good grounding and should not be underestimated. The skills developed in working with young children and their families on a day-to-day basis build a repertoire that can be transported to leadership positions. The next chapter considers specific professional development and additional education possibilities.

EARLY CHILDHOOD EDUCATORS AND PROGRAM LEADERSHIP

Program leadership beings with a clear vision that includes a unified purpose, philosophy, and values. A coherent program puts the vision into action. Early childhood educators who share a common understanding of what the vision is can use it to guide their daily decisions and actions.

Early childhood program directors and supervisors who understand the leadership roles and responsibilities are able to provide direction and support to the staff team and the operation of the program. Pedagogical leadership contributes to a working environment that encourages responsiveness. Program supervisors/directors in all early childhood settings can support and value the development, implementation, and evaluation of a coherent curriculum. They can set the stage with program practices that respect all families, provide leadership in developing a vision and philosophy to guide the setting's curriculum and pedagogy, and create a workplace that values the practice of early childhood practitioners.

Preparing for leadership in early childhood programs begins when early childhood educators become engaged in how the program is delivered. Work environments that respect the curriculum and pedagogy offer an infrastructure that supports early childhood educators and prepares them for future leadership roles.

KEY TERMS

implementation integrity   program coherence
philosophy

REFLECTION QUESTIONS

1. Based on your field placement and work experiences to date in early childhood settings, identify the characteristics of a program leader you respect and who supported you in acquiring the skills to be an early childhood educator.
2. How can early childhood educators accommodate the necessary daily routines (meals, toileting, sleep, etc.) that are part of a full-time program and still ensure that there is a curriculum and pedagogical coherence to the program?
3. What will be your role in the early childhood work force in five years? What kinds of work experiences will support your goals?
4. To get started on a personal philosophy, try completing these sentences:
   - I believe that the purpose of early child development programs are . . .
   - I believe that children learn best when . . .
   - Parents and families are important because . . .
   - A curriculum for young children should include . . .
   - The elements of a quality early learning environment are . . .
   - Parent involvement means . . .
   - The basic needs of young children are . . .
   - Qualities important for early childhood educators are . . .
5. Put together a personal philosophy and ask others to read it. Evaluate your personal philosophy. Does it state:
   - How children learn and develop?
   - What children should learn?
   - Personal core values?
6. Make a list of common daily practices and procedures in a family resource program or child care centre around snack time. Review each one and ask the following questions:
   - How does this practice/procedure contribute to achieving the program goals?
   - How useful is this practice/procedure in stimulating creativity and innovation?
   - Why is this practice/policy in place?

FOR MORE INFORMATION

1. For a short informative paper on involving children in the planning and delivery of early childhood programs, see *Exploring the Field of Listening to and Consulting with Young Children* by Alison Clark, Susan McQuail, and Peter Moss of the Thomas Coram Research Unit.

   www.dfes.gov.uk/research/data/uploadfiles/RB445.doc

2. Every two years the *Canadian Child Care Federation's Award for Excellence in Child Care* honours individuals who have made an outstanding contribution to the field of child care. It recognizes achievements in caregiving, new initiatives, quality, research, education, policy, and advocacy.

   www.cccf-fcsge.ca/aboutus/excellence_en.html

3. The *Thomson Nelson ECE Resource Centre* is intended to enhance the teaching and learning experience for both instructors and students. The website provides extensive and helpful resources in many different criteria related to early childhood education.

   www.ece.nelson.com

CONTINUOUS LEARNING

CHAPTER OUTLINE

Joan Kunderman

The ECE diploma program we offer at Red River College is a start—and a good start—at preparing early childhood educators to work with young children and their families. But professional early childhood educators need to continue their education—either by pursuing a degree program or by continually participating in professional development. We must continue to push ourselves to raise the bar on quality. Adequate programs that are safe and clear are not good enough. Early childhood educators have the unique opportunity and privilege to influence child development and population health through the provision of quality programs.

Red River College had introduced a number of innovative delivery models that have made post-secondary education more accessible to Manitoba's early childhood community. Since 1971 when the ECE diploma program was first offered at Red River College, the program has continuously evolved to remain current and to meet the learning needs of emerging early childhood programs. When the provincial government increased its requirements for educational qualifications for program staff in regulated child care centres, Red River College moved specialized courses to post-diploma programs and increased the focus on child development, curriculum, and professionalism in the ECE diploma program. When the federal government established the Aboriginal Child Care initiative, Red River College developed many partnerships with First Nations communities for community-based training in rural and remote communities. Red River College offers post-diploma programs (Studies in Aboriginal Child Care, Studies in Special Needs Child Care, or Infant Care). With experience and this additional professional education, a number of graduates move on to positions as directors of child care centres or in early childhood intervention services.

The two-year ECE diploma program is also delivered through an ECE Workplace model in an attempt to relieve the shortage of trained ECEs in Manitoba and meet the needs of the community, students, and the centres. This delivery model educates and trains individuals who have worked in a licensed early childhood program for two years or more. Students attend classes two days a week and work in their centres the remaining three days. Currently, the Manitoba government provides a substitute grant to the centres and students continue to receive a full-time salary.

Red River College graduates may transfer their ECE diploma credits to university studies. The college has several articulation agreements with universities enabling graduates to obtain credits toward degrees in the areas of developmental studies, family studies, child and youth care and human services.

After the release of the Early Years Study in 1999, we were able to join forces with Dr. Fraser Mustard and his colleagues to produce a core curriculum resource that translates recent scientific findings in young children to a flexible, learner-friendly core multimedia resource. The government of Manitoba has purchased copies of the resource for all regulated child care programs and parent–community coalitions.

I am proud of all that we have done at Red River College to support pre-service preparation and continuous learning within the early childhood work force. But we need to develop pedagogical leadership within early childhood programs. We can support and supplement such leadership—but we cannot replace it. This is the challenge the field faces right now.

Source: Interview with Joan Kunderman. Joan Kunderman was chairperson of Community Services, including the Early Childhood Education program at Red River College in Winnipeg, Manitoba, which offers a two-year ECE diploma program, from 1974 to December 2007.

Chapter Objectives

This chapter will:

1. Identify Canada's early childhood work force.
2. Consider how professional development and education opportunities support early childhood programs.
3. Describe what a learning organization is and how it operates.
4. Review specific activities that build an effective learning organization.
5. Describe how to establish a continuum of learning in early child development programs.

FROM SKILLS TO LEADERSHIP

Learning and skill development fuels leadership in early childhood programs. Early childhood educators who are confident about their abilities to work with young children and families, who are continually challenging their own knowledge base, and who are open to new ideas are the program leaders who inspire others. They set examples and provide models of what quality programming looks like. They bring out the best among their peers.

Post-secondary ECE programs include both theoretical and practical knowledge to prepare the early childhood work force. They provide a solid foundation in the practice of early childhood education, but ECE certificate, diploma, and even degree programs are only a beginning. Later in this chapter we will look at how ECE programs are delivered in post-secondary institutions. Here we will consider skill areas that ECE graduates and employers would like to boost (Beach et al., 2004). The evidence is clear. At the core of an early childhood learning organization is a skilled and competent early childhood work force that understands children's early development and learning, and families' and communities' participation in early learning and development. The challenge for the early childhood sector is to increase the skill and knowledge level of the early childhood work force and to increase the quality of early learning and care that children experience.

People are the key factor in quality child care experiences for children. Repeated studies arrive at the same conclusion. Competent early childhood educators are related to better outcomes for children (Arnett, 1989; Burton et al., 2002; Burchinal et al., 2002; Cost, Quality & Outcomes Study Team, 1995). The quality of an early child development program is largely determined by the characteristics of the interactions between individual children and the early childhood staff, the knowledge and skill base staff have, and their environment (NICHD Early Childcare Research Network, 2002; National Research Council, 2001).

Continuous learning benefits young children and families. Improvements in our skill areas also increase the ability to lead and guide others.

Skills in Working with Children with Special Needs

In a Canadian study (Beach et al., 2004), students in ten ECE programs located across Canada reported that they felt well-prepared to work with "typical children" but indicated that they felt less prepared to work with children with special needs, professionals in other educational and social service settings, parents, and other adults in their work environment. Over 90 percent of students felt very well prepared to work with typical children, but fewer than 20 percent felt very well prepared to work with children with special needs.

Successful inclusion of children with special needs depends on the overall quality of the child care centre. A high-quality child care program is more likely to successfully include children with a variety of disabilities than a centre with lower quality (Lero et al., 2006). In-house capacity for inclusion is most likely to be found in child care centres that have a well-supported staff team with its own capacity to keep including children with disabilities, build on training opportunities, and incorporate new information. Outside resources and consultation help, but it is the quality of the centre in the first place that is the key element. Quality begets quality—high-quality centres are better able to make use of additional resources and information.

Knowledge About Cultural and Linguistic Diversity

Several recent reviews have recommended that post-secondary ECE programs need to be more culturally appropriate and sensitive to diversity (Beach et al., 2004; Doherty et al., 2000; OECD, 2004). Programs such as Aboriginal Head Start (which incorporates more than 30 Inuit and First Nations languages) provide a more direct focus on cultural and linguistic diversity (McQuaid et al., 2002).

Researchers in Canada have studied the participation of newcomer families in regulated child care programs. They have found that early childhood educators are often unaware of the disconnect between their program goals and childrearing values and those of newcomer, minority families (Bernhard, 1995; Bernhard et al., 1998). The conclusions recommend that more content on cultural diversity should be included in post-secondary ECE programs.

PROFESSIONAL EDUCATION AND DEVELOPMENT

There is agreement among early childhood students, program directors, and provincial/territorial directors that the early childhood work force needs more preparatory training and ongoing professional development.

Post-Secondary Education

More education is better. Increased post-secondary education in early childhood development, education, and care is related to increased quality child care and better child outcomes. Research studies report consistent and significant associations between higher staff education levels and quality programs and outcomes for children:

- The longitudinal NICHD Early Child Care Research Network study considered the effects of child care staff or home-based caregiver education on child care quality and the effects of child care quality on child outcomes. Researchers found that educational attainment predicted staff or caregiver behaviour, which in turn predicted children's social and cognitive development. Staff and caregivers with higher levels of ECE-related education were more likely to provide quality care and learning environments (NICHD Early Childhood Research Network, 2002).

- The "You Bet I Care!" study of quality in Canadian child care centres reported that higher-quality centres were associated with staff who had post-secondary ECE credentials (Goelman et al., 2000). The related study of regulated family child care reported that increased quality environments were associated with higher levels of caregiver education. The study concluded that quality improvements are likely in regulated child care settings if all staff have post-secondary ECE qualifications (Goelman et al., 2000).

- A Canadian study of school-age child care also reported that higher quality was associated with higher levels of director and staff education (Mills et al., 2002).

- Ongoing professional development and upgrading is necessary to stay current with the latest in child development knowledge and to implement new pedagogy or curriculum that may be introduced at a provincial level, such as the "Jouer c'est magique" curriculum in Quebec.

College ECE programs prepare individuals for early childhood programs.

- Recent American studies conclude that at least some of the staff in centre-based programs should have university degrees that include early child development and education studies, in order to increase the quality of preschool programs and, in turn, improve child outcomes prior to entry into Grade 1 (Barnett, 2003; Blau, 1999; Burton et al., 2002; Howes et al., 1998; Whitebook, 2003; Zill et al., 2001).

Early childhood programs can improve the quality of their centres by increasing the staff levels of education, particularly in areas related to child development and early childhood education pedagogy. In Canada, overall educational levels have been rising among staff working in early childhood care and education programs (Beach & Flanagon-Rochon, 2007), but the rate of increase of educational attainment for the child care work force lags behind the rate of increase across all occupations. A Canadian 1984 survey of child care staff in regulated centres found that, compared to the average Canadian worker, child care workers in licensed centres were well educated (Cooke et al., 1986). More recent figures, however, suggest that the gap is closing. Over the past two decades, the overall increase in the educational attainment of the child care work force has not kept pace with the overall increases found across all occupations. This is in spite of increased awareness of the importance of ECE qualifications and, in some jurisdictions, increased qualification requirements.

Early childhood programs can encourage staff without post-secondary early childhood professional education to pursue part-time opportunities. Supportive measures such as scheduling work to allow for attending continuing education classes and financial contribution towards the cost of courses can make a difference. Programs can encourage staff with entry-level early childhood education qualifications to pursue further opportunities, including degree-level or graduate studies.

A number of provinces have introduced initiatives to address the shortage of qualified early childhood educators, especially where the supply of trained staff is not sufficient for centres to meet legislated training requirements. Initiatives to increase access to professional education and facilitate qualified early childhood educators were discussed in Chapter 2.

Barriers to Post-Secondary Education

The early childhood work force continues to identify barriers to accessing post-secondary early childhood education programs and professional development opportunities. Front-line staff point to time and cost factors, lack of information about what is available, and a lack of recognition of informal, nontraditional learning and the inability to transfer credits and credentials across institutions and jurisdictions (Beach Flanagon-Rochon, 2007).

The cost of post-secondary education to obtain either an early childhood credential or a university degree and the distance from such a program is a barrier to access for many potential students. Reports on recruitment and retention issues in Canada have concluded that the high cost of post-secondary ECE programs in relation to low remuneration levels is a significant disincentive to either enter or remain in the child care sector (Miller & Ferguson, 2003; Beach et al., 2004; Beach & Flanagon-Rochon, 2007). The same reports point to the lack of available programs in more remote regions of the country. There are concerns about cost and geographic issues in every province and territory.

Recognizing Informal Learning

Individuals working in family child care or child care centres who did not have post-secondary ECE qualifications identified in focus groups that they want recognition for what they do know and have learned outside of formal academic settings. A recent American review of research about staff qualifications that recommends a four-year degree requirement for some of the staff recognizes that staff may have acquired the necessary knowledge and skills and should be granted an equivalency status (Barnett, 2003). Newcomers to Canada may have related credentials acquired in other countries that are not recognized or perhaps understood in Canada.

Prior Learning and Recognition (PLAR) has the potential to accommodate both the needs of individuals working in child care who have experience but no recognized academic credentials, and the needs of the child care sector to improve the overall skills of the work force. PLAR works particularly well in combination with distance education programs and with learners who are currently working in early childhood settings and/or have other related experience.

Professional Development

Professional development promotes professional learning and is essential to creating an early childhood learning organization. Some forms of professional development are more effective than others in affecting the practice of early childhood education and promoting young children's optimal early development.

For example, talking at large groups of early childhood educators in order to expose them to new ideas is not the most effective approach, and it can squander the goodwill of staff to participate in professional development opportunities—particularly if it takes place outside regular work hours. Often, professional development is fragmented and incoherent and fails to build on existing knowledge and skills.

Generally, research indicates that professional development is more likely to promote professional learning if it is sustained and intensive rather than one-time sessions (National Research Council, 2001). Early childhood educator knowledge and skills are improved when professional development:

- focuses on child development and early learning content;
- is coherent with day-to-day life in early childhood settings; and
- gives early childhood educators an opportunity for "hands-on work" or practical application.

Professional Development Materials

Early childhood organizations, post-secondary education institutions, and early child development research units are producing a considerable amount of material (print, electronic, and video) aimed at individuals working with young children and families. Other materials are targeted to parents of young children. However, it is unclear how much is reaching the early childhood work force.

Early childhood educators and even post-secondary education early childhood education programs are not always aware of or making use of materials produced in Canada that may be more culturally appropriate than texts and visual materials from the United States (Beach et al., 2004).

Conferences offer early childhood educators opportunities to meet and network.

Accessing Professional Development Opportunities

Between 1991 and 1998, the proportion of child care staff who had taken part in professional development activities over the preceding 12 months decreased from 87 percent to 76 percent (Doherty et al., 2000). The most common reasons given were cost and inability to obtain release time. Of course, the inability to take off time is often related to the cost of staff replacement or lost income. This is consistent with findings from surveys of staff in family support programs. Professional development days are built into the annual schedule for kindergarten teachers, and additional support may be available for individuals who wish to pursue special projects.

EARLY CHILDHOOD PROGRAMS AS LEARNING ORGANIZATIONS

Early childhood educators can benefit from learning from each other about how to adapt to a changing environment and put what we know into daily practice. The "learning organization" has emerged as a concept that brings together many of the key

Beyond Our Borders

CONSULTATIVE GROUP ON EARLY CHILDHOOD CARE AND DEVELOPMENT

The Consultative Group on Early Childhood Care and Development (CGECCD) is a diverse consortium of agencies, donors, nongovernmental organizations, and foundations that links with regional-based early childhood care and development (ECCD) networks comprising individuals and organizations involved in programming, research, policy-advocacy, monitoring, and evaluation for young children (birth to age eight) at risk in the Majority World (the world's developing regions). It provides information and resources for early childhood programs in Canada and around the world.

The CGECCD Secretariat—in partnership with the other members of the consortium and regional networks—works actively to identify gaps, critical issues, and emerging areas of need and interest related to early childhood care and development for its work in awareness-raising, advocacy, and dissemination, and to seek out new partners.

Activities include:

- synthesis, critical review, and sharing of the lessons, findings, and impact from practice and research across regions;
- strengthening of regional networking, capacity-building, outreach, and activities; and
- strengthening and/or establishment of more effective links with others working in health, social welfare, community development, adult literacy, and basic education.

CGECCD believes that it is critical to promote a more diverse and creative range of ECCD activities that link different sectors, are more inclusive, and better address children's needs and circumstances in the context of the family and/or community.

Sources: CGECCD, 2004; Evans et al., 2000.

---

features of groups and organizations trying to take what they know from each other and put it into action in real-life situations (Senge, 1990; Keating & Hertzman, 1999).

The concept of a learning organization can be applied in early childhood programs. Clear goals, the active participation of all in achieving them, continuous improvement based on reliable feedback, and effective communication and collaboration are the key features that can create early childhood learning organizations.

Learning is not restricted to the individual acquisition of knowledge or skills (such as learning to assess children's motor development using a checklist). Learning organizations focus on building a collective understanding or shared knowledge based on

Innovations

BEST START MATERNAL, NEWBORN, AND EARLY CHILD DEVELOPMENT RESOURCE CENTRE

Best Start (see www.beststart.org/resources/index.html) is a resource centre that seeks to enhance the capacity of service providers (including early childhood educators) to implement effective health promotion programs for expectant and new parents (including both mom and dad), newborns, and young children.

Best Start began in 1992 as a unique demonstration project. Two sites were selected to develop and implement interventions to promote the health of women and families, before, during, and after pregnancy. Following this demonstration period, the Ontario government funded the resource centre to build on the lessons learned during the demonstration period and provide support to communities across the province. In 2000–01 the mandate expanded to include early child development, and it is now known as Best Start: Ontario's Maternal, Newborn and Early Child Development Resource Centre.

Best Start is central and a core part of the Ontario Prevention Clearinghouse (OPC), which is Ontario's longest-standing health promotion organization.

Best Start has prepared a number of resources (see www.beststart.org/resources/index.html) that can be used by early childhood educators to support young children's and families' health and well-being.

Source: www.beststart.org/resources/index.html.

what we can learn from each other and our experiences. Early childhood learning organizations are capable of adapting and learning from experience as well as from individual expertise.

According to Peter Senge (1990, p. 3), learning organizations are "organizations where people continually expand their capacity to create the results they truly desire, where new and expansive patterns of thinking are nurtured, where collective aspiration is set free, and where people are continually learning to see the whole together."

What does a learning organization look like? Peter Senge (1990) describes five components of successful learning organizations. Each one can be developed separately but each one is also a vital dimension to the others' success.

- *Systems thinking* is the understanding of how an organization is part of a dynamic system, not an isolated program. By understanding interdependency and change, it becomes easier to understand the consequences of different actions. Systems tend towards growth or stability over time.
- *Personal mastery* is finding a balance between what individuals want to achieve and the current state of their lives. Learning to manage the tension between vision and

reality can expand people's capacity to make better choices, and to achieve more of the results that they have chosen.

- *Building shared vision* is an emphasis on coordinated group effort toward shared goals rather than an emphasis on individual achievement. The shared vision of an early child development program needs to be clear and consistent. When goals are vague or when consensus is low, early childhood educators may feel comfortable with the autonomy they have to pursue their own unique interests. Others may just take care of the basics and not much more. Individual autonomy can reduce the ability to support optimal early child development. In contrast, shared goals can maximize efforts through collective reinforcement. Shared vision focuses on mutual purpose. People learn to nourish a sense of commitment in an early child development program by building shared images of the type of program they would like to create and the principles and guiding practices by which they hope to get there.

- *Mental models* are based on reflection and inquiry skills. By developing an awareness of the attitudes and perceptions that influence thought and interaction, individuals can avoid jumping to negative conclusions, particularly about possible change. By continually reflecting upon, talking about, and reconsidering internal pictures, people can gain more capability in governing their actions and decisions.

- *Team learning* is based on group interaction, the cornerstone of the practice of early childhood education. Techniques like dialogue and skillful discussion enable early childhood staff teams to mobilize their energies and ability greater than the sum of individual members' talents and abilities. Members of a learning organization team are in alignment with each other.

An early childhood program that is a learning organization recognizes that change is a continuous process. It welcomes the tension of competing ideas linked to cooperative activity.

There are no blueprints or how-to manuals. In fact, the best way to become a learning organization is to just start behaving like one and learn from the experience. Daniel Keating (Keating & Hertzman, 1999) identified four key principles that can guide early child development programs that want to be learning organizations and to be part of communities and societies that are serious about improving children's development and well-being:

- *Invest in the core infrastructure.* To be successful, any enterprise must invest in the infrastructure to keep it going. In an early child development program, infrastructure is the administration and management that supports the daily program. Early childhood educators and other staff can be active participants in creating a vibrant learning community that is attuned to how children are learning and developing. The front line of daily experiences is vital to organizing resources (time, space, people, and things) to create the best possible environments for young children. But imagining that front line can self-organize to provide optimal programming without adequate resources and supports is not realistic. Creating a learning organization will not "save" money. It may cost more. Increased investments do not mean steady state funding for the status quo. Some activities will challenge the accepted practices and even beliefs of a program.

- *Network available resources and ingenuity.* One of the hallmarks of a learning organization is the ability to network existing resources in order to maximize their benefits. What we often find is the coordination of resources within and among early child development programs doesn't happen. This is sometimes called the "silo" effect. Within an early childhood program, in spite of limited resources, each program area will outfit itself with the same basic equipment, rather than pool resources and work out an arrangement to share larger pieces of equipment (e.g., sand and water tables) or play materials (e.g., Lego). Within a neighbourhood, a family resource program, a home visiting program, and a child care centre may exist alongside each other, and each mounts its own outreach strategy—organizing open houses, producing pamphlets, and creating websites.

- *Focus on the core dynamics.* Early childhood programs should be driven by what we know about early brain development and the kinds of relationships and environments that shape that development. In an early childhood learning organization, every decision about where and how to invest financial or human resources needs to take the core dynamics of human development into account.

- *Monitor the outcomes.* One of the major drawbacks of well-intentioned early child development programs is that their impact is not monitored. Early childhood educators, administrators, parents, and others often do not know if their efforts made a difference. Chapter 3 included an overview of different ways to measure early child development. A learning organization is continually paying attention to the impact of its actions. Are children benefiting? How? What about their families?

Taken together, the four principles can point us in the direction of what it takes to be an early childhood learning organization.

Making It Happen

The concept and principles of learning organizations and the potential for early childhood learning organizations can be overwhelming. How can early childhood educators who are just beginning their careers and program directors who are running small programs begin to build learning organizations? Small steps can build up to dynamic professional learning communities among the staff in an early childhood program or among staff working in different programs in the same community. These small steps can leverage the value of other continuing education and professional development opportunities that may be available to early childhood educators.

Adult Learners

Early childhood educators are adult learners (Cranton, 2003). One of the challenges we all face as adult learners is how to take knowledge and translate it into practice. It is especially difficult to take new information and knowledge that we have learned from a text or in a classroom lecture and apply it in the context of a busy room filled with young children and adults.

Connecting with Experience Early childhood educators bring plentiful experiences to new learning opportunities. Connecting new learning to previous experiences respects what we already know and helps us incorporate new information and bridge theory to practice. For example, we all have our own stories about our childhoods that help us bridge theory about child development to our practice.

Collaborative Learning Early childhood educators encourage young children to construct their knowledge and understanding of the world through active play with each other. In fact, learning through play is a bottom-up approach. Play provides a platform for discussion, negotiation, and consensus. This is **collaborative learning.** Knowledge is constructed through discussion and consensus rather than transferred or acquired from others. According to (Bruffee, 1993, cited in Cranton, 2003, p. 3), "Collaborative learning assumes instead that knowledge is a consensus among the members of a community of knowledgeable peers—something people construct by talking together and reaching agreement." As adult learners, early childhood educators benefit from collaborative learning situations. Rather than just a lecture about dealing with behaviour challenges, early childhood educators may learn more through discussion with peers, which leads to new perspectives and new strategies to try out. Collaborative learning works best when learners bring a knowledge base to the discussion and have access to resources that feed the discussion.

Self-Directed Learning Adult learners who set their own goals, find resources, and carry out projects are taking responsibility for their own learning. There is transfer of new knowledge into practice. Early childhood educators need to develop the capacity to generate their own learning projects. Continuous learning is supported by learners who know how to learn and make it part of daily practice. Early childhood programs can encourage self-directed learning by encouraging staff to take ownership for the physical environment, program planning, and daily documentation. A truly child-centred learning environment is facilitated by early childhood educators who are self-directed learners who continually observe, question, and try things out.

Dialogue

Early childhood programs can foster inquiry and dialogue, making it safe for people to share openly and take risks. The term *dialogue* comes from a Greek word—*dialogos. Dia* means "through" and *logos* means the "word" or "meaning." The original meaning of dialogue was the "meaning passing or moving through, a free-flow of meaning between people" (Senge, 1990, p. 240). Dialogue can be contrasted with *discussion,* which has the same roots as *percussion* and *concussion,* meaning "to break apart." Covey (1991) compares discussion with a ping-pong game where we are hitting the ball back and forth, each trying to "win" the game. In contrast, dialogue offers a "win–win" form of communication. In dialogue, people learn to listen to one another, to hear each other's ideas without judgment. People find out what is on each other's minds without coming to any conclusions.

Dialogue is a basic process for building a common understanding. By letting go of disagreement, a group is able to build a shared perspective. It provides a tool for confronting assumptions and talking about feelings and building common ground.

Early childhood educators can improve professional dialogue with each other by listening more.

Dialogue can lead to new levels of coordinated action, without the artificial often-tedious process of creating action plans.

Early childhood educators can practise dialogue with colleagues. It is one way to impact the relationships and interactions among a staff team. Here are some guidelines to get started:

- Suspend certainties.
- Listen to your listening.
- Slow down the inquiry.
- Be aware of thought.
- Maintain peripheral attention.
- Speak from your heart, the moment, your experience, and point of view.
- Listen from the point of view of the group, the community, and the collective.
- Appreciate the silence—consider, reflect, and think before speaking.
- Assume that the ideas and observations of others come from a desire to contribute.
- Welcome differences of opinion, as they will serve to increase your acceptance of diversity, awareness, and understanding.
- Watch out for problem solving, disagreeing, and asking too many questions.

- Avoid agendas or elaborate preparations that tend to inhibit the free flow of conversation.
- Speak to the centre of the group, not to other individuals, to create common meaning, not a set of person-to-person dynamics.

A meeting chair or leader in an early child development program can support a dialogue process by implementing the following steps:

1. *Check in.* Give every participant an opportunity to simply speak for a minute from personal experience about what he or she is thinking, feeling, or has noticed. The process facilitates the individual being able to connect to current experience and relax. Gently keep the process moving so that one individual does not monopolize.
2. *Surface assumptions.* The dialogue leader or facilitator should be aware of his or her own assumptions.
3. *Display assumptions so that others can see and hear them.*
4. *Invite and offer inquiry.* Invite others to see new dimensions in what individuals are thinking and saying, and offer to do the same for them.
5. *Listen reflectively.* Model the above guidelines.
6. *Check out.* Offer an opportunity for participants to close the session with a brief statement or word that captures their current thinking or feeling.

Supervisors/directors can encourage ongoing, daily dialogue with staff members and among staff members that can help resolve concerns and celebrate successes. It is an opportunity for the supervisor to offer feedback that is proactive and positive and to deal with problems when they arise.

Constructive discussion includes specific feedback about concerns and problems. Supervisors should raise issues and focus the dialogue on resolving the immediate problem. Staff members can be encouraged to be active participants who contribute their perceptions and solutions.

Constructive discussion combined with clearly formulated policies, procedures, and job descriptions helps to reduce serious performance problems.

Staff meetings are valuable opportunities to promote a professional learning organization in an early child development program. Planning the purpose and desired outcomes and ensuring that the discussion stays on track are critical to their success. Meeting times can support dialogue in addition to practical information sharing and networking.

Review the discussion about meetings in Chapter 4 and consider how these guidelines for board of directors or advisory committee meetings can be applied to staff meetings.

Managing Change

Change is a fact of life in early childhood environments (and just about everywhere else) and is central to early childhood learning communities. In fact, the only thing we know for sure about the future may be that there will be change in our environments. Early childhood programs that expect change are more likely to embrace new developments and benefit from new opportunities. They are willing to be uncomfortable and to be challenged by new ideas, policies, and events.

At the same time, acceptance of change must bring critical thinking to new propositions and directions. Not all change is good change—in early childhood programs, the weather, or the stock market. An early childhood program that has established itself as a learning community (or part of one) is more likely to have the capacity to assess changes on the horizon and discern which to embrace and which to reject. Other changes are inevitable, so they must be managed.

Not only do early childhood educators have to be good at checking things off daily lists of things to do, but they also have to be good at managing change. Managing change means being comfortable with chaos. There are two types of chaos—the chaos of creativity and the chaos of over-creation and incompletion (Allen, 2004).

Chaos means disorder or turmoil. The process of creating anything brings some level of chaos. Creating is moving from the unknown to the knowable. A day may be planned based on all of the "known" things you intend to do—a group time centred on a particular storybook, scheduled outdoor time to follow time at learning centres carefully set up to offer opportunities to explore specific materials to achieve specific learning objectives, and daily care routines scheduled to meet the needs of children for nutrition, toileting, and sleep.

Then a child arrives, excited about the caterpillar she has found and carefully carried into the program. A parent arrives with her elderly mother and both are planning on joining the group for the morning. Grandma has come from outside of Canada and is puzzled by the idea of a child care centre but clearly wants to understand and contribute something to her grandchild's daily life at the centre. The centre cook arrives and tells you that lunch will be a little late—problems with defrosting today's main course for lunch. Early childhood educators who are attuned to the children and families they work with want to respond to what the children and families bring to the program. They create daily experiences based on the child's needs, dispositions, and interests. They want to incorporate the richness that parental and family involvement brings. And they must accept that there will always be glitches in daily food preparation, functioning of the plumbing, and weather forecasts.

Early childhood educators have to incorporate the unknown into their day, which often creates a different daily experience than what was planned. It's the ability to manage and integrate the chaos of the unknown quickly that gives early childhood educators a leading edge in becoming creative practitioners who are fully engaged in a continuum of learning.

Many early childhood educators are faced with the chaos of incompletion. When there are many tasks and activities undone or half completed, they distract and make it very difficult to be creative. Time is spent in reacting to the turmoil in an attempt to get some sense of control over it or developing strategies to avoid dealing with the stress of the surrounding chaos. Neither one of these approaches leaves much room for excitement or creativity when new things show up, because each new unknown adds to the pile of stress.

It's 9:00 A.M. and three-year-old Ayesha arrives excited about the worm she picked up on the way to the preschool program. If finding a container for the worm becomes a 15-minute exercise as you move the half-finished, abandoned papier-mâché balloons from on top of the box that contains—well many things and maybe a container, but

From the Past

LEARNING FROM THE PLAY OF YOUNG CHILDREN

At the end of the nineteenth century, Froebel kindergartens were gaining popularity in North America. The following excerpt reveals the emphasis placed on observing the actions of young children rather than simply provide rote skill-building tasks:

> It happens, therefore, that the kindergarten gives great attention to the sequence of studies, the educational value of each exercise, and to the correct method of directing the pupil's own efforts without stunting them by officious help. In all these things she, the good kindergartner, continually follows the lead of Froebel, and ever finds new significance in his profound thoughts, expressed, as they often are by him, in the form of obscure hints or inadequate expositions.
>
> The existence in every community of a coterie of zealous students of Froebel, composed of teachers and mothers of young children, will tend to draw large numbers of the instructors of older children and youth into the study of the mental evolution of children. Then will follow an educational era of good methods in all grades of schools. We shall not find then, as we do now, a teacher permitted to overdo one branch of study to such an extent as to arrest development on some elementary plane, and destroy aspiration for more perfect instruments of knowledge and for deeper depths of thought.

Source: Susan Blow, Symbolic Education: A Commentary on Froebel's "Mother Play" *1898, Vol. XXVI of International Education Series (New York: D. Appleton & Co.), p. ix.*

maybe not. The table where the play dough is set out is now covered with egg cartons and whatnot. Ayesha is losing interest in waiting and is becoming upset as her mother has to go and nothing has happened with the worm. But then there are last week's clay sculptures that were to be painted—in fact, a couple of children have asked about them, but they were forgotten under the box of whatnot until now. The clay sculptures are now on top of last week's paintings that were to be hung on the walls as soon as the Halloween paintings come down. It is December 2. Ayesha's worm becomes a stressor, not a challenge that elicits creativity. There are too many undone things in the environment to allow for creativity and new learning.

Part of making chaos the catalyst for creativity is having things in order, knowing what needs to be done, and knowing that there is a system in place for making sure that things get done.

Embracing change requires confident and competent leadership.

PROFESSIONAL RECOGNITION, ORGANIZATIONS, AND NETWORKS

Professional associations at the national, provincial/territorial, and local levels support the early childhood work force. They carry out a range of professional education and development activities. Professional organizations and networks encourage continuous learning and can complement an early childhood program's professional development strategy. Go to www.cfc-efc.ca/startup/orgs.htm for a comprehensive listing of national, provincial, and territorial organizations. Often ECE students are offered special rates to join these organizations. It is an opportunity to find out more about the early childhood work force network in your community.

The professional recognition of early childhood educators by provincial governments is becoming more common in Canada. Provincial/territorial professional organizations have taken on tasks related to professionalism and continuous learning, including voluntary **certification**, development of **codes of ethics**, consultation with governments on issues related to **equivalency validation** of early childhood education **credentials**, and appropriate course content for professional education programs. These tasks are often associated with self-governance.

Voluntary Certification

Voluntary certification recognizes and endorses the educational qualifications and, sometimes, the performance levels of early childhood educators, regardless of their work setting. It is a mechanism to monitor standards of practice and to promote both the quality of early childhood education and care services and the professionalism of the early childhood work force.

Three provincial professional organizations offer voluntary certification to their members: the Association of Early Childhood Educators of Ontario (AECEO), the Early Childhood Professional Association of Alberta (ECPAA), and the Certification Council of Early Childhood Educators of Nova Scotia (CCECENS).

There are limitations to the voluntary certification processes in Canada. Only a small proportion of early childhood educators in each province are certified. Although in some early childhood education and care programs, certification is recognized and valued, there is little overall recognition or motivation to become certified, as it is not required. In both Alberta and Ontario the ECE educational qualification establishes eligibility and, therefore, provides the standards of practice to be assessed. In Nova Scotia the process has introduced an assessment of an early childhood educator's practice based on criteria established by other practitioners. Unfortunately, the automatic renewal in certification in the three provinces fails to provide a mechanism to ensure that early childhood educators' knowledge remains current (Doherty, 1997).

Self-Governance

The **self-governance** of a profession refers to its authority to establish bodies to regulate its members and their practice through certification, standards of practice, discipline, and requirements for professional education. Self-governance recognizes bodies outside government or organizations that represent the economic or professional development interest of practitioners. The recognition is embedded in legislation.

The Association of Early Childhood Educators, Newfoundland, became Canada's first self-governing organization that is recognized by government. The Certification Council of Early Childhood Educators, Nova Scotia; the Association of Early Childhood Educators, Ontario; and the Early Childhood Educators of British Columbia have proposed legislated or mandated self-regulatory bodies, which would regulate early childhood educators within each of the provincial jurisdictions. To date, the proposals have not been adopted.

In 2007, the Ontario government set up a transition council to establish the College of Early Childhood Educators, a self-regulating professional body. Members of the college will be required to meet entry standards and continuing competence in order to be licensed with the college. It is anticipated that certification and licensing with the college will be required in regulated early childhood settings (Ministry of Children and Youth Services, 2005; Government of Ontario, 2007).

Government Recognition of Credentials

Governments may issue credentials to graduates from ECE certificate, diploma, and degree programs. Credentials can by issued by the government, as a licence or classification, or they may be issued by a professional organization, as **voluntary recognition** or certification (Bertrand & Michals, 2006):

- In British Columbia, early childhood educators are required to have a government licence to be recognized as qualified staff in a regulated child care centre or preschool. To be eligible for the licence to practise, early childhood educators must have an ECE academic qualification and documented work experience.
- In Alberta, the Day Care Staff Qualifications Office manages the day care certification process: reviewing training and determining level of certificate based on the training level.
- In Saskatchewan, early childhood educators must apply to Saskatchewan Learning (provincial education department for certification).
- Manitoba Child Day Care classifies all early childhood educators who work in licensed child care centres.
- The P.E.I. Child Care Facilities Board is responsible for determining the qualifications of staff who work in licensed child care/early childhood education programs and issuing supervisor's and staff certificates.

EARLY CHILDHOOD EDUCATORS AND PROFESSIONAL DEVELOPMENT

Early childhood educators who bring a depth of knowledge about early child development and parenting, and the programs that can support both, are ready to be active participants in early childhood learning organizations. Early childhood programs can be learning organizations that challenge early childhood educators to participate in a cycle of continuous learning about young children, their families, and the kinds of environments that benefit them.

Effective learning organizations invest in the core infrastructure, network available resources and ingenuity, focus on the core dynamics, and monitor the outcomes. An early childhood program that actively promotes a learning organization can leverage the individual knowledge and expertise of early childhood educators. Training, education, and professional development can increase the personal mastery and depth of knowledge that individual early childhood educators are able to contribute to a learning organization.

The early childhood work force can use professional development and education to strengthen the capacity of early childhood programs to be dynamic learning organizations. An early childhood program workplace can be a learning organization that challenges practice and welcomes debate. Professional growth comes from continuing to ask the questions and explore answers. Early childhood educators who take on the challenge will probably find their work more rewarding and satisfying. As an individual early childhood educator, you can use professional development and further professional education to increase your knowledge base.

KEY TERMS

certification
code of ethics
collaborative learning
constructive discussion

credential
equivalency validation
self-governance
voluntary recognition

REFLECTION QUESTIONS

1. Think about the following questions:

   - What does school readiness really mean?
   - What makes for a high-quality learning experience for a three- or four-year-old? What about a one-year-old?
   - Why don't many early childhood programs work together as well as they could?
   - How can parents be a more integral part of daily programs?

   How might these questions be raised for discussion among early childhood educators working together in a program?

2. Do you expect to be working in the early childhood sector in five years after graduation? Why or why not?

FOR MORE INFORMATION

1. *Society for Organizational Learning.* Dr. Peter Senge is the founding chairperson for the Society for Organizational Learning. It is a global network of communities, institutions, and regions that are committed to applying the principles of Senge's vision on learning organizations.

   www.solonline.org/

2. The *Thomson Nelson ECE Resource Centre* is intended to enhance the teaching and learning experience for both instructors and students. The website provides extensive and helpful resources in many different criteria related to early childhood education.

   www.ece.nelson.com

ADVOCATING FOR CHILDREN, FAMILIES, AND COMMUNITIES

Kerry McCuaig

Delivery of early childhood services in Canada (outside Quebec) does not meet the needs of children, families, or communities. There are not enough programs. Rural and remote communities, children with special needs, and families with non-traditional work hours are woefully underserved. High costs form another barrier. Overall quality is mediocre, unable to support children's optimal early development and learning. There is no unifying policy or funding framework for early childhood. Services streams operate in isolation of one another, with no supporting infrastructure for resource, curriculum, and human resources development or planning, monitoring, or evaluation.

Today if a government wants to invest in the early years, it confronts the competing demands of the child care, kindergarten, and parenting support sectors. Transforming this desperate patchwork into a cohesive system offers many advantages. Program consolidation would create a foundation for effective public funding.

A single program—delivered by a consistent set of early childhood professionals, with the same expectations—eliminates the many disruptions that young children confront as they move from caregiver to kindergarten and onto the next caregiver. We recognize that so many changes are unsettling to a child in Grade 4, yet this is a typical day for a kindergarten-aged child. A single program offers ready access to parenting resources.

Some communities are not waiting for senior governments to act and have taken steps to integrate local services, often establishing a working model and then inviting others to replicate their efforts or join in. Some sites, for example, have begun by integrating a few kindergarten classes with child care and parenting programs before adding more rooms. Others have proceeded on a school or community-wide basis. Each community needs to determine the scale that best meets their readiness.

Source: Interview with Kerry McCuaig. Better Child Care Education/Toronto First Duty.

Chapter Objectives

This chapter will:

1. Describe specific actions to put what we know about early childhood education into action for young children, their families, and their communities.
2. Identify personal and collective approaches to advocating for early childhood programs and its work force.
3. Recognize the role of early childhood organizations and broader coalitions in advocating for early childhood programs.
4. Evaluate strategies for building an early childhood system that is responsive to children, families, and communities.

Early childhood programs can make a difference to children, strengthen families, and transform communities. Early childhood educators can use their knowledge and professional experience to advocate for early childhood programs that are high quality and available to young children and their families. In the *Early Years Study 2: Putting Science Into Action* (McCain et al., 2007), the Council for Early Child Development outlines an action plan to build an early childhood system. It is adapted in this chapter to present an action plan for early childhood educators.[1]

The action plan is founded on evidence that:

- Infancy and early childhood is the first and most critical phase of human growth; a child's earliest experiences shape brain development. Genes interact with experiences creating a dynamic that affects lifelong health, learning, and behaviour.
- Early childhood programs benefit children, parents, communities, and society through improved outcomes and enhanced quality of life for children. Effective programs are holistic, comprehensive, flexible, high quality, and supported by a shared vision, a common framework, and sufficient resources.
- Neighbourhood schools are the natural location for quality early childhood centres in every community—centres that involve children, parents, and the community; that revolve around the power of play; that provide full-time, full-year options, nutrition, links to home-based and specialized services, and are staffed by a skilled, competent, and fairly compensated work force.
- Community early child development reporting tracks progress and provides knowledge to communities and accountability for social investments in an early childhood system.
- Investing in early childhood is *boldly* investing in Canada's future.

HARNESS THE EVIDENCE

Early experiences play a significant role in children's social, emotional, intellectual, and physical development. Early childhood educators can accurately and passionately convey the findings from neuroscience and developmental research, economic analyses, and relevant studies of academic achievement, health, and behaviour to policymakers and the public.

The importance of early child development may seem obvious based on the synthesis of knowledge across disciplines. Nevertheless, many individuals still question whether the early years really have a profound effect on lifelong learning, behaviour, and health—and whether investments in early childhood programs are beneficial to young children.

The new frameworks of understanding about early child development synthesize research findings from developmental psychology, epidemiology, neuroscience, and education (Mustard, 2002). We also need stronger institution capabilities to build linkages among the social and biological sciences and to transfer the integrated knowledge into everyday use. The significance of brain development in early childhood and its implications for the future health and stability of a globalized world needs to become popularized.

Ensuring optimal outcomes in children's early development should be of interest to all families, communities, and governments. It is the core business of early childhood

---

1. M. McCain, F., Mustard, and S. Shanker (2007), Chapter 1, *Early Years Study 2*. Toronto: Council for Early Child Development. Adapted with permission.

educators. It is based on knowledge about early child development that is being constantly refreshed and growing in size and complexity. The challenge is to make it accessible and available to the public without compromising the rigours of science and professional practice.

Keep Up to Date

Early childhood educators can be powerful messengers, but the message has to be accurate and current. Fortunately, new technology and the Internet shorten the distance between new research findings and directions and their appearance in professional material and popular publications. The Internet provides reliable sources and practical applications for wide audiences.

The following are four examples of reliable Canadian resources that use the Internet and multimedia technology to "harness the evidence" about early childhood:

- *The Science of Early Child Development* (see www.scienceofecd.com) is a resource curriculum that uses multimedia and interactivity to make research come "alive." The resource consists of five modules—developmental health, brain development, genetics and experience, coping and competence, and communicating and learning. It was created by the Early Childhood Education program at Red River College in partnership with Founders' Network and the Atkinson Centre for Society and Child Development at the University of Toronto. It is a powerful tool for professors and trainers, and for early childhood educators, advocates, and administrators.

- The *Encyclopedia on Early Childhood Development* (see www.excellence-earlychildhood.ca/home.asp?lang=EN) is produced by the Centre for Excellence in Early Childhood Development and funded by the Public Health Agency of Canada. It is a source for policymakers, planners, and service providers offering a compendium of texts written by leading experts on topics related to the social and emotional development of young children, from conception to age five. A simplified synthesis of topics provides key knowledge to practitioners and parents, answering why the topic is important, what is the most up-to-date knowledge about it, and what can be done to improve services, policies, and research.

- The *ECD Review* (see www.earlychilddevelopment.ca) provides a review of current early child development articles, reports, events, and book reviews maintained by the Council for Early Child Development. It is an eclectic selection of material from Canada and elsewhere that is a quick take on what is new in the science, policy, and practice of early childhood.

- *Early Childhood Education and Care in Canada* (see www.childcarecanada.org) provides cross-Canada data and information on early childhood programs and policies together with associated demographic information. In particular, detailed provincial/territorial profiles on regulated child care include numbers of spaces, standards and regulations, monitoring, funding, history, and regular developments. There is also specific information on services for children with special needs and Aboriginal early childhood programs. It is the only overview of the early childhood sector available in Canada. New data are compared to data in earlier editions (since 1992) to reveal trends in early childhood programs over the past 15 years.

The Internet has opened up opportunities for early childhood educators to stay current with research developments.

Share, Apply, and Act on the Science of Early Child Development

Early childhood educators who understand what we know about early child development can demonstrate how to put that knowledge into action in their daily practice. They become models of how to use the knowledge to set up environments and interactions with children that nurture and stimulate all areas of development. They also demonstrate how to communicate respectfully with parents and other family members.

The science of early childhood development needs to be shared and is an appropriate topic for gatherings from conferences and boardrooms to community meetings and book clubs. Early childhood educators who are knowledgeable and keep abreast of new research and practices are able to provide access to information and guide discussions with parents and others in the community. Some possibilities include:

- Giving workshops and presentations to practitioners' groups, including teachers, other early childhood educators, family physicians, and those working in public health, child welfare, and social services.

- Partnering with local high schools to support inclusion of early child development in biology and family life courses.
- Finding opportunities to work with the media to improve the quality of information in electronic and print publications.

Packaging the Message

Mechanisms to carry the message about early childhood need to balance the rigours of the science with accessible formats. Dissemination strategies must also recognize the different applications of the science and the practice for educators, policymakers, practitioners, parents, and the public.

Messages about mothers working, early brain development, and school readiness have bombarded the public media over the past decade (McCain et al., 2007; Bales, 2005; Shonkoff & Phillips, 2000; OECD, 2006). Often the message is polarizing (e.g., mothers at home versus mothers at work) or leads to the schoolification or pathologization of early childhood (OECD, 2006), as discussed in Chapter 1. Schoolification refers to the downward extension of school expectations into early childhood—getting children ready for school translates into early academics. Pathologization of childhood refers to children as "problems" waiting to be found and needing to be fixed.

Innovations

MESSAGES TO FRAME DISCUSSIONS ABOUT EARLY CHILDHOOD PROGRAMS

Communication experts have suggested that we need to "reframe" the early childhood message to nurturance, community child, opportunity, community/child exchange, and the future. In fact, these messages move away from messages that are more directly related to the science. Are they more effective?

1. *Nurturance.* Young children need milk to grow strong bones and they need nurturance to feed optimal development. In order to develop and grow socially and intellectually, children need a stimulating environment that feeds their curiosity, consistent relationships that build their sense of security, and interactions with friends to learn how to get along with others.

2. *Community child.* Children come in contact with many people in many different settings as they grow. Parents may be a child's first teachers, but they aren't a child's only teachers. Child care providers, early childhood educators, teachers, doctors, neighbours, and coaches influence children as well. Children learn a lot in the early years. They learn respect for others, right

from wrong, and how to get along with each other. All the people they come in contact with help influence this learning. Parents who provide security, early childhood educators and teachers who encourage curiosity, coaches who teach them how to get along with others, and counsellors who help them recognize right from wrong—all these people connect with children in ways that influence their long-term development.

3. *Opportunity*. Parents want to provide the best for their children. Very young children need more than love to develop intellectually, socially, and emotionally. They need stimulation. Some communities can afford quality early childhood programs while others may not have that opportunity. It is only fair that all children, regardless of income or family circumstances, have the best possible opportunity to achieve. That means supporting quality early childhood programs for all children, basic health care, and community supports like good libraries, playgrounds, parenting coaches, and programs for new parents.

4. *Child/community exchange*. Children cost their families and communities a great deal when they are young, but they give back even more, in both emotional and material support, down the road. Children bring joy to the home and pride to the community, they provide security in old age, and they carry forward our dreams. Those who nurture children perform an important social function and should be celebrated. Children should be the focus of community sharing.

5. *Future*. Children are our future—the future of families, communities, and the nation. They are us, and we must do all we can to give them the hearts, minds, and souls they will need to carry our work forward and to make the world a better place. When we give them the nurturance they need to grow, the experiences they need to discover, and the friends and teachers they need to expand their horizons, we shape the future.

Sources: Shonkoff & Phillips, 2000; Bales, 2005; National Scientific Council on the Developing Child, 2007.

FOSTERING CONNECTIONS WITH AND BETWEEN COMMUNITIES

Communities are important. They are where families live, practitioners work, and public policy hits the road and comes to life. Communities benefit from strong early childhood programs. Good early childhood programs, schools, and services build vibrant communities that draw knowledge workers.

Public spaces in neighbourhoods that are child-friendly build social capital.

Each community is unique and has diverse cultural, linguistic, and socioeconomic characteristics. Each has its own array of challenges and assets, making a "one-size fits all" approach to early childhood programming a missed chance to effectively match resources with local needs. Yet communities share common challenges and opportunities. Exchanges among communities build energy, expertise, and accelerate action.

A community's capacity for early childhood includes all its resources that are or should be linked with early child development programs—schools, child care programs, family support, hospitals and other health services, social services, recreational programs, libraries, colleges and universities, and so on. Communities that come together to build on their strengths create social capital. Universal touch points can be used within communities to connect families with young children to neighbourhood resources in an effort to develop and expand their social networks.

Ensuring quality programming and integrating various programs into an accessible and parent-friendly system will need to involve a number of community and government players, taking an incremental approach and building on progress over time. It takes time for people to understand why an integrated system for early childhood is needed and how it can be organized.

Building Community Networks

As discussed in Chapter 1, raising the social capital of communities raises social cohesion—the level of trust and sharing, a recognition that we are all responsible in some sense for each other, and that we all share a responsibility for the next generation. Socially cohesive neighbourhoods are better places to live, characterized by less crime and isolation, more public and community spaces, and greater volunteerism and intergenerational reciprocity. There is also some evidence that regions with a large measure of social cohesion tend to be stronger and better able to cope with the challenge of changing economic and social pressures.

Community-driven initiatives do make a difference and local leadership and flexibility are essential to respond to diverse geographic, cultural, and ethnic realities. But the playing field between communities is not level. Timely and effective interventions by governments are essential if regional and ethno-cultural inequities are to be addressed.

Early childhood and other community development measures support communities learning about what does and doesn't work in their neighbourhoods and allows them to compare results with others.

INFLUENCE PUBLIC POLICY

The research evidence related to what we now know about early experienced-based brain development on later human development and the returns on investment in early development have significant implications for the way governments set policies and allocate their resources.

Community experience, combined with scientific evidence, equips decision makers with the tools needed to set policies and allocate resources.

How new investments, policies, and programs are introduced is equally important to communities. Piecemeal actions do not work. New resources for one early childhood stream can create competition between programs. In an effort to leave their mark, some governments have wiped out existing programs to create their own new ones. Imposed planning and network models can destabilize those that have been operating effectively. The mobilization of communities to accept new initiatives, only to have the proposal downsized or withdrawn, creates fatigue and apathy. These policy blunders validate the *Early Years Study* premise that consolidating the early years assets of communities

 ## Beyond Our Borders

EXPERIMENTS WITH COMMUNITY-BASED EARLY CHILDHOOD INITIATIVES

Comprehensive early childhood initiatives in the United States and the United Kingdom hold great promise to expand supports for children and families and improve the delivery of existing services, but only if they are supported by public policies that make adequate investments, maintain consistent standards, and sustain investments in multiple strategies to support children and families. Experimentation with community-based initiatives designed to respond to local needs for early childhood programs has underlined the need for strong public policies.

"With sufficient resources, a clear vision, collaborative leadership and reasonable expectations, state-driven community planning initiatives are a strategy that can make a difference for children and families" (Children's Defense Fund, 2002, p. 2).

Source: Children's Defense Fund, 2002, Bringing It Together: State-Driven Early Childhood Initiatives, *p. 2.*

create both social cohesion and a base for new investments. In this scenario, there are no winners and losers, only more and better programming for families.

Role of Local Governments

Depending on the jurisdiction, local governments may be excluded from a mandated role in early childhood service provision. Nevertheless, regional authorities can be strong and effective partners, in both advocating for children with higher levels of government and using their powers to remove barriers and support creative community initiatives. There is a consensus between business and local government regarding infrastructure investment in transportation, housing, and energy efficiencies. Urban renewal and expansion is an opportunity to link capital and social development. Children's programs must be included when planning infrastructure needs. School boards, municipalities, and community agencies can lay the groundwork for more effective program delivery for young children and families.

Professional Organizations and Coalitions

Canadian early childhood organizations and associations at the national, provincial/ territorial, and local levels support the early childhood work force and advocate for its recognition. As discussed in Chapter 9, these organizations are related to professionalism and a range of professional education and development activities. They can also have a significant role in advocating for public policies that promote an early childhood system that is grounded in quality—for children, their families, and the early childhood workforce.

Early childhood organizations and **coalitions** with those in related sectors can contribute to public policies for an early childhood system. But all too often, sector protectionism conspires to block a consensus on how to pull together piecemeal and underfunded programs into a coherent and comprehensive system of early childhood programs. Sometimes coalitions that cross sectors and share a common vision can broker agreement around a common policy agenda.

The Canadian Child Care Advocacy Association (CCAAC) is a coalition of advocates working together for the right of all children to access a quality child care system supported by public funding. It includes a board of directors representing provinces and territories and representatives from sectors that support universal child care. Its Council of Child Care Advocates was established to bring together the provincial/ territorial board members and sectoral representatives from the CCAAC's partners in the social justice movement. The sectoral representatives bring voices from families and parents, the labour movement, the anti-poverty movement, the disability movement, the immigrant and visible minority community, and other groups. The role of the Council of Child Care Advocates is to advise the CCAAC on **advocacy** policies, strategies, and campaigns.

Changing Public Policy

Canada's current public policy mix on early childhood programs (outlined in Chapter 2) is piecemeal and inadequate in responding to the needs of young children and their families (OECD, 2004; Friendly & Beach, 2005; McCain et al., 2007). Influencing new public policy is central to establishing a stable early childhood system. Here are some guidelines:

1. Provide policymakers and politicians with evidence and current science policy tools, and relevant contacts.
2. Establish a long-term vision and broad public policy agenda to improve early child development.
3. Promote interdepartmental responsibility for early child development and parenting programs. Cross-departmental collaboration from finance, health, education, and social services is essential.
4. Recommend public investment, private support, and community incentives to promote the establishment of a system of early child development and parenting programs. Investments in early child development should be placed in a public policy structure that embraces all sectors that relate to human development, including health, education, and community services. A greater proportion of public investment is needed at the front end of human development—before expensive remedial services are needed.

Code Blue (see www.buildchildcare.ca/background/aboutcodeblue) is a Canada-wide campaign to build a comprehensive pan-Canadian child care system. The campaign brings together national, provincial, and territorial child care organizations, labour, women's, and social justice groups, along with Canadians from all walks of life.

Code Blue works with federal, provincial, territorial and local elected officials, coalition partners, families, and the child care community. Its goal is to build a universal, inclusive, comprehensive, high-quality, community-based child care system that is accessible and provides early learning and development opportunities for all children.

Code Blue is campaigning for:

- Restored multi-year federal funding so the provinces and territories can begin building child care systems.
- Federal child care legislation that lays out the principles of a pan-Canadian child care system.
- Effective income supports for families, in addition to quality child care.
- Dedicated capital transfers for community-based child care services.

CULTIVATE LEADERS

Key influencers can provide critical leadership and motivation in mobilizing societies to raise the awareness of, and investment in, early childhood programs. Dynamic leaders take on social problems by bringing together people and resources to work towards a shared vision and to create viable solutions for their community. They catapult issues into the public realm and galvanize support. Leadership comes from different places and includes mayors, educators, health practitioners, church officials, businesspeople, and parents themselves. Leaders who are influential and who do not have a direct self-interest are often most effective in carrying the message forward.

Innovations

CANADIAN LEADERS SPEAKING OUT FOR EARLY CHILD DEVELOPMENT

David Dodge is an economist and Governor of the Bank of Canada. His position has given him considerable insight into the link between economic and human development:

> [W]ith a small cohort of children to replace those retiring over the next two decades, it is more important than ever that the human capital of these children be developed as fully as possible if we are to raise the productivity of a future smaller labour force.

Charles Coffey is the former executive vice-president of government relations for RBC Financial Group:

> More business leaders must step up to the plate when it comes to investing in the future generations—business leaders need to occupy seats at early childhood forums. They need to hear and discuss research findings—the business case. They need to hear . . . that employers increasingly find the availability of good early childhood programs is critical to the recruitment and retention of parent employees.

Thomas d'Aquino is chief executive and president of the Canadian Council of Chief Executives. His ten-point plan to strengthen Canada's economic base starts with families and communities:

> If Canada is to succeed in forging a creative economy, we cannot afford to waste the talents of a single Canadian. In this context, Canada needs to reduce the financial burden of raising children and preparing them for productive lives as global citizens. The federal government should start by reducing the steep clawback provisions of the Canada Child Tax Benefit that penalize families with modest incomes and by providing new support for child care. . . .

In 1997, Quebec cabinet minister Pauline Mourais convinced her cabinet colleagues to adopt a bold new family policy with $5-per-day children's centres at its core. These centres serve 65 percent of children up to age four and are an established part of Quebec's social infrastructure:

> I took a chance. Don't wait for every detail to be in place before moving ahead.

Roy Romanow is the former premier of Saskatchewan and chair of the Royal Commission on the Future of Health Care in Canada (Romanow Report, 2000–2002) that investigated the sustainability of universal health care in

Canada. He uses his stature to popularize the need for early childhood programs to improve health outcomes:

> Good early learning and developmental supports are essential to improving all of the so-called "determinants of well-being" and a life well-lived.

The Honourable John Godfrey chaired many federal posts but has made the welfare of children central to whatever portfolio he has held. In 1999 he proposed the development of an early childhood care and education program as a national project:

> The goal of that National Project would be to make Canada the best country in the world for the care and nurturing of young children. If we could say that Canada had the best prenatal programs, the lowest rates of child abuse, and the best early childhood care and education programs, all of which culminated in the best rates of school readiness . . . not only will we reduce child poverty, we will also dramatically improve literacy rates, creating a solid base for future economic growth, and for employment success in the new economy.

Ted Whitehead is the head of the Canadian Association of Principals:

> It is to our collective advantage to promote the understanding of early brain development research ... and to ensure the values of early child development become embraced as an integral component of the education of every child, just as traditional schools are currently.

Source: McCain et al., 2007. Early years study 2: Putting science into action. Toronto: Council for Early Child Development.

Promote Champions for Early Childhood Programs

Many policymakers and influencers acknowledge the problem of Canada's scattered approach to early child development programs, but it remains a marginal issue without significant public agreement about how best to proceed.

Business needs to understand that short- to long-term measures to reduce disparity by enhancing early childhood development are an effective business strategy. Failure to come to terms with this issue not only affects the bottom line; it can move countries to the end of the line.

Business is a powerful sector, with the capacity to influence government policy and public opinion. History has proven time and time again that shifts or changes in public policy don't usually *take off* until the business community rallies behind them.

But business is not the only important player. Public institutions such as health and education are reluctant to release their grip on the public purse. Yet the sustainability of valued public programs such as education and health are dependent on healthy child development. It is therefore in the self-interest of these sectors to provide leadership promoting a comprehensive approach to early childhood development, and to cooperate in breaking down the barriers that stand in the way of a comprehensive systems approach.

Early childhood leaders can be central in drawing together and informing leaders from other sectors. Knowledge and professional wisdom are needed to make the compelling case for an early childhood system and convince potential leaders that this is not a marginal issue but one that is central to a prosperous and just society (McCain et al., 2007). Possible actions include:

1. Involve elected officials or high-profile personalities who are able to speak publicly about the benefits of early childhood development and program integration. Perhaps start by inviting them to speak at annual general meetings or neighbourhood events. Be sure to invite participants from all political parties.
2. Look for parent leaders and involve them from the start. Parents of young children are busy people coping with multiple demands. But they are also some of the most effective spokespeople for early childhood programs. They have passion and know what a difference a good program makes to their daily lives.
3. Partner with the business, union, and voluntary sectors to raise awareness and understanding about the early child development knowledge framework.
4. Help communities identify and involve "social entrepreneurs"—dynamic leaders in their communities who can mobilize people and resources to work towards an early childhood system.
5. Work closely with interested media, providing background materials and leads on emerging stories. Newspaper columnists and electronic media commentators who become interested in and knowledgeable about the early childhood agenda become champions who can access a broader audience.

MONITOR RESULTS

Communities need to know how their children are doing and if they are making a difference in early child development outcomes. By measuring, analyzing, and interpreting early child development and community-level data and information, communities can effect change and reduce gaps among different groups of children. Close monitoring is necessary to ensure all children have the opportunities to meet their full potential.

We now have the capability to measure how well young children are doing at various stages of their development. Birth outcomes, preschool developmental tools, and the Early Development Instrument (EDI), a teacher report of children's readiness for school learning (see Chapter 3), provide child outcome data that can be combined with other community-level information about resources and neighbourhood characteristics.

Population data and longitudinal studies, such as the National Longitudinal Survey of Children and Youth in Canada or the British Cohort Studies, provide population-level data that is useful to track trends and consider local data in a larger context.

Data collection and analysis need to be properly resourced. Poor data is worse than no data. While no data means no problem and no action, poor data creates big problems and bad actions.

Communities need to know how their children are doing and if community environments are making a difference in early child development outcomes. By measuring, analyzing, and interpreting community-level information, communities can effect change and reduce gaps among different groups of children. Data collection and monitoring provides information so agencies can avoid duplication, provide services more effectively, and utilize the specialties of each partner to the greatest effect.

Close monitoring is necessary to ensure that all children have the opportunities to meet their full potential, and to measure how well young children are doing at various stages of their development. Birth outcomes, preschool developmental tools, and the EDI provide child outcome data that can be combined with other community-level information about resources and neighbourhood characteristics. Population data and longitudinal studies provide population-level data that are useful to track trends and consider local data in a larger context. Community data can be used to track and create change. Quality data collection and reporting is important to public accountability and building trust. The public is prepared to support early childhood initiatives but they need to be assured that funding is producing the intended affects.

Quality matters. Small children cannot be compensated for the opportunities lost to a poor program. Programs must be monitored. It is important to track both program quality and children's progress. Indicators able to demonstrate that early childhood programs are having a positive impact on children's development will enhance support for public investments. Assessment must be scientifically based and free from immediate political demands. Adopting the same quality monitoring instruments allows comparisons and provides consistent messages to parents.

Local primary schools can be excellent locations for early childhood programs.

Regular transparent evaluation processes involving all participants are indispensable tools. They reflect both successes and challenges and document progress for participants. Staff is particularly encouraged when improved outcomes for clients can be demonstrated.

Service providers must commit to program quality. Poor programs compromise children's futures and alienate parents and the public. If insufficient resources make this impossible, operators and staff have an obligation to take decisive action to inform the public.

Join Up Existing Early Childhood Programs

Reorganizing existing early childhood and family support services is indispensable to the success of new public policy initiatives and an early childhood system. Increased investments in early childhood development are unlikely to fulfill their potential under the current service delivery status quo. Child care, family support programs, and kindergarten urgently request increases from governments and other funders to expand the quantity and quality of available services. The price for such increased resources for these programs could be reduced if early childhood programs moved from independent and overlapping services toward a seamless system (Gallagher et al., 2004).

Improved communication and coordination between sectors is a starting point, but systemic change comes through **service integration** (McCain et al., 2007). Integrating early childhood programs puts science into action in communities for children. Where successful early childhood service systems exist, they are integrated.

There is growing consensus about what an ideal comprehensive early childhood system would look like. The *Early Years Study* (McCain & Mustard, 1999, p. 20) recommended "a first 'tier' program for early child development, as important as the elementary and secondary school system and the post-secondary education system. The system should consist of community-based centres operating at the local level and linked to local schools within a provincial framework."

Research indicates that it is harder to integrate than start new programs (Corter et al., 2006). Different cultures, identities, professional training, and so forth, are real. Still, all early childhood services have as their core mandate the well-being of children and families. This approach, fuelled by the scientific evidence, is the driver behind integration. Integration needs to happen on a system level, but progress can be made neighbourhood by neighbourhood, program by program.

Service integration is not a cost-saving exercise. It is designed to use existing resources more effectively to the benefit of children and their families. It also provides a solid foundation for new investments. Early childhood programs must be holistic and available and include the core functions of child development, nonparental care, and parenting involvement and support. Specialized services are most effective when wrapped around a core system of universally accessible early childhood and parenting centres. The benefits for children who are at risk because of social or developmental delays are limited if problems are not identified until after they have become biologically embedded or if there is no site to deliver the interventions.

At the beginning stages, it is important to allow sufficient time for all partners to thoroughly understand their community, its needs, and the work of the various agencies. This information lays the groundwork for a common vision. As such, integration is both a process and a product. Mutual trust, willingness, and commitment of the partners are the most important drivers of successful service integration. Once these are in place, many challenges can be overcome.

Early childhood service integration involves a transformation of culture, methodologies, and schedules. Making change requires leadership. At the program level, this involves vision, charisma, and also decision-making power. In short, not only the agreement, but the time and enthusiasm of participating leaders are necessary.

Agencies justifiably seek increased funding to improve service quality and access, but new funding must be accompanied by reorganization. Agencies, users, professionals, and unions must be consulted, but they also have a responsibility to break down barriers to integration.

Private funders can ensure their allocations support a comprehensive approach to service delivery rather than fostering fragmentation.

Each group has a similar mission: to help children (most often with special needs or limited opportunities) master the skills and knowledge needed to adapt effectively to kindergarten at age five. Each group has its own history and has developed more or less independently of the others. Because the groups developed independently, they have overlapping personnel preparation programs, evaluation efforts, and data systems.

First Duty is a program delivery model that is constructed by joining up existing early childhood programs (Corter et al., 2006). The First Duty framework consists of five core elements: governance, access, early learning environments, early childhood staff, and parent participation. Specific program indicators and benchmarks that move from coexistence to integration are included in the Indicators of Change, a tool that monitors the progression of integration across the five elements. It is described in the Innovations box on pages 262–263.

Local Governance

A local governance structure is responsible for program policies, resource allocation, service planning and monitoring, and human resource decisions. Integrated local governance brings together community partners: schools, child care, family support, health, and other specialized services into a single governing body, responsible for financial, human resource, and operational/program decisions.

Integrated decision-making creates a single entity that provides opportunities for joint planning, enables the creation of a comprehensive system at the local level, and reduces service duplication/gaps. By planning together, service providers can efficiently use resources to do what makes sense for the families and children in the community.

To be sustainable, changes are required as to who makes decisions and how they're made. They must be made by consensus according to a bigger plan, rather than arbitrarily. Staff persons at all levels need to be engaged in the process. Leadership comes from the top down (direction-policies, legislation, etc.), but also from the bottom up (front-line staff taking on new joint initiatives).

Who should be at the table? Leading representatives of the core partners—child care, school, and family supports, as well as other partners working with children and families in the community. What should you look for? Decision makers—those with commitment, expertise, and the ability to influence others.

Innovations

TORONTO FIRST DUTY INDICATORS OF CHANGE

Toronto First Duty set out to create a new integrated early childhood service delivery system. The First Duty *Indicators of Change* is a management tool that guides, tracks, and assesses the progress a site is making towards the integration of programs (child care, early childhood education, family support programs, and kindergarten) that are linked to early intervention, community and public health, and social services.

A unique set of program indicators define specific activities and practice for each of the key elements (local governance, seamless access, early learning environment, staff team, and parent participation). A total of 19 indicators track the progress that First Duty sites are making towards implementing the five core elements.

SUMMARY OF KEY ELEMENTS AND INDICATORS

1. Local Governance

   A local governance structure is responsible for program policies, resource allocation, service planning and monitoring, and human resource decisions.

Indicator 1.1	Program mandate, policy, and practices
Indicator 1.2	Service planning and monitoring
Indicator 1.3	Allocation of financial resources
Indicator 1.4	Human resources

2. Seamless Access

   Seamless access is available to an expanded and comprehensive early learning and care program, providing a continuum of supports and services to all families and young children prenatally to six years.

Indicator 2.1	Capacity
Indicator 2.2	Child care provision and affordability
Indicator 2.3	Intake, enrollment, and attendance

3. Learning Environment

   High-quality learning environments combine learning expectations, activities, and routines from existing kindergarten, early childhood education/child care, and parenting/family support programs.

Indicator 3.1	Curriculum framework and pedagogical approach
Indicator 3.2	Daily routines and schedules

Indicator 3.3   Use of space

Indicator 3.4   Children's development and progress

Indicator 3.5   Program quality

4. Early Childhood Staff Team

Develop an early childhood staff team that works together to deliver and achieve program goals.

Indicator 4.1   Program planning and implementation

Indicator 4.2   Behaviour guidance/child management

Indicator 4.3   Roles and responsibilities

Indicator 4.4   Staff development

5. Parent Participation

Parent participation in children's early learning and development should be increased through direct involvement in programs, planning, and decision-making.

Indicator 5.1   Parent input and participation in programs

Indicator 5.2   Parenting capacity

Indicator 5.3   Relationships with families

Benchmarks

For each of the program indicators, benchmarks track progress along a continuum of coexistence to coordination, collaboration, and integration. The benchmarks are organized on a five-point scale from 1 (coexistence) to 5 (integration). They set out the details of the Toronto First Duty vision and outline the predicted, incremental steps that move towards the goal of service integration.

Source: Bertrand et al., 2006. Evidence-based Understanding of Integrated Foundations for Early Childhood. Toronto: Atkinson Centre at OISE/UT.

Involve parents from the start. Look to child care boards and school parent councils for parent leaders. Preparation is required to build consensus—getting acquainted, setting goals, and mapping your community are starting points.

Seamless Access

Seamless access is available to an expanded and comprehensive early learning and care program, providing a continuum of supports and services to all families and young children, prenatally to six years.

The goal of seamless access is to provide a common program for all children up to age six and their families, regardless of the parents' work, family, or socioeconomic status. Services will be responsive to children with special needs and to the community's culture. Families will be linked to early intervention, community health, and social services, as required.

It may seem easier to address service gaps by starting new programs rather than joining existing services and activities, but research indicates it is less effective and adds to the existing patchwork. Often the advent of new programs creates destabilization in others. Integration maps a plan to capture all a community's existing early childhood service assets by blending them into a single program with a common mandate.

Early Learning Environment

High-quality learning environments combine learning expectations, activities, and routines from existing kindergarten, early childhood education/child care, and parenting/family support programs.

Children's learning environment is built on the physical setup, activities, routines, and interactions that are offered within their early learning programs. These are based on specific values, approaches, and sets of expectations that are established to better support children's learning.

The learning environment is where children and families experience the integrated program. Linking the activities provided by the partners and developing a common pedagogical approach provides a consistent learning and care environment for children and more accessible entry for parents. A joint commitment to the application of effective practices enhances quality and therefore children's developmental opportunities.

Integrated early childhood programs bring together the goals, values, and expectations of the three core services in a child's life to create a secure and consistent environment that accommodates his or her individual learning needs, while supporting parents in their parenting role.

Currently, early childhood service programs work in parallel ways, creating a huge number of transitions for young children. This number of transitions would not be considered acceptable for children in the older grades. Program approaches and philosophies are often different and create inconsistencies that reduce their positive impact in the lives of children and their families.

When early childhood services set up common goals and agree on common approaches, professionals can extract the best practices from each sector and create a program where positive impact is magnified.

Early Childhood Staff Team

Develop an **early childhood staff team** that works together to deliver and achieve program goals. Currently, programs often work within their own program boundaries even when they are located in the same building. They share limited information with each other, if they share at all. Professionals who work with children and families are often limited by their program resources and mandate when they are trying to respond to changing family needs.

The core staff team in integrated early childhood programs includes kindergarten teachers, early childhood educators, parenting workers or facilitators, as well as educational assistants and early childhood assistants. In addition, the core team works with the support of professionals who provide specialized services within each community (e.g., cultural interpreters, nurses, resource teachers, social workers, etc.).

Working as one team allows members to share knowledge, resources, expertise and information to create a seamless program continuum. Program goals, expectations, and new strategies can be developed to further support children and families and to provide greater flexibility.

The process of bringing diverse professionals and individuals is greatly facilitated when there is a certain structure in place that supports the team and when clear common goals are established. We all need to know *why* we are coming together (identify benefits of collaboration), establish common goals, and clarify roles and responsibilities.

Both research and our own experience show us that when people work together the results are always greater than the sum of the individual efforts. More can be accomplished together.

Staff members need to know that when they start working more closely with their multidisciplinary team their efforts will be supported by their managers and supervisors, and opportunities for getting to know each other will be provided as part of the process.

Parent Participation

Parent participation in children's early learning and development should be increased through direct involvement in programs, planning, and decision making.

From Coexistence to Integration

The integration of early childhood programs progresses along a continuum of coexistence to communication, coordination, collaboration, and integration (see Figure 10.1).

■ Figure 10.1

From Coexistence to Integration

Level 1: Coexistence

Level 1 describes practices in early childhood and family programs that are located in the same building or neighbourhood, but operate as separate and distinct services.

- Programs located in same building or neighbourhood
- Families make separate arrangements to participate

Examples:

- Child care, kindergarten, and family centre located in school building
- Public Health offers parenting programs in local school or child care facility

(continued Figure 10.1)

Level 2: Communication

Benchmark level 2 describes individual programs that share information with one another.

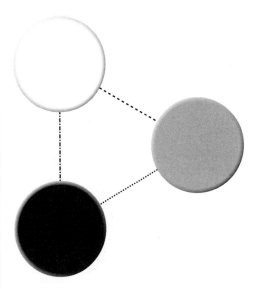

- Share program plans and behaviour guidance strategies
- Provide information to families about one another's programs

Examples:

- Child care ECEs and kindergarten teachers know one another and talk on a regular basis
- Regular exchange of newsletters among family resource programs and school
- Child care and family support program staff visit one another's centres
- Public health nurse provides information about neighbourhood early childhood programs to new parents

Level 3: Coordination

Level 3 indicates some specific joint activities that merge human resources, space, and/or materials to offer new, or enhance existing, program opportunities.

- Joint family night and field trips
- Public Health early identification takes place at school kindergarten registration
- Work together to reduce number of transitions the child makes in a day
- Provide joint events for families
- Bring children and parents/caregivers together for joint activity
- Children choose from activities across programs
- New program activity based on existing resources (e.g., staff, space, or equipment) and expertise

Examples:

- Regular joint storytime/music group
- Community kitchen
- Preschool curriculum planned by kindergarten teachers and ECD staff

(continued Figure 10.1)

Level 4: Collaboration

Benchmark level 4 describes an expansion of joint TFD activities and a clear influence on the operation of the original partner programs (kindergarten, child care, and family support).

- Common activities expanded
- Partner organizations influenced by collaborative activities
- Joint roles and responsibilities emerge

Examples:

- Child care centre and kindergarten class merge in common space with a joint staff team (ECE and kindergarten teacher)
- Family resource program offers ongoing early childhood education program with option of regular or occasional non-parental care

Level 5: Integration

Benchmark level 5 describes full integration of existing and expanded programs into an integrated early learning and care program delivery system within a defined neighbourhood or community.

- Single identity
- One curriculum and pedagogical approach
- Common program policies and practices
- Core staff team
- Seamless participation
- Full-time, half-day, regular part-time, and occasional
- Child- and family-focused
- All children and families can participate
- Single funding envelope

Example:

- Toronto First Duty

Source: Bertrand, 2007.

EARLY CHILDHOOD EDUCATORS AND ADVOCACY

This chapter lays out six strategic directions and a number of specific actions for early childhood educators to put what we know about early childhood development and programs into action for children and their families and communities. Early childhood educators understand how children develop and what environments best support that early development.

Early childhood educators have a unique perspective and opportunity to personally advocate for early childhood programs and for the early childhood work force as part of their daily practice. As you integrate theoretical frameworks, research findings, and your own daily experiences to guide your interactions with young children and their families, you are demonstrating why early childhood programs and early childhood educators are beneficial.

Early childhood educators can work together with each other and with other groups in organizations and coalitions that advocate for investments and policies for an early childhood system. A shared policy agenda that is bold in its scope but still practical within the immediate social, economic, and political context is more powerful in influencing public policy and investment than divergent calls for different kinds of actions. Professional organizations and coalitions provide a meeting place for early childhood educators to formulate policy proposals and evaluate new government initiatives. You can become part of the policy agenda dialogue by participating in organizations and coalitions, taking part in debates about options, and evaluating strategies for building an early childhood system that is responsible to children, families, and communities. When coalitions represent a broad spectrum of interested groups and sectors (including business groups, labour, social services, and the education and health sectors), the voices of early childhood educators contribute to maintaining a focus on what we know about early child development.

In advocating for an early childhood system that respects and adequately compensates an early childhood work force, early childhood educators have to become comfortable with the uncomfortable. You will need to speak about what is important to those who do not understand.

KEY TERMS

advocacy

coalition

early childhood staff team

service integration

REFLECTION QUESTIONS

1. Think about field placement or work experiences in early childhood programs. Can you name typical opportunities to share information about early child development with parents who are picking up their children?
2. Elissa is three years old and attending the Squire Early Childhood Program. Sophia (Elissa's mother) asks you if Elissa should attend a six-week summer school readiness program so that she is ready to start junior kindergarten in the fall. What is your response?
3. The local Rotary Club president is interested in supporting early childhood. He heard Dr. Fraser Mustard speak about the importance of early brain development at a seminar last year and is setting up a special committee to determine a specific early childhood program project. You are invited to participate on the committee and provide early childhood expertise. At the first meeting, there is enthusiasm for

a project to start up a neighbourhood health and developmental screening program on Saturday morning at the local shopping mall. You know that the local public health department works closely with family resource programs and child care centres in the area to identify children with developmental problems. What do you suggest to the committee?

4. The local child care coalition group is mounting a campaign to promote free use of space located in school buildings for child care programs. The provincial government has declared that kindergarten and Grades 1 to 3 class sizes will be limited to a maximum of 20 children. What is the potential conflict between these two initiatives?

5. Can good coordination become the enemy of an integrated early childhood system? How?

FOR MORE INFORMATION

1. *Toronto First Duty Early Childhood Services Integration Guide* is intended for community leaders, service providers, systems managers, and the front-line staff who deliver early childhood services in various fields, including child care, education, family support, and health and social services. It is assumed that those using the guide are already familiar with the benefits of early childhood service integration and want a primer on the process.

   www.toronto.ca/firstduty/guide/index.htm

2. Find out more about the integration of early childhood education and kindergarten programs in Canada and elsewhere from the *Integration Network Project*.

   www.inproject.ca

3. The Ontario Coalition for Better Child Care advocates for accessible, quality, nonprofit, early childhood programs and work environments. Several on-going projects support early childhood educators advocates.

   www.childcareontario.org

4. The *Thomson Nelson ECE Resource Centre* is intended to enhance the teaching and learning experience for both instructors and students. The website provides extensive and helpful resources in many different criteria related to early childhood education.

   www.ece.nelson.com

APPENDIX: DOWNTOWN SQUIRE EARLY CHILDHOOD CENTRE

SAMPLE 4.1 BYLAW 1

BE IT ENACTED AS A BYLAW OF <u>Downtown Squire Early Childhood Centre</u>
(hereinafter called "the Corporation") as follows:

1. HEAD OFFICE

As provided in the Letters Patent, the Head Office of the Corporation shall be at
<u>409 Front Street, Quesceville</u>, in the Province of Ontario.

2. MEMBERS

Members of the Corporation shall consist of

    (1)   the parent(s) or guardian(s) of a child admitted to the Corporation;

    (2)   community members who are reside in <u>Quesceville</u>.

Each member in good standing shall be entitled to one vote on each question arising at any special or general meeting of the members.

3. FEES

No dues or fees for membership shall be payable by members.

4. RESIGNATION & TERMINATION

A member may terminate her/his membership by tendering her/his resignation in writing to the board of directors. Family unit from which there is a child enrolled in the Corporation's child care centre shall automatically terminate upon such child ceasing to be enrolled in the child care centre.

5. ANNUAL MEETING

The annual meeting of the members shall be held at the head office of the Corporation or elsewhere in Ontario and at such time as the board of directors may designate but not more than fifteen (15) months after the last preceding annual meeting.

At the annual meetings there shall be presented a report of the board of directors on the affairs of the Corporation and the auditor's report thereof, and such other information or reports relating to the Corporation's affairs as the board of directors may determine.

6. GENERAL MEETING

A general meeting of the members of the Corporation may be called at any time by the board of directors or on the written requisition of not less than one-quarter (1/4) of the members of the Corporation. A requisition for a general meeting shall include a copy of any motion to be presented at such meeting. Within thirty (30) days of the receipt of such requisition the board of directors shall hold the meeting.

7. NOTICE

The Notice of the time and place of a meeting and the general nature of the business to be transacted thereat shall be delivered or mailed by prepaid post to each member and the auditor of the Corporation at least seven (7) days before the day on which the meeting is to be held, directed to such address as appears on the books of the Corporation, or, if no address is given therein, then to the last address known to the Secretary.

8. VOTING

At any meeting of members, each member shall be entitled to one vote and such right to vote may be exercised by a proxy for such member, duly appointed in writing.

9. ADJOURNMENTS

Any Corporation or Directors meeting may be adjourned at any time and from time to time and such business may be transacted at such adjourned meetings as might have been transacted at the original meeting from which such adjournment took place. No notices shall be required of any such adjournments. Such adjournments may be notwithstanding that no quorum is present.

10. QUORUM OF GENERAL MEETINGS

One-fifth (1/5) of the membership present in person shall constitute a quorum at any meeting of the members.

11. POWERS

The affairs of the Corporation shall be managed by a board of directors, which may exercise all such powers and do all such acts and things as the Corporation is allowed by its charter. The board of directors may appoint such agents and engage such employees as it shall deem necessary from time to time and such persons shall have such authority and shall perform such duties as shall be prescribed by the board of directors at the time of such appointment.

12. NUMBER OF DIRECTORS

The board of directors shall consist of eleven (11) directors as follows:

    (a) nine (9) of whom shall be members who are elected by members of the Corporation;

    (b) one (1) of whom shall be a staff member of the First Ave. Public School and shall be an ex officio director; and

    (c) one (1) of whom shall be the centre director of the Townsville Community Centre and shall be an ex officio director.

13. TERM

The term of office of a director shall be from the date of her/his election or appointment until the annual meeting next following or until a successor is elected or appointed. Directors shall be eligible for re-election or re-appointment at the annual meeting of members following the annual meeting at which they were first elected or appointed.

14. REMOVAL OF DIRECTORS

A director shall cease to be a director of the Corporation upon any of the following events:

    (a) she/he ceases to be a member of the Corporation;

    (b) she/he becomes bankrupt;

    (c) she/he resigns as director by notice in writing to the Secretary of the Corporation and such resignation, if not effective immediately, becomes effective in accordance with its terms;

(d) an order is made declaring her/him to be mentally incompetent person or incapable of managing her/his own affairs;

(e) upon a resolution passed by at least two-thirds (2/3) of the votes cast at a General Meeting of members of which notice specifying the intention to pass a resolution removing such director from office has been given;

(f) death.

If the members of the Corporation remove an elected director from office pursuant to paragraph 15(e) above, they may, by a majority of votes cast at such meeting, elect another director in her/his stead for the remainder of her/his term.

15. VACANCIES
If a vacancy shall occur on the board, the remaining directors, if constituting a quorum as defined in article 18, may appoint a qualified person to fill the vacancy. In the absence of a quorum, the remaining directors shall forthwith call a meeting of members to fill the vacancy. If the number of directors is increased, a vacancy or vacancies on the board to the number of the authorized increase shall thereby be deemed to have occurred which may be filled in the manner herein provided.

16. REMUNERATION
As provided in the letters patent, the directors shall serve as such without remuneration, and no director shall directly or indirectly receive any profit from her/his position as a director; provided that a director may be paid reasonable expenses incurred by her/him in the performance of her/his duties.

17. QUORUM
A majority of the directors shall form a quorum for the transaction of business.

18. PLACE AND NOTICE OF MEETINGS
The board of directors may hold its meetings in any place in Ontario. Meetings of the board of directors shall be held at such place and time and on such day as the President or any four (4) directors may determine and the Secretary shall call meetings when directed or authorized by the President or any four (4) directors. Notice of every meeting so called shall be given to each director not less than forty-eight (48) hours before the time when the meeting is to be held but notice of a meeting shall not be necessary if all the directors are present or if those absent waive notice of such meeting. The board of directors may designate certain places, times, and days for regular meetings of the board and such regular meetings may be held without notice. A meeting of the board of directors may also be held without notice immediately following the annual meeting of members.

19. VOTING
Questions arising at any meeting of the board shall be decided by a majority of votes. In the case of an equality of votes, the chairperson of the meeting shall be entitled to a casting vote.

20. PROCEDURE
There shall be the following standing committees made up of not less than three persons. Each committee shall be chaired by a board member who shall report regularly to the board of directors. Board members shall be appointed to a committee not later than the second meeting of the board following the annual general meeting. Committees shall be open to other members of the Corporation who are not board members.

Unless otherwise specified by the board of directors, each such committee shall have power to fix its quorum, to elect its chair from the board members, and to regulate its procedure.

21. FINANCE COMMITTEE
There shall be a finance committee whose function shall be to ensure the centre's financial viability by overseeing finances and preparing recommendations and reports for the board of directors' meetings. The Treasurer and at least one other board member shall be on the finance committee.

22. PERSONNEL COMMITTEE
There shall be a personnel committee whose function shall be to ensure that the board and staff are able to work together, by establishing and monitoring personnel policies, hiring and monitoring the performance of the supervisor, responding to staff grievances, and recommending changes in the salary scale, benefits, and working conditions to the board of directors. The President and at least two other board members shall be on the personnel committee.

23. AD HOC COMMITTEES
The board of directors may elect or appoint ad hoc committees to perform such duties as it may prescribe from time to time. Unless otherwise specified by the board of directors, each such committee shall have power to fix its quorum, to elect its chair from the board members and to regulate its procedure.

24. OFFICERS
The officers of the Corporation shall consist of a President, a Vice-President, a Secretary, and a Treasurer, and such other officers as the board of directors may by bylaw determine. One person may hold more than one office. The officers shall be elected by the board of directors from among their number at the first meeting of the board after the annual election of such board of directors, provided that in default of such election, the incumbent shall hold such office until her/his successor is elected.

25. PRESIDENT
The President shall be the chief executive officer of the Corporation. She/he shall also, when present, preside as president of all meetings of the board and of the members. Without limiting the generality of the foregoing, she/he shall sign all bylaws, and special resolutions with the Secretary. She/he shall be a member of the personnel committee.

26. VICE-PRESIDENT
The Vice-President shall in the absence of the President perform the duties of the office of the president. The Vice-President is charged with general external relations and the coordination of activities with other organizations in the child care field.

27. SECRETARY
The secretary shall give or cause to be given notices of all meetings of the board of directors and of the members, and shall have the charge of the seal, minute book, registers and other corporate documents except as otherwise determined by the board.

28. TREASURER
The Treasurer shall monitor the books of account and accounting records of the Corporation and shall be responsible for the care and custody of the funds and in vestments of the Corporation. The Treasurer shall be a member of the finance committee.

29. DELEGATING DUTIES OF THE OFFICERS

In case of the absence or inability to act of the Vice-President, Secretary, or Treasurer, the directors may delegate all or any of the powers of such officer to any other office or to another director for the time being.

30. INDEMNIFICATION OF DIRECTORS AND OFFICERS

Every director and officer and her/his heirs, executors and administrators, and estate and effects, respectively, shall from time to time at all times, be indemnified and saved harmless out of the funds of the Corporation, from and against:

(a) all costs, charges, and expenses whatsoever that she/he sustains or incurs in or about any action, suit, or proceeding that is brought, commenced, or prosecuted against her/him for or in respect of any act, deed, matter, or thing whatsoever, made, done, or permitted by her/him, in or about the execution or the duties of her/his office; and

(b) all other costs, charges, and expenses that she/he sustains or incurs in or about or in relation to the affairs of the Corporation, except such costs, charges, or expenses as are occasioned by her/his own willful neglect or default.

31. AUDITORS

At the annual meeting of the Corporation there shall be appointed an auditor or auditors for the ensuing year. No person shall be appointed as an auditor of the Corporation who is a Director, officer, or employee of the Corporation or who is a partner or employee of any such Director, officer, or employee. The report of the auditor(s) shall be submitted at the Annual General Meeting of the Corporation and shall be open to inspection by any member of the Corporation.

32. CHEQUES

All cheques or other orders for the payment of money and notes or other evidence of indebtedness shall be signed by such one or more officers or other persons and in such manner as the board of directors may from time to time specify.

33. INSTRUMENTS

Contracts, documents, or any instruments in writing requiring the signature of the Corporation, shall be signed by any two (2) officers and all contracts, documents, and instruments in writing so signed shall be binding upon the Corporation without any further authorization or formality. The directors shall have power from time to time by resolution to appoint an officer or officers on behalf to sign specific contracts, documents, and instruments in writing. The directors may give the Corporation's power of attorney to any registered dealer in securities for the purposes of transferring and dealing with any bonds, debentures, or other securities of the Corporation. The seal of the Corporation when required may be affixed to contracts, documents, and instruments in writing signed as aforesaid or by any officer or officers appointed by resolution of the board of directors.

34. FINANCIAL YEAR

Unless otherwise ordered by the board of directors, the financial year of the Corporation shall terminate on the 31st day of December in each year.

35. CUSTODY OF SECURITIES

All investments of the Corporation or documents of title thereto shall be lodged for safekeeping with such chartered bank, trust company, or other depository as the Corporation may from time to time determine. Such investments and documents of title may be registered in the name of a nominee or held in bearer form.

36. BOOKS AND RECORDS

The directors shall see that all necessary books and records of the Corporation required by the bylaws of the Corporation or by any applicable statute or law are regularly and properly kept.

37. ENACTMENT AND AMENDMENT OF BYLAWS

Bylaws of the Corporation may be enacted, repealed, amended, or altered subject to the provisions of the Corporation.

38. INTERPRETATION

In these Bylaws and in all Bylaws of the Corporation hereafter passed unless the context otherwise requires, words importing the feminine gender shall include the masculine gender, and vice versa.

Certified true copy of Bylaw No. 1 enacted by the directors of <u>Downtown Squire Early Childhood Centre</u> on the <u>12</u> day of <u>November, 1989</u> and confirmed by all the members on the same date which Bylaw is still in full force and effect.

DATED this <u>15</u> day of <u>December 1990</u>.

_____   _____
President   Secretary

SAMPLE 4.2   OBJECTS AND SPECIAL PROVISIONS FOR DOWNTOWN SQUIRE EARLY CHILDHOOD CENTRE

Objects:

To provide nonparent care arrangements, an early learning environment for children aged _0 to 10 years_, and support to families in Quesceville, Ontario.

Special Provisions:

a. The corporation shall be carried on without the purpose of gain for its members and any profits or other accretions to the corporation shall be used in promoting its objects.

b. The corporation shall be subject to the _Charities Accounting Act_ and the _Charitable Gifts Act._

c. The directors shall serve as such without remuneration and no director shall directly or indirectly receive any profit from their positions as such, provided that directors may be paid reasonable expenses incurred by them in the performance of their duties.

d. The borrowing power of the corporation pursuant to any bylaw passed and confirmed in accordance with section 59 of the _Corporations Act_ shall be limited to borrowing money for current operating expenses, provided that the borrowing power of the corporation shall not be so limited if it borrows on the security of real or personal property.

e. If it is made to appear to the satisfaction of the Minister, upon report of the Public Guardian and Trustee, that the corporation has failed to comply with any of the provisions of the _Charities Accounting Act_ or the _Charities Gifts Act_, the Minister may authorize an inquiry for the purpose of determining whether or not there is sufficient cause for the Lieutenant governor to make an order under subsection 317(1) of the _Corporations Act_ to cancel the letters patent of the corporation and declare them to be dissolved.

f. Upon the dissolution of the corporation and after payment of all debts and liabilities, its remaining property shall be distributed or disposed of to charities registered under the _Income Tax Act_ (Canada) of Canada.

g. To invest the funds of the corporation pursuant to the _Trustee Act._

OR

To invest the funds of the corporation in such manner as determined by the directors, and in making such investments the directors shall not be subject to the _Trustee Act,_ but provided that such investments are reasonable, prudent, and sagacious under the circumstances and do not constitute, either directly or indirectly, a conflict of interest.

h. For the above objects, and as incidental and ancillary thereto, to exercise any of the powers as prescribed in the _Corporations Act_, or by any other statutes or laws from time to time applicable, except where such power is limited by these letters patent or the statute or common law relating to activities.

i. For the above objects, and as incidental and ancillary thereto, to exercise any of the powers as prescribed in the _Corporations Act_, or by any other statutes or laws from time to time applicable, except where such power is limited by these letters or the statute or common law relating to charities.

SAMPLE 4.3 DOWNTOWN SQUIRE EARLY CHILDHOOD CENTRE BOARD OF DIRECTORS' LEGAL OBLIGATIONS, POLICIES, AND PROCEDURES

The board of directors of the <u>Downtown Squire Early Childhood Centre</u> will be informed of their legal responsibilities and obligations, are legally responsible for governing <u>Downtown Squire Early Childhood Centre</u>, and may be liable for misusing or neglecting their legal duties.

Procedures:

1. The board of directors' handbook outlines board members' responsibilities and obligations. It is updated and reviewed with all new board members and as part of the annual board orientation and the board performance review.

2. Board members are expected to use their particular level of skill, knowledge, and personnel experience in carrying out their responsibilities.

3. Board members will declare a conflict of interest if there is a conflict or a perceived conflict between the interests of <u>Downtown Squire Early Childhood Centre</u> and personal interests.

4. Board members will declare a conflict of interest if they stand to benefit financially directly or indirectly from the actions of <u>Downtown Squire Early Childhood Centre</u>.

5. Board members know the Bylaws of <u>Downtown Squire Early Childhood Centre</u> and are expected to be familiar with licensing and other regulatory requirements outlined in the board of directors' handbook.

6. Board members are expected to attend meetings regularly and review all reports and correspondence from licensing and other regulatory authorities.

7. Make personnel and financial decisions based on knowledge and professional counsel if appropriate.

8. Board members are expected to make decisions that protect against any form of discrimination to staff, children, or families.

SAMPLE 6.1   EARLY CHILDHOOD PROGRAM STAFF JOB DESCRIPTION

Job Title: PROGRAM STAFF

Qualifications:

Two-year early childhood education diploma or equivalent that is approved by the provincial licensing process is required.

Responsibilities:

Provide a care and education program for young children and their families in a group setting under the direction of the program director.

1. Plan, implement, and review children's experiences in accordance with the program's philosophy and program goals.

   - Provide a daily balance of active/quiet, indoor/outdoor, and individual/group activities.

   - Establish and carry out a daily schedule that incorporates child-directed activity, care routines, and transition times.

   - Organize space, equipment, and materials prior to activities.

   - Assist children in expressing themselves by listening and responding with questions or comments that extend conversations.

   - Use a variety of teaching techniques including modelling, observing, questioning, demonstrating, reinforcing, and bridging.

   - Set up daily routines to take advantage of embedded learning opportunities.

   - Plan and carry out experiences that promote children's understanding of their own and others' culture and value system.

   - Plan and carry out activities that promote problem-solving play (pretend play, creative and constructive play, and games with rules play).

   - Organize physical and social environment to extend and expand child-directed play experiences.

   - Recognize and build on emergent and early literacy and numeracy activities. Encourage children's representation of their experiences.

   - Represent and document children's activities—photos, display of children's drawings and printing, portfolios, videos.

   - Provide experiences and play materials that actively promote anti-racist and nonsexist interactions and attitudes.

   - Participate in short- and long-term planning and the annual program review.

2. Individualize the curriculum.

   - Seek out opportunities to recognize and celebrate new developmental achievements.

   - Encourage and assist each child in carrying out daily routines.

- Provide daily opportunities for each child to choose to be alone.

- Engage each child individually each day.

- Observe how children use the materials and interact with each other and adults.

- Use observations to expand play, and plan activities that recognize individual differences.

- Work with resource staff and other specialists to plan, carry out, and review individual program plans.

- Initiate referrals or additional services for children and parents/guardians if there are concerns about the course of development.

3. Guide children's behaviour to promote autonomy and positive self-concept.

- Set reasonable behaviour expectations consistent with the centre's philosophy and policies.

- Provide positive guidelines such as re-directing, positive language, and reinforcement.

- Immediately address problem behaviour without labelling the child.

- Follow behaviour guidance policies established by the centre.

4. Ensure the child's environment is healthy and safe.

- Follow the centre's procedures for maintaining health records, hygienic routines, universal precautions, and administering medication and first aid.

- Report all accidents, injuries, and illnesses to the supervisor or designate and record such incidents in the daily log, playground log, and as a serious occurrence, if necessary.

- Monitor the indoor and outdoor environments for hazards.

- Update daily on children's allergies and other special conditions.

- Establish enjoyable daily eating routines.

- Attend to children's physical needs for diapering, toileting, eating, and sleeping, with respect and as promptly as possible.

- Report all incidents of suspected child maltreatment.

- Release children only to persons authorized by the parents/guardians.

5. Encourage and support active family involvement.

- Seek out opportunities to recognize and respect family's childrearing practices and expert knowledge about their children.

- Complete daily information charts appropriate for the age group.

- Discuss the program's daily events with family members at drop-off and pick-up times.

- Guide families to activities that will allow them to participate in their children's early learning and development.

- Accommodate the family instructions for daily care routines whenever possible.

- Encourage family members to spend time and to participate in the program throughout the day.

6. Contribute to the ongoing operation of the centre.

- Follow licensing and other regulatory requirements.
- Carry out the responsibilities of the supervisor as the designate when requested.
- Attend regular staff meetings.
- Maintain confidentiality of all information related to the centre's children, families, and staff.
- Participate in the annual performance review process.
- Plan and carry out annual plan for staff development.
- Keep up-to-date with early childhood education and advocacy developments.
- Maintain regular attendance and punctuality.

SAMPLE 6.2   PARENTING WORKER JOB DESCRIPTION

Job Title: PARENTING WORKER

Qualifications:

Two-year early childhood education diploma or equivalent that is approved by the provincial licensing process is required or a university degree in social work or related field. Minimum three years' experience working with families with young children.

Responsibilities:

1. Encourage and support active family participation.

   - Seek out opportunities to recognize and respect family's childrearing practices and expert knowledge about their children.

   - Guide families to activities that will allow them to participate in their children's early learning and development.

   - Accommodate the family instructions for daily care routines whenever possible.

   - Use a variety of coaching techniques, including modelling, observing, questioning, demonstrating, reinforcing, and bridging.

2. Plan, implement, and review children's experiences in accordance with the program's philosophy and program goals.

   - Provide a daily balance of active/quiet, indoor/outdoor, and individual/group activities that is responsive to the arrivals and departures of children.

   - Organize space, equipment, and materials prior to activities.

   - Assist children in expressing themselves by listening and responding with questions or comments that extend conversations.

   - Use a variety of coaching techniques including modelling, observing, questioning, demonstrating, reinforcing, and bridging.

   - Set up routines to take advantage of embedded learning opportunities.

   - Plan and carry out experiences that promote children's understanding of their own and other's cultures and value systems.

   - Plan and carry out activities that promote problem-solving play (pretend play, creative and constructive play, and games with rules play).

   - Organize physical and social environment to extend and expand child-directed play experiences.

   - Recognize and build on emergent and early literacy and numeracy activities. Encourage children's representation of their experiences.

   - Represent and document children's activities—photos, display of children's drawings and printing, portfolios, videos.

- Provide experiences and play materials that actively promote anti-racist and nonsexist interactions and attitudes.
- Seek out opportunities to recognize and celebrate new developmental achievements.
- Observe how children use the materials and interact with each other and adults.
- Use observations to expand play, and plan activities that recognize individual differences.
- Initiate referrals or additional services for children and parents/guardians if there are concerns about the course of development.

3. Outreach to families in the community to ensure program's participants represent the neighbourhood.
- Recruit families through the local school, community health centre, and recreation centre.
- Arrange transportation for participants as necessary to enable them to attend activities.
- Promote, publicize, and disseminate information about the program.

SAMPLE 6.3 SUPERVISOR JOB DESCRIPTION

Job Title: SUPERVISOR

Qualifications:

Minimum two-year Early Childhood Education diploma (or equivalent as defined in the provincial/territorial regulations). Five years' experience in child care settings.

Job Summary:

To ensure the development and management of the procedures required for carrying out the policy decisions of the board of directors for the fulfillment of the goals and objectives of the centre.

Job Duties:

1. Ensure that the centre complies with all legal requirements.

   - Arrange for sufficient staffing of the centre to meet requirements in the *Day Nurseries Act*.

   - Recognize, document, and take action in case of suspected abuse, illness, or accident, reporting the incident as a serious occurrence.

   - Inform the board of all visits and reports from licensing authorities.

   - Submit annual changes in board membership and Bylaws to the annual corporation report.

   - Renew insurance coverage each year.

   - Submit information required for provincial licence annual renewal.

2. Provide the board of directors with support to make informed decisions.

   - Provide a supervisor's report at each board meeting and at the annual general meeting.

   - Prepare background information on issues as required by the board for policy development.

   - Assist the board in planning committee, board, and annual general meetings.

   - Distribute minutes and reports from meetings.

3. Ensure that operational policies established by the board of directors are implemented.

   - Establish a waiting list system, which is updated twice a year.

   - Enroll children on the priority basis set by the board.

   - Establish and update children's records, including registration forms, medical records, and permission forms.

   - Establish a system to record arrivals and departures of children each day.

   - Establish and review logbook daily, monitoring consistent use by staff and parents/guardians.

   - Carry out and document daily playground inspection.

   - Establish, carry out, and review monthly, seasonal, and annual playground inspections.

- Ensure daily medication forms are signed and medication is administered and documented properly.

- Prepare and distribute monthly newsletter to families.

- Meet all new parents enrolling their children in the centre and review the family handbook, introduce staff, and provide a tour of the centre.

- Review family handbook, updating policies and procedures as changes occur.

- Review weekly menus for compliance with centre policies and the *Day Nurseries Act.*

- Maintain updated information on individual children's diet.

- Establish daily charts for each program room, appropriate for the age group.

- Arrange parent program staff meetings and interviews as requested by either parents or staff.

4. Ensure that the curriculum for children and families meets policies established by the board of directors.

- Review the program yearly in consultation with program staff and parents/guardians and prepare summary report with recommendations for the board.

- Act as a resource to program staff in planning program experiences and environment to support all areas of children's development, coping, and competence and emerging literacy skills.

- Review daily and weekly program plans.

- Observe and participate in daily routines and activities regularly (minimum, once weekly) in each group.

5. Ensure ongoing supervision of centre staff and implementation of centre's personnel policies.

- Update job descriptions to reflect centre policies and responsibilities.

- Maintain complete staff files.

- Appoint a designate in case of supervisor's absence.

- Interview and hire new staff in consultation with personnel committee.

- Recommend staff members for permanent status or dismissal after probation period.

- Provide orientation for new staff members.

- Carry out annual performance reviews with all staff members.

- Update staff handbook yearly.

- Plan and hold monthly staff meetings.

6. Ensure accurate financial information is available to the board of directors.

- Maintain complete, accurate financial records including parent fee statements, receipts for fees, payroll, bank deposits, bank statements, and petty cash, and submit promptly to the bookkeeper.

- Assist the finance committee in preparing annual operating budget with updated information of municipal and provincial funding guidelines.

- Submit annual budget to municipality (or DSSAB).

- Provide fee invoices to parents/guardians the last week of each month and submit invoice to municipality for subsidy payment.

- Prepare monthly financial status reports from bookkeeper's statement and present to the finance committee.

- Submit salary deductions to Canada Revenue Agency.

- Implement financial spending and fee collection policies.

- Purchase services, supplies, and equipment as needed within the budget guidelines.

- Seek out and apply for any available grants.

7. Promote the centre in the community.

- Prepare annual fact sheet on the centre and distribute to community groups.

- Establish and maintain coordination and collaboration with other community programs that work with the program's families.

- Consider response to community needs for additional family and child programs.

SAMPLE 6.4   DOWNTOWN SQUIRE EARLY CHILDHOOD CENTRE PERSONNEL HANDBOOK, TABLE OF CONTENTS

SAMPLE 7.1   DOWNTOWN SQUIRE EARLY CHILDHOOD CENTRE'S FEE COLLECTION POLICY AND PROCEDURES

Policy:

Downtown Squire Early Childhood Centre will collect child care fees in a consistent, equitable manner to ensure the financial viability of the centre.

Procedures:

1. Fees are due on the first day of each month for that month. There are no deductions for absences or statutory holidays.

2. A four-week fee deposit is required when children are enrolled in the centre. The fee deposit will be applied to the fees for the last four weeks children are enrolled in the centre, providing a two-week notice of withdrawal is given.

3. The monthly fee is set by the board of directors and renewed annually. Parents are responsible for paying the full monthly fee unless a child care fee subsidy is obtained from _____.

4. If a fee subsidy is obtained from _____, the monthly fee paid by the family is based on the assessed daily fee contribution. Parents/guardians are responsible for fulfilling all the requirements of the _____ necessary to maintain the subsidy. If parents/guardians become ineligible for child care subsidy, they are responsible for paying the full monthly fee or for withdrawing their child(ren).

5. Parents/guardians who are late paying their fees will be charged a fine of 2 percent of the outstanding balance. The supervisor will advise the Board of Directors of fees that are outstanding for more than two months. The supervisor may negotiate alternative payment arrangements with parents but must communicate the arrangements to the Board.

REFERENCES

Alberta Association for Accreditation of Early Learning and Care Services. (2006). Accreditation Overview, www.abccaccred.ca/index.php?option=com_content&task=view&id=2&Itemid=10, accessed May 16, 2006.

Ali, M. (2005). Effects of migration on parenting capacity of newcomer parents of young children. *Research connections Canada: Supporting children and families.* Ottawa: Canadian Child Care Federation.

Ali, M.A., Taraban, S., & Gill, J.K. (2003). *Unaccompanied/separated children seeking refugee status in Ontario: A review of documented policies and practices.* CERIS Working Paper Series #27.

Allen, D. (2004). *Getting Things Done.* New York: Penguin Books.

Arnett, J. (1989). Caregivers in day care centers: Does training matter? *Journal of Applied Developmental Psychology, 10*(4), 541–552.

Arnold, C. (2004). Positioning ECCD for the 21st century. *Coordinators' notebook, 28,* pp. 1–5.

Arnup, K. (1994). *Education for motherhood: Advice for mothers in twentieth-century.* Toronto: University of Toronto Press.

Astington, J.W. (1993). *The child's discovery of the mind.* Cambridge, MA: Harvard University Press.

Astington, J.W. (2004). *Why language matters for theory of mind.* London: Oxford University Press.

Astington, J., & Pelletier, J. (1996). The language of the mind: Its role in teaching and learning. In D.R. Olson and N. Torrance, eds., *The handbook of education and human development: New models of learning, teaching, and schooling,* pp. 593–619. Cambridge, MA: Blackwell Publishers Ltd.

Bakan, A.B., & Kobayashi, A. (2000). "Employment Equity Policy in Canada: An Interprovincial Comparison." Paper prepared for the Status of Women Canada's Policy Research Fund Initiative on the Integration of Diversity into Policy Research, Development and Analysis, www.swc-cfc.gc.ca/pubs/pubspr_e.html, accessed December 19, 2006.

Bales, S. (2005). Talking Early Child Development and Exploring the Consequences of Frame Choices, *FrameWorks Message Memo.* Washington, DC: The FrameWorks Institute.

Ball, J. (2005). Early childhood care and development programs as hook and hub for inter-sectoral service delivery in First Nations communities. *Journal of Aboriginal Health, 1*(2), 36–50.

Barnett, S. (2003). Better teachers, better preschools: Student achievement linked to teacher qualifications. *Preschool Quality Matters,* March 2003. National Institute for Early Education Research, Rutgers University.

Barnett, S., Brown, K., & Shore, R. (2004). The universal vs. targeted debate: Should the United States have preschool for all? *Preschool Policy Matters,* April 2004.

Barnett, S., Yarosz, D., Thomas, J., & Hornbeck, A. (2006). *Educational Effectiveness of a Vygotskian Approach to Preschool Education: A Randomized Trial.* New Jersey: National Institute for Early Education Research.

Battle, K., Torjman, S., & Mendelson, M. (2006). *More than a name change: The Universal Child Care Benefit.* Ottawa: Caledon Institute of Social Policy.

Beach, J., Bertrand, J., & Cleveland, G. (1998). *Our childcare workforce: From recognition to remuneration: More than a labour of love.* Ottawa: Child Care Human Resources Steering Committee.

Beach, J., Bertrand, J., Forer, B., Michal, D., & Tougas, J. (2004). *Working for Change: Canada's Child Care Workforce.* Prepared for the Child Care Human Resources Sector Council. Ottawa: Child Care Human Resources Sector Council.

Beach, J., & Flanagon-Rochon, K. (2007). *Training strategy project: Final report.* Ottawa: Child Care Human Resource Sector Council.

Beauvais, C., & Jenson, J. (2002). *The well-being of children: Are there neighbourhood effects?* Ottawa: Canadian Policy Research Networks.

Bennett, J. (2004). *Starting strong: Curricula and pedagogies in early childhood education and care.* Paris: Directorate for Education, OECD.

Bergen, D. (2002). The role of pretend play in children's cognitive development. *Early Childhood Research and Practice,* Spring 2002.

Berk, L., & Winsler, A. (1995). *Scaffolding children's learning: Vygotsky and early childhood education.* Washington, DC: National Association for the Education of the Young Child.

Bernard van Leer Foundation. (2000). The Effectiveness Initiative: Creating an environment for learning. *Early Childhood Matters 96,* 1–20.

Bernhard, J.K. (1995). The changing field of child development: Cultural diversity and the professional training of early childhood educators. *Canadian Journal of Education, 20*(4), 415–436.

Bernhard, J.K. (2003). Toward a 21st century developmental theory: Principles to account for diversity in children's lives. *Race, Gender, and Class, 9*(4), 45–60.

Bernhard, J., Freire, M., & Mulligan, V. (2004). *Canadian Parenting Workshops.* Toronto: Chestnut.

Bernhard, J.K., Landolt, P., & Goldring, L. (2006a). *Transnational, multi-local motherhood: Experiences of separation and reunification among Latin American families in Canada.* CERIS Policy Matters #24, http://ceris.metropolis.net/PolicyMatter/2006/PolicyMatters24.pdf, accessed April 15, 2006.

Bernhard, J.K., Lefebvre, M.L., Chud, G., & Lange, R. (1997). The preparation of early childhood educators in three Canadian areas of immigrant influx: Diversity issues. *Canadian Children, 22*(1), 26–34.

Bernhard, J.K., Lefebvre, M.L., Murphy Kilbride, K., Chud, G., & Lange, R. (1998). Troubled relationships in early childhood education: Parent-teacher interactions in ethnoculturally diverse settings. *Early Education and Development, 9*(1), 5–28.

Bernhard, J.K., Lero, D., & Greenberg, J. (2006b). *Diversity, equity and inclusion considerations to be presented to Best Start Vision and Implementation Joint Work Group.* Toronto: Best Start Early Learning Panel.

Bertrand, J. (1990). *Child care management guide.* Toronto: Ontario Coalition for Better Child Care.

Bertrand, J. (2007). *Toronto First Duty indicators of change.* Toronto: Atkinson Centre, OISE/UT.

Bertrand, J., & Corter, C. (2007). *Quality in early learning and care in Ontario: Measuring up: A review of the literature.* Toronto: Ontario Coalition for Better Child Care.

Bertrand, J., & Michals, D. (2006). Preliminary literature review: Training strategy project. Unpublished paper.

Blatz, W., Millichamp, D., & Fletcher, M. (1935). *Nursery education and practice*. New York: William Morrow & Co.

Blau, D. (1999). The effects of child care characteristics on child development. *The Journal of Political Economy, 106*(1), 786–822.

Bloom, P. (1992). Looking inside: Helping teachers assess their beliefs and values. *The Child Care Exchange.* November 1992, 11–13.

Bloom, P. (1997). *A great place to work: Improving conditions for staff in young children's programs*, rev. ed. Washington, DC: NAEYC.

Bloom, P. (2000). *Circle of influence implementing shared decision making and participative management*. Lake Forest, IL: New Horizons.

Boyce, W.T., & Keating, D.P. (2004). Should we intervene to improve childhood circumstances? In D. Kuh & Y. Ben-Shlomo, eds., *A life course approach to chronic disease epidemiology*. Oxford, England: Oxford University Press.

Bradshaw, D. (1997). Front line profile. *Ideas,* December 1997, 19.

Braun, S., & Edwards, E.P. (1972). *History and theory of early childhood education*. Worthington, OH: Charles A. Jones.

Brooks-Gunn, J. (2003). Do you believe in magic? What can we expect from early intervention programs? *Social Policy Report,* Volume XVII, Number I. Chicago: Society for Research in Child Development.

Bruffee, K.A. (1993). *Collaborative learning, higher education, interdependence and the authority of knowledge.* Baltimore; London: Johns Hopkins University Press.

Burchinal, M.R., Roberts, J.E., Hooper, S., & Zeisal, S.A. (2000). Cumulative risk and early cognitive development: A comparison of statistical risk models. *Developmental Psychology, 36*(6), pp. 793–807.

Burchinal, M.R., Howes, C., & Kontos, S. (2002). Structural predictors of child care quality in child care homes. *Early Childhood Research Quarterly, 17,* 87–105.

Burton, A., Young, M., Belim, D., Whitebook, M., & Broach, L. (2002). *Inside the pre-K classroom: A study of staffing and stability in state-funded prekindergarten programs.* Washington, DC: Center for the Childcare Workforce.

Cameron, C. (2004). *Building an integrated workforce for a long-term vision of universal education and care.* London: Day Care Trust.

Canadian Child Care Federation. (2006). *Policy brief on school age child care.* Ottawa: Canadian Child Care Federation.

Canadian Intergovernmental Conference Secretariat. (2000). *Early childhood development agreement.* Ottawa: Government of Canada.

Canadian Teachers Federation. (n.d.). *Teaching in Canada,* www.ctf-fce.ca/en/, accessed November 21, 2006.

Carr, M., & May, H. (2000). Te Whaariki: Curriculum voices. In H. Penn, ed., *Early Childhood Services: Theory, policy and practice*, pp. 53–73. Philadelphia: Open University Press.

Carr, M. (2001). *Assessment in early childhood settings: Learning stories.* London: Paul Chapman Publishing.

Carver, J., & Carver, M.M. (1996). *Basic principles of policy governance.* San Francisco, CA: Jossey-Bass Publishers.

Case, R., Griffin, S., & Kelly, W. (1999). Socioeconomic gradients in mathematical ability and their responsiveness to intervention during early childhood. In D. Keating & C. Hertzman, eds., *Developmental health and the wealth of nations,* pp. 125–149. New York: Guilford Press.

Child & Youth Health Network for Eastern Ontario. (2005). *Middle childhood matters.* Ottawa: CYHNEO.

Child and Youth Office for BC. (2005). *Healthy child development in British Columbia: From words to action.* Victoria: Child & Youth Office, BC.

Child Care Human Resources Sector Council. (2006). *Occupational standards for child care administrators.* Ottawa: CCHRSC.

Childcare Resource and Research Unit. (2000). *Early childhood care and education in Canada: Provinces and territories 1998.* Toronto: University of Toronto, Centre for Urban and Community Studies, Childcare Resource and Research Unit.

Children's Defence Fund. (2002). *Child care matters.* Washington, DC: CDF.

Chumak-Horbatsch, R. (2004). Linguistic diversity in early childhood education: Working with linguistically and culturally diverse children. *Canadian Children, 29*(2), 20–24.

Clark, D. (2002). Risk management plans in action: Is your program ready? *The Director's Link,* Winter 2002, 1–2.

Clarke-Stewart, A., & Allhusen, V.D. (2005). *What we know about childcare.* Cambridge and London: Harvard University Press.

Cleveland, G. (2007). Personal communication.

Cleveland, G., Corter, C., Pelletier, J., Colley, S., Bertrand, J., & Jamieson, J. (2006). *Early childhood learning and development in child care, kindergarten and family support programs.* Toronto: Atkinson Centre at OISE/UT.

Cleveland, G., & Krashinsky, M. (2003). *Fact and fantasy: Eight myths about early childhood education and care.* Toronto: Childcare Resource & Research Unit, University of Toronto.

Consultative Group on Early Childhood Care and Development. (2004). ECCD Rights and Investments. *Coordinators Notebook,* no. 28.

Cook, C., & Willms, J.D. (2002). Balancing work and family live. In J.D. Willms, ed., *Vulnerable children.* Edmonton, AB: University of Alberta Press.

Cooke, K., London, J., Edwards, R., & Rose-Lizee, R. (1986). *Report on the Task Force on Child Care.* Ottawa: Status of Women Canada.

Corbett, B. (1989). *A century of kindergarten education in Ontario.* Mississauga: The Froebel Foundation.

Corter, C., Bertrand, J., Pelletier, J., Griffin, T., McKay, D., Patel, S., & Ioannone, P. (2004). *Early findings: Toronto First Duty.* Toronto: Atkinson Centre at OISE/UT.

Corter, C., Bertrand, J., Pelletier, J., Griffin, T., McKay, D., Patel, S., & Ioannone, P. (2006). *Evidence-based understanding of integrated foundations for early childhood.* Toronto: Atkinson Centre at OISE/UT.

Corter, C., Bertrand, J., Pelletier, J., Griffin, T., McKay, D., Patel, S., & Ioannone, P. (2007). *Toronto First Duty: Final report.* Toronto: Atkinson Centre at OISE/UT.

Corter, C., & Pelletier, J. (2004). The rise and stall of parent and community involvement in school. *Orbit, 34*(3), 5–20.

Corter, C., & Pelletier, J. (2005). Parent and community involvement in schools: Policy panacea or pandemic? In H. Bascia, A. Cumming, A. Datnow, K. Leithwood, & D. Livingstone, eds., *International handbook of educational policy*. Dordrecht, Netherlands: Springer.

Cost, Quality & Outcomes Study (1995). *Cost, quality and child outcomes in child care centers*. Denver, CO: Economics Dept., University of Colorado at Denver.

Covey, S. (1991). *Principle-centered leadership*. New York: Simon & Schuster.

Cox, R. (2005). *Making family child care work: Strategies for improving the working conditions of family childcare providers*. Ottawa: Status of Women Canada.

Cranton, P. (2003). From knowledge to practice: Wiley Coyote crashes again. In B. Dietze & B.Crossley, eds., *Outdoor play in early childhood education and care programs*. Ottawa, ON: Canadian Child Care Federation.

Dickinson, P. (2005). *International Curriculum Framework Survey*. Prepared for the Best Start Expert Panel on Early Learning.

Dodge, D. *Human capital, early childhood development, and economic growth: An economist's perspective*. Address to the Sparrow Lake Alliance, May 2003.

Doherty, G. (1997). Zero to six: The basis for school readiness. Research paper, Applied Resources Branch. Ottawa: Human Resources Development Canada.

Doherty, G. (2000). Issues in Canadian child care: What does the research tell us? *Research Connections Canada, 5*, 5–106.

Doherty, G. (2001). Targeting early childhood care and education: Myths and realities. Occasional Paper Number 15. Toronto: Child Care Research and Resource Unit, University of Toronto.

Doherty, G. (2003). *Occupational standards for child care practitioners*. Ottawa: Canadian Child Care Federation.

Doherty, G. (2005). *International policies, practices and implications for quality and human resources*. Background Paper for Best Start Expert Panel on Quality and Human Resources. Toronto: Ministry of Children and Youth Services.

Doherty, G. (2007). *Conception to age six: The foundation of school-readiness*. Paper prepared for The Learning Partnership's Partners in Action—Early Years Conference. January 26, 2007. Toronto: The Learning Partnership.

Doherty, G., Friendly, M., & Beach, J. (2003). OECD thematic review of early childhood education and care: Canadian Background Report, Canada.

Doherty, G., Lero, D.S., Goelman, H., LaGrange, A., & Tougas, J. (2000). *You bet I care! A Canada-wide study on wages, working conditions, and practices in child care centres*. Guelph, ON: Centre for Families, Work and Well-Being, University of Guelph.

Epstein, J., & Sanders, M. (2002). Family, school, and community partnerships. In M.H. Bornstein, ed., *Handbook of parenting*, 2nd ed. (Vol. 5: Practical issues in parenting). Mahwah, NJ: Lawrence Erlbaum Associates.

Epstein, J.L. (1995). School/family/community partnerships: Caring for the children we share. *Phi Delta Kappan, 76*, 701–712.

Epstein, J.L. (2005). School-initiated family and community partnerships. In T. Erb, ed., *This we believe in action: Implementing successful middle level schools*, pp. 77–96. Westerville, OH: National Middle School Association.

European Commission Child Care Network. (1996). *Quality in early learning and child care services: Papers from the European Commission Childcare Network (2004)*. Toronto: Childcare Resource and Research Unit, University of Toronto.

Evans, J., Myers, R., & Ilfeld, J. (2000). *Early childhood counts*. Washington, DC: World Bank Institute.

Ferguson, E., & McCormick, T. (2001). *Maximizing child care services: The role of owners and boards*. Halifax: Child Care Connections, and St. Catharines: Early Child Care and Development Centre.

Frankel, E.B. (2004). Supporting inclusive care and education for young children with special needs and their families: An international perspective. *Childhood Education, 80,* 310–316.

Friendly, M. (2000). *Child care and Canadian federalism in the 1990s: Canary in a coal mine*. Toronto: Childcare Resource and Research Unit, University of Toronto.

Friendly, M. (2006). *Canadian early learning and child care and the Convention on the Rights of the Child*. Occasional paper 22. Toronto: Childcare Resource and Research Unit, University of Toronto.

Friendly, M., & Beach, J. (1998). *Early childhood care and education in Canada: Provinces and territories*. Toronto: Childcare Resource and Research Unit, University of Toronto.

Friendly, M., & Beach, J. (2005). *Early childhood education and care in Canada, 2004*. Toronto: Childcare Resource and Research Unit, University of Toronto.

Friendly, M., & Beach, J. (2007). *Early childhood education and care in Canada, 2004*. Toronto: Childcare Resource and Research Unit, University of Toronto.

Friendly, M., Beach, J., & Turiano, M. (2002). *Early childhood education and care in Canada: Provinces and territories, 2001*. Toronto: Childcare Resource and Research Unit, Centre for Urban and Community Studies, University of Toronto.

Friendly, M., Doherty, G., & Beach, J. (2006). *Quality by Design*. Toronto: Childcare Resource and Research Unit, University of Toronto.

Fullan, M. (2001). *Leading in a culture of change*. San Francisco: Jossey-Bass.

Fullan, M. (2002). *Leadership and sustainability: System thinkers in action*. Boston: Harvard Business School Press.

Galinsky, E. (2006). *The economic benefits of high quality early childhood programs: What makes the difference?* Washington, DC: Committee for Economic Development.

Galinsky, E., Bond, J.T., & Friedman, D.E. (1993). *The changing workforce: Highlights from the national study*. New York, NY: Families and Work Institute.

Gallagher, J., Clifford, R., & Maxwell, K. (2004). Getting from here to here: To an ideal early preschool system. *Early Childhood RO,* Spring 2004, 6(1).

Gestwicki, C. (1995). *Home, school, community relations*, 3rd ed. Albany, NY: Delmar Publishers.

Goelman, H. (2004). Down under is on top in early childhood programs. *Toronto Globe and Mail,* September 6.

Goelman, H. (2006). *Seven myths about child care*. Vancouver, BC: Human Early Learning Partnership.

Goelman, H., Doherty, G., Lero, D., LaGrange, A., & Tougas, J. (2000). *You bet I care! Caring and learning environments: Quality in child care centres across Canada*. Guelph: Centre for Families, Work and Well-Being, University of Guelph, Ontario.

Goelman, H., & Hertzman, C. (n.d.). *What the EDI IS and IS NOT.* Vancouver, BC: Human Early Learning Partnership.

Goleman, D. (2000). Leadership that gets results. *Harvard Business Review,* 78(2), 78–93.

Gopnik, A., Meltzoff, A., & Kuhl, P. (1999). *The scientist in the crib: Minds, brains and how children learn.* New York: William Morrow & Co., Inc.

Gordon, M. (2005). *Roots of empathy.* Toronto: Thomas Allen Publisher.

Gott, C., & Wilson, J. (2004). *Rural voices for early childhood education and care: Final report.* Longbow Lake, ON: Rural Voices.

Government of Canada (2007). *Welcome to the Parliament of Canada.* Ottawa. Accessed March 15, 2007. http://www.parl.gc.ca/common/index.asp?Language=E.

Government of Ontario (2007). *Early Childhood Educators Act.* Toronto.

Greenspan, S., & Shanker, S. (2004). *The first idea: How symbols, language and intelligence evolved from our primate ancestors to modern humans.* Cambridge, MA: Da Capo Press.

Health and Welfare (1973). *Status of child care.* Ottawa: Government of Canada.

Heinick, K. (2004). *Women, power and politics.* Toronto: Ontario Coalition for Better Child Care.

Helburn, S., Culkin, M., Morris, J., Morcan, N., Howes, C., Phillipsen, L., Bryant, D., Clifford, R., Cryer, D., Peisner-Feinberg, E., Burchinal, M., Kaga, S., & Rusticic, J. (1995). *Cost, quality & child outcomes in child care centres.* University of Colorado, University of California, University of North Carolina, and Yale University, Bloomington, IN: Phi Delta Kappa Educational Foundation.

HELP. (2005). *Community mapping toolbox.* Vancouver, BC: Human Early Learning Partnership.

Hertzman, C. (2002). *Early development in Vancouver: Report of the Community Asset Mapping Project.* Vancouver: HELP, UBC.

Hewes, J. (2004). *Full-day Head Start: Early intervention in centre-based child care.* Edmonton, AB: Grant McEwen College.

Ho, E.S., & Willms, J.D. (1996). Effects of parental involvement on eighth-grade achievement. *Sociology of Education, 69,* 126–141.

Howe, N., Jacobs, E., & Fiorentino, L. (2000). The curriculum. In L. Prochner and N. Howe, eds., *Early childhood care and education in Canada.* Vancouver: UBC Press.

Howes, C., Galinsky, E., Shinn, M., Gulcar, L., Clements, M., Sibley, A., Abbott-Shim, M., & McCarthy, J. (1998). *The Florida child care quality improvement study: 1996 report.* New York: Families and Work Institute.

Irwin, S. (2005). *Child care inclusion practices, profiles and principles.* Sydney, NS: SpeciaLink.

Irwin, S.H., Lero, D.S., & Brophy, K. (2004). *Inclusion: The next generation in child care in Canada.* Wreck Cove: Breton Books.

Janus, M., & Offord, D. (2000). Readiness to learn at school. *Isuma, 1*(2), 71–75.

Janus, M. (2006). Measuring community early child development. *The CAP Journal, 14*(3).

Jappel, C., & Tremblay, R. (2005). *Quality counts.* Montreal: Institute for Research on Public Policy.

Johnson, L., & Mathien, J. (1998). *Early childhood education services for kindergarten age children in four Canadian provinces: Scope, nature and future models.* Ottawa: Caledon Institute of Social Policy.

Kagan, S. (1998). *Examining Children's Readiness for School: Progress Over the Decade — A Report to the National Education Goals Panel*. Washington, DC: National Education Goals Panel.

Kagan, S., & Kauerz, K. (2006). Preschool programs: Effective curricula. In R.E. Tremblay, R.G. Barr, and R. DeV. Peters, eds., *Encylopedia on early childhood development*. Montreal: Centre of Excellence for Early Childhood Development.

Kagan, S.L. (2005). A conversation with Sharon Lynn Kagan. In M.R. Jalongo and J.P. Isenberg, eds., *Exploring your role: A practitioner's introduction to early childhood education*. Columbus, OH: Merrill/Prentice Hall.

Kagan, S.L., & Lowenstein, A.E. (2004). School readiness and children's play: Contemporary oxymoron or compatible option? In E.F. Zigler, D.G. Singer, and S.J. Bishop-Josef, eds., *Children's play: The roots of reading*, pp. 59–76. Washington, DC: Zero to Three Press.

Kagan, S., & Britto, P. (2005). *Going global with indicators of child development*. UNICEF Final Report. New York, NY: UNICEF.

Keating, D. (1998). Enhancing learning readiness: The family and the preschool child. *Transition*. Ottawa: Vanier Institute.

Keating, D., & Hertzman, C. (1999). *Developmental health and the wealth of nations*. New York: Guilford Press.

Kershaw, P. (2007). Measuring up: Federal, BC and Alberta family benefits in international context. *Choices, 13*(2), 1–41.

Kershaw, P., Irwin, L., Trafford, K., & Hertzman, C. (2006). *The British Columbia atlas of child development*, 1st ed. Vancouver: Human Early Learning Partnership.

Kontos, S., & Fiene, R. (1987). Child care quality, compliance with regulations, and children's development. In D. Phillips, ed., *Quality in child care: What does the research tell us?* pp. 57–80. Washington, DC: National Association of the Education of Young Children.

Kouzes, J., & Posner, B. (2002). *The leadership challenge*. San Francisco, CA: Jossey-Bass.

Kyle, I., & Kellerman, M. (1998). *Case studies of Canadian family resource programs. Supporting families, children and communities*. Ottawa: Canadian Association of Family Resource Programs.

Lapierre, L., & Sherman, A. (1979). *To herald a young child: The report of the commission of inquiry into the education of the young child*. Toronto: Ontario Public School Men Teachers' Federation.

Lero, D.S., Irwin, S.H., & Darisi, T. (2006). *Partnerships for inclusion—Nova Scotia: An evaluation based on the first cohort of child care centres*. Guelph: Centre for Families, Work and Well-Being.

Liebert, R., & Sprafkin, J. (1988). *The early window: Effects of television on children and youth*. New York: Allyn and Bacon.

Maggi, S., Irwin, L., Siddiqi, A., Poureslami, I., Hertzman, E., & Hertzman, C. (2005). *Analytic and strategic review paper: International perspectives on early child development*. Vancouver: Human Early Learning Partnership, UBC.

Mahon, R. (2001). A welfare state restructuring and changing gender relations: The politics of family policy in Sweden and Canada. In B. Fox, ed., *Family patterns, gender relations*, pp. 524–545. Oxford: Oxford University Press.

Mahon, R. (2004). *Early child learning and care in Canada: Who rules? Who should rule?* A discussion paper prepared for national conference on child care in Canada. Child Care for a Change. Winnipeg, November 12–14, 2004. Ottawa: Canadian Council on Social Development.

Malcolmson, J. (2004). *Synergy: Integrated approaches in family support.* Ottawa: FRP Canada.

Malcolmson, M. (2002). *Putting the pieces together: A conceptual framework of family support practice.* Ottawa: Canadian Association of Family Resource Programs.

Manitoba Child Care Association & Canadian Child Care Federation. (2006). *Feasibility study on voluntary accreditation of Manitoba's licensed child care services* Winnipeg, MB: MCCA.

Matthews, H., & Ewen, D. (2006). *Reaching all children? Understanding early care and education participation among immigrant families.* Washington: Centre for Law and Social Policy (CLASP).

McCain, M., & Mustard, F. (1999). *Early years study.* Toronto: Government of Ontario.

McCain, M., Mustard, F., & Shanker, S. (2007). *Early years study 2: Putting science into action.* Toronto: Council for Early Child Development.

McCuaig, K. (2004). *From patchwork to framework: A child strategy for Canada.* Ottawa: Child Care Advocacy Association of Canada.

McQuaid, S., Chaulk, P., & Smith, N. (2002). *"For Our Educators": A study of the early childhood education sector.* Prince Edward Island: Early Childhood Development Association of PEI.

Mill, D., Jacobs, E.V., & Jennings, M. (2002). *Innovative programs in school-age care.* Report for Human Resources Development Canada. Ottawa.

Miller, C., & Ferguson, E. (2003). *Attracting and keeping qualified staff in Canadian child care.* Halifax: Child Care Connections Nova Scotia.

Ministry of Child and Youth Services. (2005). *Background on college of early childhood educators.* Toronto: MCYS.

Ministry of Children and Youth Services. (2006). *Ontario's Best Start action plan: A progress report,* www.children.gov.on.ca/NR/CS/BestStart/ProgressReport.pdf, accessed December 9, 2006.

Ministry of Social Affairs and Health. (2004). Early childhood education and care in Finland. *Brochures of the Ministry of Social Affairs and Health,* 14.

Mort, J. (2004). *The EDI impact study—BC school districts: Embracing young children and their families,* www.earlylearning.ubc.ca/documents/EDIImpactStudy.pdf.

Moses, L., & Carlson, S. (2004). Self-regulation and children's theories of mind. In C. Lightfoot, C. Lalonde, M. Chandler, eds., *Changing concepts of psychological life,* pp. 127–148. New Jersey: Lawrence Erlbaum Associates Inc.

Moss, P. (2006). Farewell to childcare? *National Institute Economic Review, 195* (January 2006), 70–83.

Moss, P., & Cameron, C. (2002). *WP6: Care work and the care workforce: Report on stage one and state of the art review.* London: Thomas Coram Research Unit, Institute of Education, University of London.

Mujis, D., Aubrey, C., Harris, A., & Briggs, M. (2004). How do they manage? Research on leadership in early childhood. *Journal of Early Childhood Research, 2*(2), 157–169.

Mustard, J.F. (2002). Early child development and the brain: The base for health, learning, and behavior throughout life. In M.E. Young, ed., *From early child development to human development*. Washington, DC: The World Bank.

Mustard, J.F. (2006). *Early child development and experience-based brain development: The scientific underpinnings of the importance of early child development in a globalized world.* Washington, DC: Brookings Institute.

Nabuco, M., & Sylva, K. (1996). *The effects of three early childhood curricula in Portugal on children's progress in first year primary school.* London: Institute of Education, University of London.

NAEYC. (2005). *Screening and assessment of young English-language learners.* Washington, DC: National Association for the Education of Young Children.

NAEYC & NAECS/SDE (National Association of Early Childhood Specialists in State Departments of Education). (1990). *Guidelines for appropriate curriculum content and assessment in programs serving children ages 3 through 8.* Joint position statement. Washington, DC: NAEYC.

National Research Council. (2001). *Eager to learn: Educating our preschoolers* (Committee on Early Childhood Pedagogy of the Commission on Behavioral and Social Sciences and Education). Washington, DC: The National Academies Press.

National Scientific Council on the Developing Child. (2005). *Excessive Stress Disrupts the Architecture of the Developing Brain.* Working Paper No. 3., www.developingchild.net/reports.shtml, accessed October 21, 2006.

National Scientific Council on the Developing Child. (2007). *The science of early childhood development: Closing the gap between what we know and what we do.* Boston: Center on the Developing Child at Harvard University.

Neuman, S., & Dickinson, D. (2001). *Handbook of early literacy research.* New York: Guilford Press.

Newmann, F.M., King, M.B., & Youngs, P. (2000). Professional development that addresses school capacity: Lessons from urban elementary schools. *American Journal of Education, 108*(4), 259–299.

NICHD Early Child Care Research Network. (2002). Early child care and children's development prior to school entry: Results from the NICHD Study of Early Child Care. *American Educational Research Journal, 39*, 133–164.

NICHD, Early Child Care Research Network. (2005). *Child care and child development: Results from the NICHD study of early child care and youth development.* The Guildford Press, New York, NY.

Oberhuemer, P. (2005). International perspectives on early childhood curriculum. *International Journal of Early Childhood, 37*(1), 27–37.

Oldershaw, L. (2002). *A national survey of parents of young children.* Toronto: Invest in Kids.

Ontario Children's Health Network & Ontario College of Family Physicians. (2005). *Report of the Expert Panel on the 18 Month Well Baby Visit.* Toronto: Ministry of Children and Youth Services.

Ontario Coalition for Better Child Care. (2003). *Pay equity.* Toronto: OCBCC.

Ontario Ministry of Community & Social Services. (1990). *Children first.* Toronto: Queen's Printer for Ontario.

Ontario Ministry of Education. (1985). *Report of the Early Primary Education Project*, p. 116. Toronto: Ontario Ministry of Education.

Orellana, M.F., Thorne, B., Chee, A.E., & Lam, W.S.E. (2001). Transnational Childhoods: The participation of children in processes of family migration. *Social Problems, 48*(4), 572–591.

Organisation for Economic Co-operation and Development & Statistics Canada. (2000). *Literacy in the information age: Final report of the international adult literacy survey.* Paris: OECD.

Organisation for Economic Co-operation and Development (OECD). (2001). *Starting strong I.* Paris: OECD Secretariat.

Organisation for Economic Co-operation and Development (OECD). Directorate for Education. (2004). *Early childhood care and education policy: Canada country note.* Paris: OECD.

Organisation for Economic Co-operation and Development (OECD). (2006). *Starting strong II.* Paris: OECD Secretariat.

Osburn, D.K. (1991). *Early childhood education in historical perspective.* Athens, GA: The Day Press.

Pacini-Ketchabaw, V., Bernhard, J.K., & Freire, M. (2001). Struggling to preserve home language: The experiences of Latino students and families in the Canadian school system. *Bilingual Research Journal, 25*(1&2), 115–145.

Pelletier, J. (2002). Parents come to kindergarten: A unique junior kindergarten program for four-year-olds and their families. FINE Harvard Family Research Project, www.gse.harvard.edu-hfrp/projects/fine/reosources/digest/parent.html.

Pelletier, J., & Brent, J. (2002). Parent participation and children's school readiness: The effects of parental self-efficacy, cultural diversity and teacher strategies. *International Journal of Early Childhood, 34*, 45–60.

Pence, A. (2006). Reconceptualizing early childhood. *Research Connections*, 13. Ottawa: Canadian Child Care Federation.

Premier's Council on Health, Well-Being and Social Justice. (1994). *Yours, mine and ours: Ontario's children and youth phase one.* Toronto: Queen's Printer for Ontario.

Prentice, S. (2001). *Changing child care: Five decades of child care advocacy and policy in Canada.* Halifax: Fernwood Publishing.

Prochner, L. (2000). A history of early education and child care in Canada, 1820–1966. In L. Prochner and N. Howe, eds., *Early childhood care and education in Canada.* Vancouver: UBC Press.

Putnam, R.D. (2000). *Bowling alone: The collapse and revival of American community.* New York: Simon & Schuster.

Ramey, C.T., Campbell, F.A., Burchinal, M., Skinner, M.L., Gardner, D.M., & Ramey, S.L. (2000). Persistent effects of early childhood education on high risk children and their mothers. *Applied Developmental Science, 4*(1), 2–14.

Raymond, Jocelyn. (1991). *The nursery years.* Toronto: University of Toronto Press.

Reeves, K. (2002). *2002 status report on Canadian family resource programs.* Ottawa: FRP Canada.

Rodd, J. (1996). Towards a typology of leadership for the early childhood professional of the 21st century. *Early Childhood Development and Care, 120*, 119–126.

Rodd, J. (1998). *Leadership in early childhood: the pathway to professionalism.* New York, NY: Teachers College Press.

Rolfe, H. (2005). Building a stable workforce: recruitment and retention in the childcare and early years sector. *Children and Society, 19*(1), 54–65.

Rolfe, H., Metcalf, H., Anderson, T., & Meadows, P. (2003). *Recruitment and Retention of Childcare, Early Years and Playworkers: Research Study*, Research Report 409. London: National Institute for Economic and Social Research.

Rose, R., & Ouellet, E. (2000). *Making family child care work: Strategies for improving the working conditions of family childcare providers.* Ottawa: Status of Women.

Roskos, K., & Christie, J. (2004). Examining the play-literacy interface: A critical review and future directions, pp. 95–124. In E. Ziegler, D. Singer, and S. Bishop-Josef, eds., *Child's play: The roots of reading.* Washington, DC: Zero to Three Press.

Royal Commission on Learning. (1994). *For the love of learning: Report of the royal commission on learning: A short version.* Toronto: Queen's Printer for Ontario.

Rush, E. (2006). *Child care quality in Australia.* Discussion Paper Number 84. Manuka, Australian Capital Territory: The Australian Institute.

Rushowy, K. (2007). Sharing, learning together: Kids get benefit of involved parents at country's oldest co-op nursery, now in 70th year. *The Toronto Star,* April 26, 2007, p. 12.

Russell, L., & Morrow, E. (1978). Co-operative day care, in K. Gallagher Ross, ed., *Good day care: Fighting for it, getting it, keeping it.* Toronto: The Women's Press.

Rutter, M., & Rutter, M. (1993). *Developing minds: Challenge and continuity across the life span.* London, England: Penguin Books.

Sammons, P., Siraj-Blatchford, I., Sylva, K., Melhuish, E., Taggart, B., & Elliot, K. (2005). Investigating the effects of pre-school provision: Using mixed methods in the EPPE research. *International Journal of Social Research Methodology, 8,* 207–224.

Schulz, P. (1978). Day care in Canada: 1850–1962. In *The good day care book.* Toronto: The Women's Press.

Schwebel, D.C., Rosen, C.S., & Singer, J.L. (1999). Preschoolers' pretend play and theory of mind: The role of jointly constructed pretence. *British Journal of Developmental Psychology, 17*(3), 333–348.

Schweinhart, L. (2006). Preschool programs. In R.E. Tremblay, R.G. Barr, and R.DeV. Peters, eds., *Encylopedia on Early Childhood Development.* Montreal: Centre of Excellence for Early Childhood Development.

Schweinhart, L.J., Barnes, H.V., & Weikart, D.P. (2005). *Significant benefits: The High/Scope Perry preschool study through Age 27.* High/Scope Educational Research Foundation.

Schweinhart, L., & Weikart, D. (1993, Summer). Changed lives, significant benefits: The High/Scope Perry preschool project to date. *High/Scope Resource,* 10–14.

Senge, P. (1990). *The fifth discipline: The art and practice of the learning organization.* New York: Doubleday.

Shaffer, D., Wood, E., & Willougby, T. (2005). *Developmental psychology: Childhood and adolescence.* Toronto: Thomson Nelson.

Shonkoff, J. (2000). Science, policy, and practice: Three cultures in search of a shared mission. *Child Development, 71*(1), pp. 181–187.

Shonkoff, J., & Meisels, S. (2000). *Handbook of early childhood intervention,* 2nd ed. Cambridge: Cambridge University Press.

Shonkoff, J., & Phillips, D. (2000). *From neurons to neighborhoods.* Washington, DC: National Academy Press.

Siraj-Blatchford, I., Sylva, K., Muttock, S., Gilden, R., & Bell, D. (2002). *Researching effective pedagogy in the early years*. London: Department for Education and Skills.

Smith, A. (2005). Integrating Care and Education in New Zealand. Presentation at The Unhurried Day: Learning and Caring Seamlessly. Toronto, Integration Network Project, Institute Child Study, University of Toronto.

Social Development Canada, Public Health Agency of Canada and Indian & Northern Affairs Canada. (2005). *Early childhood development and early learning and child care activities and expenditures, 2003–2004*. Ottawa: Government of Canada. http://www.socialunion.ca.

Statistics Canada. (2004). *Canadian Social Trends,* No. 72. Ottawa: Government of Canada.

Statistics Canada. (2006). Women in Canada: A gender-based statistical report, Ottawa, ON: Author.

Stevenson, J. (1990). Co-operative nursery schools. In I. Doxey, ed., *Child care and education: Canadian dimension*. Toronto: Nelson Publishing.

Sutherland, N. (1976). *Children in English-Canadian society: Framing the 20th century consensus*. Toronto: University of Toronto Press.

Sylva, K., Melhuish, E., Sammons, P., Siraj-Blatchford, I., Taggart, B., & Elliot, K. (2003). *The Effective Provision of Pre-School Education (EPPE) Project: Findings from the Pre-School Period*. London, England: Institute of Education, University of London and SureStart.

Sylva, K., Melhuish, E.C., Sammons, P., Siraj-Blatchford, I., & Taggart, B. (2004). The Effective Provision of Pre-School Education (EPPE) Project. *Technical Paper 12—The Final Report: Effective Pre-School Education*. London: DfES/Institute of Education, University of London.

Sylva, K., & Wiltshire, J. (1993). The impact of early childhood education on children's later development. *European Early Childhood Education Research Journal, 1,* 17–40.

Tabors, P.O., & Snow, C.E. (2001). Young bilingual children and early literacy development. In S.B. Neuman and D.K. Dickinson, eds., *Handbook of early literacy research*. New York: Guilford Publications.

Talan, T., & Bloom, P. (2004). *Program administration scale: Measuring early childhood leadership and management*. New York: Teachers College Press.

Thomas, E. (2006). Readiness to Learn at School among Five-year-old children in Canada. Children and Youth Research Papers Series. Ottawa: Statistics Canada.

Tougas, J. (2004). Child care in Quebec. Discussion Paper prepared for the Canadian Council on Social Development's National Conference on Child Care in Canada, Winnipeg, November 12–14, 2004.

Turcotte, M. (2007). Time spent in family during a typical workday 1986–2005. *Canadian Social Trends*. Statistics Canada Catalogue No. 11-008. pp. 2–11.

UNESCO. (1998). *Early childhood development: Laying the foundations of learning*. New York: UNESCO.

UNESCO. (2002). *Framework for Action on Values Education in Early Childhood*. New York, NY.

United Nations. (1991). *Convention on the rights of the child*. Ottawa: Human Rights Program Department of Canadian Heritage.

Valimaki, A-L., & Lindberg, P. (2004). *National curriculum guidelines on early childhood and care in Finland*. Helsinki, 26 August 2004, pp. 24–25.

Weber, E. (1984). *Ideas influencing early childhood education*. New York: Teachers' College.

Weiss, H., Caspe, M., & Lopez, M. (2006). Family involvement in early childhood education. *Family Involvement Makes a Difference*. Harvard Research Project No. 1 in a series.

Whitebook, M. (2003). *Early education quality: Higher teacher qualifications for better learning environments—A review of the literature*. Berkeley, CA: Center for the Study of Child Care Employment.

Whitebook, M., Sakai, L., & Howes, C. (1997). *NAEYC accreditation as a strategy for improving child care quality*. Washington, DC: National Center for the Early Childhood Workforce.

Williams, R., Biscaro, A., & Van Lankveld, J. (Unpublished) *Part 1: Getting it right at 18-months, Making right for a lifetime. The importance of the new 18-month checklist*.

Willms, J.D. (2002). *Vulnerable children*. Edmonton: University of Alberta Press.

Wilson, L. (2005). *Partnerships: Families and Communities in Early Childhood Development*. Third Edition. Toronto: Thomson Nelson.

Wolf, T. (1990). *Managing a nonprofit organization*. New York: Prentice Hall Press.

Wright, J.C., & Huston, A.C. (1999). Effects of educational TV viewing of lower income preschoolers on academic skills, school readiness, and school adjustment one to three years later: A report to Children's Television Workshop.

Wright, M. (2000). Toronto's Institute of Child Study and the teachings of W.E. Blatz. In L. Prochner and N. Howe, eds., *Early childhood care and education in Canada*, pp. 96–114. Vancouver: University of British Columbia Press.

Yau, M. (1995). *Refugee students in Toronto schools: An exploratory study*. Toronto: Research Department of Toronto Board of Education.

Young, M.E., ed. (2002). *From early child development to human development: Investing in our children's future*. Washington, DC: The World Bank.

Young, M.E., ed. (2007). *Early child development from measurement to action*. Washington, DC: The World Bank.

Young, N. (1994). *Caring for play: The school and child care connection*. Toronto: Exploring Environments.

Ziegler, E., Singer, D.G., & Bishop-Josef, S.J. (2004). *Child's Play: The roots of reading*. Washington, DC: Zero to Three Press.

Zill, N., Resnick, G., Kim, K., Hubbell McKey, R., Clark, C., Pai-Samant, S., Connell, D., Vaden-Kieran, M., O'Brien, R., & D'Elio, M. (2001). *Head Start FACES: Longitudinal findings on program performance, third progress report*. Washington, DC: Research, Demonstration, and Evaluation Branch & Head Start Bureau, Administration on Children, Youth and Families, U.S. Department of Health and Human Services.

PHOTO CREDITS

This page constitutes an extension of the copyright page. We have made every effort to trace the ownership of all copyrighted material and to secure permission from copyright holders. In the event of any question arising as to the use of any material, we will be pleased to make the necessary corrections in future printings. Thanks are due to the following authors, publishers, and agents for permission to use the material indicated.

Chapter 1. 7: Karen Struthers/Shutterstock **8:** Courtesy of Osvalda Matos Vieira **14:** Stephen Coburn/Shutterstock

Chapter 2. 33: Zsolt Nyulaszi/Shutterstock **37:** Losevsky Pavel/Shutterstock **45:** Ingrid Crowther **50:** Andrey Stratilatov/Shutterstock **55:** © 2007 JupiterImages and its Licensors. All Rights Reserved. **68:** Jaimie Duplass/Shutterstock

Chapter 3. 80: Ingrid Crowther **82:** Anita Patterson Peppers/Shutterstock **87:** © 2007 JupiterImages and its Licensors. All Rights Reserved.

Chapter 4. 106: Ingrid Crowther **116:** Sandy Matos **123:** Sandy Matos

Chapter 5. 131: Ingrid Crowther **137:** Ingrid Crowther **138:** Ingrid Crowther **140:** Ingrid Crowther **145:** Dean Sanderson/Shutterstock

Chapter 6. 155: Ingrid Crowther **168:** Sandy Matos **174:** Sandy Matos

Chapter 7. 181: Sandy Matos **185:** Sandy Matos **193:** © 2007 JupiterImages and its Licensors. All Rights Reserved.

Chapter 8. 202: Ingrid Crowther **215:** © 2007 JupiterImages and its Licensors. All Rights Reserved.

Chapter 9. 227: Sandy Matos **230:** Sandy Matos **236:** Sandy Matos

Chapter 10. 249: Sandy Matos **252:** Zsolt Nyulaszi/Shutterstock **259:** Jaimie Duplass/Shutterstock

Cover: © 2007 JupiterImages and its Licensors. All Rights Reserved.

Section Opener 1. 1: © 2007 JupiterImages and its Licensors. All Rights Reserved.

Section Opener 2. 97: © 2007 JupiterImages and its Licensors. All Rights Reserved.

Section Opener 3. 197: © 2007 JupiterImages and its Licensors. All Rights Reserved.

Table of Contents vii: © 2007 JupiterImages and its Licensors. All Rights Reserved.

GLOSSARY

Aboriginal
In Canada includes First Nations, Métis, and Inuit people.

accounting
Financial record-keeping that tracks all financial transactions—income and expenditures.

accreditation
System of voluntary evaluation of excellence in early childhood programs or post-secondary education programs.

advocacy
Defending or stating the cause of another. In early childhood education, actions that support the ideas and issues of the sector.

assessment
Measurement of abilities, skills, and knowledge when referring to persons, or components when referring to environments.

at risk
Term used when concerns exist about developmental delay owing to negative environmental or physical conditions.

auspice
Type of legal governance structure that operates an organization.

capital budgets
Outlines projected expenses for large pieces of equipment and furnishings, land costs, building costs, and renovations. These are usually one-time expenses that are sometimes covered by one-time fund-raising campaigns, grants, and/or donations.

cash accounting
Method of keeping bookkeeping that records revenue when cash, cheques, or direct deposits are received, and expenses when they are actually paid.

cash disbursements
Expenses paid.

cash receipts
Revenue or money received.

certification
Professional recognition of an individual's ability to practise within an occupation.

coalition
An alliance among individuals or organizations for the purpose of a joint action for a joint purpose.

code of ethics
A statement of the responsibility and obligations of individual professionals in a particular sector that govern moral behaviour and ethical decisions.

cognition
Construction of knowledge, learning strategies, and ways of thinking and reasoning that enable children to learn about themselves, others, and the world they live in.

collaborative learning
Variety of educational approaches that involve joint thinking and exchange of information among participants.

commercial
Early childhood programs established to earn profit for their owners. Also called proprietary and for-profit.

compensation
Salary and benefits.

compensatory programs
Programs designed to ameliorate the impact of social or economic disadvantage through an enriched environment.

constructive discussion
Specific feedback and conversation about concerns and problems that focus on solutions.

cooperative

In the early childhood sector, a not-for-profit corporation that involves all families in the governance structure and may involve family participation in the operation of the program.

credentials

Professional qualifications from recognized educational institutions, professional organizations, and/or government departments.

curriculum

Sum total of experiences, activities, and events that occur within an inclusive environment designed to foster children's well-being, learning, and development, including planned and spontaneous activities and interactions.

custodial care

Housekeeping tasks (e.g., disinfecting toys, washing dishes, cleaning, moving furniture, and taking out garbage) that are necessary to maintain a healthy environment for young children.

day nursery

Term used for child care programs in Ontario in the middle of the twentieth century.

diversity

Variety of differences that exist among children of the same age, within a program, community, culture, or country. Refers to differences and uniqueness that each child brings to the early learning setting, including values and beliefs, culture and ethnicity, language, ability, education, life experiences, socioeconomic status, spirituality, gender, and so forth.

early child development

First phase of human development that extends from conception to age six or eight years and sets the foundation for lifelong learning, behaviour, and health.

early childhood programs

Programs that are organized to provide care and learning opportunities for children from infancy through middle childhood; includes child care centres, home child care, nursery schools, school readiness programs, preschool programs, and preschool early intervention groups.

early childhood staff team

Those who provide the daily learning and care program, including early childhood educators, early childhood assistants, kindergarten teachers, educational assistants, and family support practitioners; may also include special needs service professionals if they are part of the daily program delivery.

Early Development Instrument (EDI)

Teacher-completed checklist that measures kindergarten children's readiness to learn at school in five domains: physical health and well-being, social competence, emotional maturity, language and cognitive development, and communication skills and general knowledge.

early identification

Screening and other approaches to identify the early signs or symptoms of a problem with health or child development.

early intervention

Services and strategies to prevent or treat a potential or actual early developmental problem.

early learning standards

Describes expectations for the learning and development of young children across the domains of health and physical well-being, social and emotional well-being, approaches to learning, language development and symbols systems, and general knowledge about the world around them.

early literacy

Ability to recognize and understand print (letters and simple words), make sound–letter connections, and understand the context of individual words.

emergent curriculum

Pedagogical philosophy and approach that evolves from early childhood educators' observations of children's play and exploration of that which is socially relevant, intellectually engaging, and personally meaningful leading to children's discovery, understanding, and learning. Early childhood educators follow children's leads by observing their interests and needs and then planning the learning environment.

emergent literacy
Children's use of books and writing materials to imitate reading and writing activities.

emotional maturity
Degree to which children feel at ease, act spontaneously, and show vitality and self-confidence, indicating their basic needs have been satisfied.

entitlement
A program or resource that one has a right to have and society is obligated to provide.

equity
Equal opportunity to full participation regardless of socioeconomic status, ability, ethnocultural background, language, or religion.

equivalency validation
Process to determine if ECE postsecondary education programs and/or credentials meet specified standards.

family involvement
Meaningful participation of family members in their young children's early learning and development—at home and in decisions about and/or direct participation in early childhood programs.

family support program
Family-focused program that offers activities and services to young children and their families and caregivers.

fraud
Legal misrepresentation.

functional capacities
Underlying abilities that support cognition, emotional maturity, and social capacity.

governance
Refers to the process of making decisions. Governance is the structure that has the final authority and responsibility to make decisions and set policies.

Head Start
U.S. educational program for preschoolers in families below the poverty level. Comprehensive services include education, family support through social services and parent education, and medical, dental, and nutritional services for children.

High Scope
Active learning curriculum model.

implementation integrity
Extent to which the early childhood program is focused on a clear vision and developmental goals; also called program coherence.

inclusion
Placement of individuals with special needs in classrooms with typically developing individuals, and in which special services are provided within the classroom setting; or ensuring everyone is included, regardless of socioeconomic status, cultural background, or ability.

inquiry
Process of exploring, observing, gathering information, discovery of patterns and relationships in order to understand the environment.

kindergarten
Early childhood programs usually for five-year-old children, now operated as part of most school systems. Originated by Friedrich Froebel.

Junior Kindergarten
Half-day programs for four-year-old children operated in Ontario's school system and in some Quebec at-risk communities.

literacy
Reading, writing, and oral language abilities consisting of the following components: acquiring vocabulary and language, phonological awareness, knowledge of print, knowledge of letters and words, comprehension of meaning, and awareness of storytelling, books, and other texts.

monitoring
Measurement of the impact on early child development at the community or population level.

Montessori
Specific curriculum model based on the philosophy and approach of Maria Montessori; focuses on didactic learning materials and a prepared learning environment.

not-for-profit
Term referring to programs and organizations that are incorporated as not-for-profit.

numeracy
Proficiency mainly in mathematics that involves developing confidence and competence with numbers and measures, and requiring understanding of the number system, a repertoire of mathematical techniques, and an inclination and ability to solve quantitative or spatial problems in a range of contexts.

occupational standards
Describe what a person in a defined occupation must know and be able to do in order to be considered competent in that role.

organizational chart
A visual graphic that represents the hierarchical structure of an organization.

parenting
Rearing (loving, caring, stimulating) of a child or children by a parent or other primary caregiver.

pathologization
Tendency to view children and/or families as needing to be fixed and the primary purpose of early childhood programs is to provide remediation.

pay equity
Equal pay for work of equitable (similar but necessarily the same) value.

pedagogy
Educational approach that is a deliberate process of cultivating development and learning.

peer-reviewed
Process of academic review that ensures scientific rigour.

philosophy
Statement outlining the fundamental beliefs, values, and ideals that are important to individuals. Related to early childhood education, one's ideas about how children learn, and how early childhood educators teach.

play
Activity in which children are intrinsically motivated and characterized by imagination, exploration, delight, capriciousness, and a sense of wonder that reflects the unique experience of children, and through which children express their ideas and feelings, and come to understand themselves, others, and their world.

pre-kindergarten
Early childhood programs offered by local school boards or districts for children prior to entry to kindergarten programs.

pretend play
Play that involves symbolic thinking and make-believe.

probation period
Clearly defined trial period for new employees.

program coherence
Extent to which the early childhood program is focused on a clear vision and developmental goals.

program evaluation
Process of using assessment information and other data to review the quality and effectiveness of programs in order to make decisions about change.

program standards
Indicators of quality in early learning and care programs whose success has been demonstrated by research, describing the human resources, supports, activities, and methodology needed to promote children's learning. Includes characteristics such as staff qualifications, group size, ratio, environment, materials, and supports available to children and families in order to create optimal learning environments and equitable outcomes.

public policy
Government (national, provincial, regional, or local) policies that guide programs and practices.

reflective practice
Process of thinking back over experiences with young children and their families to form questions, set goals, and grow as a practitioner.

Reggio Emilia
Early childhood programs in Reggio Emilia, Italy, that are world famous for their child-centred and extensive project approach to learning.

responsiveness
Being sensitive to a child's emotional and physical needs, and taking actions to meet those needs.

risk management plan
A written document that foresees possible risks, identifies strategies to prevent crises, and prepares for a response plan to mitigate the negative impact of emergencies and disasters.

school readiness
Social, emotional, language, cognitive, and physical development needed for an individual child to take part in school learning. Also a benchmark to measure the degree to which families, communities, early childhood programs, and public policy have supported the collective early child development of young children before transition to school.

schoolification
Tendency for early childhood programs to focus primarily on discrete skills that are identified as prerequisites to school learning.

seamless
Organization and integration of programs for young children so that they can move easily from one service (e.g., child care) to another (e.g., junior kindergarten), and the services are complementary and harmonized with one another, and contribute to healthy child development.

self-governance
Legal authority to establish entities to regulate a group of professionals and their practice.

self-regulation
Ability to regulate one's response to challenges and stresses, related behaviour, attention, emotion, and memory.

service integration
Consolidation of individual programs to provide a single program for families and young children.

social capital
Collective value of connections between people and the inclinations that arise from these networks to do things for each other.

social competence
Ability to get along with others and understand social cues.

start-up budget
Outlines the income and expenses for the initiation of a new program or program component.

symbolic thinking
Ability to use symbols to represent real objects or events.

voluntary recognition
Nonmandatory endorsement of professional credentials and/or experience.

INDEX